FINDING AND
EDUCATING
HIGH-RISK AND
HANDICAPPED INFANTS

FINDING AND EDUCATING HIGH-RISK AND HANDICAPPED INFANTS

Edited by

Craig T. Ramey, Ph.D.
Professor of Psychology and Director of Research
Frank Porter Graham Child Development Center
University of North Carolina at
Chapel Hill

and WITHDRAWN

Pascal L. Trohanis, Ph.D.
Principal Investigator and Director of TADS
Frank Porter Child Development Center
University of North Carolina at
Chapel Hill

University Park Press / Baltimore

UNIVERSITY PARK PRESS
International Publishers in Science, Medicine, and Education
300 North Charles Street
Baltimore, Maryland 21201

This book was developed by the Technical Assistance Development System (TADS), a division of the Frank Porter Graham Child Development Center of the University of North Carolina at Chapel Hill, with the assistance of Ruth A. Meyer, Former Publications Coordinator, and John A. Bernard, Editorial Assistant. TADS is located at 500 NCNB Plaza, Chapel Hill, NC 27514.

This book was prepared pursuant to contract number 300-77-0507 from the Office of Special Education, U.S. Education Department. Contractees undertaking such projects under government sponsorship are encouraged to express freely their judgment in professional and technical matters. Points of view or opinions do not, therefore, necessarily represent the Education Department's position or policy. The enclosed selections are presented for information purposes only; no endorsement is made.

Office of Special Education
Project Officer to TADS
Dr. David Rostetter

Composed by Master Composition, Inc.
Manufactured in the United States of America by The Maple Press Company

Cover photograph by Solomon Associates, Baltimore, Maryland

Library of Congress Cataloging in Publication Data

Main Entry under title:
Finding and educating high-risk and handicapped infants.
Includes index.
1. Handicapped children—United States—Identification—Addresses, essays, lectures
2. Handicapped children—Education—United States—Addresses, essays, lectures.
3. Infants—Services for—United States—Addresses, essays, lectures.
I. Ramey, Craig T. II. Trohanis, Pascal Louis
HV888.5.F54   362.4'0880542   81-16230
ISBN 0-8391-1710-8   AACR2

CONTENTS

CONTRIBUTORS

G. R. Beck
School of Medicine
University of Washington
Seattle, Washington 98195

Diane D. Bricker
Professor of Special Education
Director of Early Intervention
  Program
Center on Human Development
University of Oregon
Eugene, Oregon 97403

Marie M. Bristol
Assistant Director for
  Family Studies, CIREEH
Frank Porter Graham Child
  Development Center
300 NCNB Plaza
Chapel Hill, North Carolina 27514

James O. Cox
Technical Assistance Coordinator,
  TADS
500 NCNB Plaza
Chapel Hill, North Carolina 27514

James J. Gallagher
Director of FPG
FPG Child Development Center
Highway 54, Bypass West
Chapel Hill, North Carolina 27514

James L. Hamilton
U.S. Special Education Programs
400 Maryland Avenue, S.W.
6th and D Street
Donohoe Building, Room 3120
Washington, D.C. 20202

Alice H. Hayden
WESTAR (Western State Technical
  Assistance Resource)
Suite 215, University District
  Building JD-06
1105 45th N.E.
Seattle, Washington 98105

Anne E. Hogan
Research Assistant
Mailman Center for
  Child Development
University of Miami
Miami, Florida 33101

Frances Degen Horowitz
Professor of Human Development
  and Psychology
Department of Human
  Development and Family Life
The University of Kansas
lawrence, Kansas 66045

Sharon L. Hostler
Medical Director
Children's Rehabilitation Center
University of Virginia
School of Medicine
Route 250 West
Charlottesville, Virginia 22903

Elouise Jackson
Department of Elementary and
  Special Education
Hampton Institute
Hampton, Virginia 23668

Merle B. Karnes
Professor of Special Education
Institute for Child Behavior and
  Development
University of Illinois
403 East Healey
Champaign, Illinois 61820

Ruth A. Meyer
Former Publications Coordinator,
TADS
3336 K. Fairway Oaks Drive
Lawrenceville, Georgia 30245

Sonya Prestridge
Technical Assistance Coordinator,
TADS
500 NCNB Plaza
Chapel Hill, North Carolina 27514

Craig T. Ramey
Associate Director of FPG
Highway 54 Bypass
Chapel Hill, North Carolina 27514

David Rostetter
U.S. Special Education Programs
400 Maryland Avenue, S.W.
6th and D Street
Donohoe Building, Room 3120
Washington, D.C. 20202

Keith G. Scott
Professor of Pediatrics and
    Psychology
Mailman Center for Child
    Development
University of Miami
Miami, Florida 33101

Tanya M. Suarez
Associate Director, TADS
500 NCNB Plaza
Washington, D.C. 20202

Pascal L. Trohanis
Director of TADS
500 NCNB Plaza
Chapel Hill, North Carolina 27514

FOREWORD

Although we have only limited data on the merits of early identification and programming for the high-risk or handicapped infant, what research data we have, plus common sense, tell us that the earlier we initiate appropriate intervention programs, the greater the child's chances of developing his or her potential to the fullest. In fact, there are high-risk infants who, when provided with intervention, grow to be normal and are no longer considered in need of special programming. Even those infants who continue to be handicapped in subsequent years are generally functioning at a higher level than would be the case if careful early programming had not been available.

Programs for infants have been initiated gradually throughout the country in the last 10 years. The Special Education Program (SEP) in the U.S. Education Department must be lauded for its leadership during this period in encouraging the development, demonstration, and dissemination of exemplary practices for handicapped and high-risk infants. Through its Handicapped Children's Early Education Program (HCEEP), state and local sites not only have been encouraged to intervene early in children's lives, but they have also been provided with the funds needed to do it. The result has been service models worthy of replication. In addition, SEP has supported the development of publications such as this one, which provide information about advances and current practices useful to all who are interested in early education of special children.

Although in recent years a number of excellent publications have included information about serving infants, this book by the Technical Assistance Development System (TADS), in fulfillment of a contract with SEP, makes a unique contribution because the authors combine so many years of experience working with children, designing screening and intervention programs, and helping others to develop programs. They know what professionals entering the field or working in the field need to know, and the skills they must acquire, to work effectively with infants from birth. The result is a single-volume reference that can be used as a guide from the earliest planning stages through implementation of infant programs.

Ramey, Trohanis, and Hostler provide the reader with an introduction to the volume in Chapter 1. First, they explain the transactional model of development, which describes the interplay between genetics and environmental factors of child development. Then the authors discuss the concept of "risk," the history of the term "handicap," and various classification systems of handicapping conditions. Finally, they provide a useful review of key developments in medicine, education, public policy, and training that are improving the outlook for finding and educating high-risk and handicapped infants.

ix

In Chapter 2, Hayden and Beck provide valuable information about the "occurrence, distribution, and determinants of the conditions that threaten the health and development of the very young." They explain the difficulty of getting accurate data and leave the reader with a better understanding of the statistics of infant impairments, how the statistics are determined, and the implications of the statistics for effective practices. Their chapter contains some of the most comprehensive information available about the epidemiology of high-risk and handicapped infants.

The environments of high-risk and handicapped infants are discussed in Chapter 3 by Jackson, who sorts out what is known and what is uncertain about the effect on development of various home and institutional environments. She also questions research indicating that differences in child-rearing practices of the poor, and particularly of minority groups, are necessarily detrimental and responsible for deficits in cognitive development of young children. To reinforce her view, she cites research that does not support the above relationship. Then she makes a valid plea for cross-cultural research that is capable of distinguishing between what is functional and what is not in different child-rearing practices and between the factors affecting children that are family related and those that are attributable to society.

The focus of the authors of Chapter 4 is identification. But Scott and Hogan make the point in the very beginning that identification of the infant and appropriate intervention go hand in hand. Without an intervention program, they essentially say, why bother to identify the handicapped or high-risk infant? Then they cover in detail the major methods of identification: casefinding and referral, the use of risk registers, and screening. The discussion about appropriate and inappropriate identification is excellent. And the reader will appreciate the information about identification costs and the glossary of terms provided.

The six exemplary screening programs described by Trohanis, Meyer, and Prestridge in Chapter 5 were chosen from respondents to a national survey conducted by the authors. A review of the instrument, contained in the appendices, revealed that the questionnaire used was very comprehensive. In all probability, no other survey of programs for this segment of our population has tapped such a breadth of information. The chapter's brief review of the survey results and the program profiles are enlightening and should be helpful to researchers and practitioners alike. As an additional service to the reader, an annotated listing of all screening programs that responded to the survey is provided in the appendices.

Horowitz describes methods of assessment of high-risk and handicapped infants in Chapter 6. She stresses the complexity and plasticity of the developmental process and the difficulty of finding early measures of infant development suitable for prediction and intervention planning. She also underscores what is generally known—that measures of infant intelligence do not predict intelligence at a later date. The instruments that Horowitz describes so clearly in the chapter are those considered reliable, and she helpfully explains the best circumstances in which to use them.

Bricker, who has had many years of experience working with handicapped infants and those at risk, devotes Chapter 7 to intervention program planning. I know of no one better prepared to deal with this subject. Using a question format, she guides the reader into an understanding of the issues that must be faced by program planners and implementers, and she shares her own wealth of experience in coping with those problems that are invariably present. Especially helpful are discussions about effective transition of infants to other programs and tracking of previously enrolled infants, topics rarely dealt with in the literature.

In recent years it has become recognized that parents are, after all, the first teachers of their children and that they have a great deal to offer in reinforcing the individualized educational program developed by the professional/parent team. In Chapter 8, Bristol and Gallagher discuss the changing role of families in intervention strategies and the nature of parent-infant interactions. They also describe the adjustments that take place in the family into which a handicapped child has been born and provide excellent recommendations for practices that foster the unique role the parents can play in promoting the infant's development.

Trohanis, Cox, and Meyer have written a helpful chapter about selected exemplary intervention programs that, like the chapter about screening practices, is based upon a national survey of infant programs. The nine projects the authors describe in Chapter 9 were chosen because of their representativeness of all survey respondents as well as because they are exemplary models of effective delivery of infant services. Most of the projects are in the outreach or dissemination stage and have had their models replicated in many sites. The reader, too, may wish to replicate a given program or adapt certain project components.

There is nothing mystical about evaluation, and Suarez makes that clear in Chapter 10. She states the reasons for systematically planning the evaluation component of an infant program and does it straightforwardly and with conviction. Her down-to-earth discussion of how to plan an evaluation will be appreciated by readers who recognize the contribution evaluation makes to progress—for infants, for programs, and for the field—and have been searching for a practical method.

Finally, in Chapter 11, Rostetter and Hamilton take a closer look at some risk factors that are beyond the confines of the child and his or her family. First they discuss those risk factors associated with measurement and intervention practices; then they move on to a discussion of factors related to community, state, and federal policy. These are all factors that must be reduced or eliminated by society, its leaders, and its professionals, they argue. They conclude with sound recommendations for policy and decision making and for obtaining and committing the resources essential for child and family services.

In summary, this excellent text has the interests and concerns of the practitioner at heart. It answers so many of the questions practitioners are asking about how to identify and program for the high-risk and handicapped infant, and it translates research findings into recommendations for action. Also, the reader cannot help but be encouraged by the progress the book shares. It is clear that no one initiating programs for handicapped infants needs to feel he or she is alone, because there are many who have been blazing trails and can help newcomers move along the path more smoothly and at a faster pace.

This book should be in the library of every professional working with young children. Parents also will find it helpful in understanding the various dimensions of programming for infants; by giving them insights, it will enable them to become more effective in involving themselves in their children's educational programs. In my opinion, the book is also the best basic textbook to date for students in training to work with infants. The references that follow each chapter are themselves outstanding supplementary resources.

All of us interested in serving high-risk and handicapped infants are indebted to the authors, to TADS, and to SEP for making this publication possible. We assure you that the time and effort you have expended in sharing with us your thinking, your experiences, and your expertise, and in relating research findings to practice, will pay off in terms of helping all of us make the progress so essential to improving programming for the unserved or underserved infants who are potentially handicapped or who have identifiable handicaps.

MERLE B. KARNES
Professor of Special Education in the
Institute for Child Behavior and
Development, Graduate College
University of Illinois
Urbana-Champaign Campus

PREFACE

Increased interest in providing high quality, appropriate, and the earliest possible services to high-risk and handicapped infants created a need for a single guidebook on the planning and operating of identification and intervention programs. To meet this need, the Technical Assistance Development System (TADS) of the Frank Porter Graham Child Development Center, University of North Carolina at Chapel Hill, has produced *Finding and Educating High-Risk and Handicapped Infants.* The book was developed under a contract with the Special Education Program, U.S. Department of Education.

This text represents a collection of 11 chapters which were designed by a variety of professionals to share their expertise and ideas. The information is diverse purposefully so as to reflect the diversity of a field of inquiry, practice, and discovery that is rapidly maturing. As a consequence, the material should appeal to and be useful to various readers. For example, administrators of current or prospective infant service programs may be able to extract programmatic ideas to help them make decisions, design, or improve their practices in such aspects as assessment, curriculum, and program evaluation. In addition, faculty from institutions of higher education may desire to use this text as primary or secondary reading source for such varied courses as program planning for infant exceptional children, policy implications for young handicapped children, and services in the health care/education setting for at-risk infants. Next, state, local, and federal policy-makers may find this material useful in creating policies and procedures, program guidelines, and position papers. Finally, professionals from fields including early childhood, special education, nursing, and psychology may use this text to help clarify general issues, stimulate thinking about infant programming concerns, or locate information about particular, promising practices.

Ultimately, we hope that this volume portrays the content in both a meaningful manner and with sufficient breadth to indeed assist infant program planners and implementors.

FINDING AND EDUCATING HIGH-RISK AND HANDICAPPED INFANTS

An
Introduction

Craig T. Ramey, Pascal L. Trohanis, and
Sharon L. Hostler

A growing body of evidence documents that the effects of a handicap can be lessened, and potential handicaps often prevented, when high-risk and handicapped infants are identified early and given appropriate intervention. The beneficial effects of the intervention on development can be seen not only in the short term, but also years later (Denhoff, 1979). In light of these findings, it is imperative that all infants who need it be provided with the kind of individualized care and training that will help them achieve the fullest, most productive lives possible.

In fact, expanded effort and resource expenditure in such areas as research, training, policy development, educational intervention, and

CRAIG T. RAMEY is director of research at the Frank Porter Graham Child Development Center and professor of psychology, the University of North Carolina at Chapel Hill.

PASCAL L. TROHANIS is director of the Technical Assistance Development System (TADS) of the Frank Porter Graham Child Development Center and associate professor of education, the University of North Carolina at Chapel Hill.

SHARON L. HOSTLER is medical director of the Children's Rehabilitation Center and associate professor of pediatrics, the University of Virginia School of Medicine.

medical technology and practice do reflect increasing interest in fulfilling the mandate of providing the best start in life for every child. These thrusts, in turn, have helped increase the number of advocates and professionals concerned with designing and implementing more and better services to infants and their families. The contributed chapters in *Finding and Educating High-Risk and Handicapped Infants* represent the best of what has been accomplished.

This introductory chapter provides some background information about infant development and services that puts the other chapters in perspective. First, it describes a transactional model of development, along with its implications for education, prevention, and remediation. Then, the concepts of the normal child, the child who is high risk, and the child who is handicapped are discussed. Finally, the chapter briefly describes endeavors in many fields that are creating progress in prevention and remediation of the conditions that interfere with the development of infants and the adults they will become.

A TRANSACTIONAL MODEL OF DEVELOPMENT

Current theories of human development emphasize the dynamic interplay between the biology of an individual and the environmental forces that he or she encounters. Neither biology nor experience alone is sufficient to account for the process of development. For example, biological factors such as prematurity affect the way the infant initially behaves. But the quality of the environment to which the child is exposed will determine his or her subsequent developmental level (Parmelee, 1977).

In their influential review of perinatal risk and developmental outcome, Sameroff and Chandler (1975) noted evidence of the biological-environmental interplay for a variety of risk conditions and proposed what they called a general "transactional model" of development. In such a model, portrayed in Figure 1, the child's biological characteristics, his or her genotype, are not fully expressed at the time of conception. However, as time progresses, the genotype exerts a continuing influence on the child's phenotype, or observed status. The influence of the child's genes continues through life, affecting such phenomena as the menstrual cycle in young women or the onset in young adulthood of a degenerative disease called Huntington's chorea, which results in paralysis and mental retardation. For any point in time, the child's phenotype is the sum of the interactions of his or her genotype with experiences and the environment. Furthermore, the phenotype at any point in time will influence future interactions with the environment (e.g., being cared for in an in-

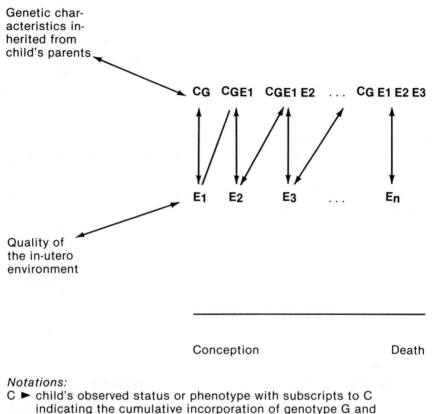

Figure 1.   A schematic diagram of a general transactional model of development.

tensive care unit for premature infants) and having encountered that environment will both alter it (e.g., a nurse's behavior) and in turn be changed by it (e.g., growing and developing more rapidly than otherwise would have been possible).

This general transactional model can be developed in more detail and used as a conceptual framework for educating high-risk and handicapped children. For example, Ramey, Zeskind, and Hunter (1981) have developed such a framework for premature infants, and Ramey and McKinney (1981) have developed one for learning-disabled children.

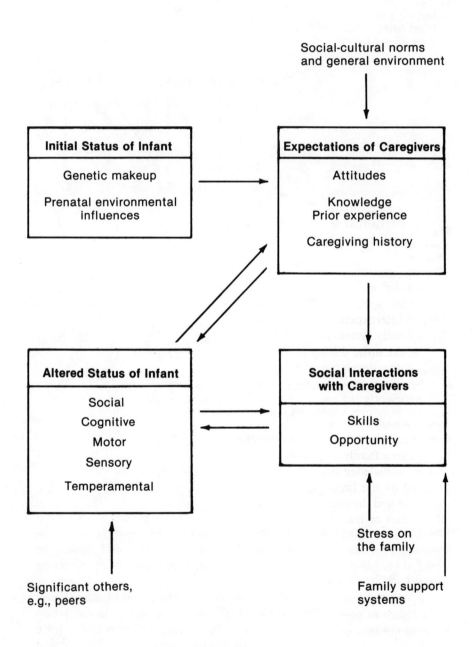

Figure 2.   One concept of infant education.

Educational Implications of the Transactional Model

In order to apply the transactional model to the education of infants, it is necessary to understand how knowledge, culture, and social values are believed to be transmitted from generation to generation. It is a process in which the infant is affected not only by its family system (or other primary system, such as an institution, to which the child belongs), but also by the broader network in which the family operates—the family's financial resources and constraints, cultural milieu, sources of stress, and sources of support.

Based on the nature of systems and networks, as described by Sarason et al. (1977), several assumptions can be made:

1. Development generally proceeds toward regularized functioning, and hence, predictability.
2. A pattern that is replicated has been reinforced.
3. A family system is an adaptation to the broader network of which it is a part.
4. The functioning of a family system can be modified, whereas the network in which it operates is more resistant to change.
5. A family, like other systems, proceeds towards increased sufficiency and interdependence of functioning.
6. A family system can most easily be changed when it is in transition, for example, during a family crisis.
7. For the developing child, the impact of proximal events declines through time and distal events increase in importance until both are sufficiently influential to be codeterminants of actions.

From the seven assumptions, it is possible to conceptualize the education of infants, represented schematically in Figure 2. The infant initially enters into a family system that has certain expectations based upon the attitudes, knowledge and prior experiences of family members, factors influenced by the broader sociocultural environment. The initial status of the infant and the expectations of the caregivers codetermine specific social interactions or transactions, which vary with the skills of those involved and the opportunities that exist for their occurrence and are affected by the stresses on the family and the supports that exist to deal with them. The transactions are the filter through which the infant's world is experienced and are causally related to alterations in the infant's social, cognitive, motor, temperamental, and sensory status. Through time, significant others, such as peers and other extrafamilial persons, come to exercise an increasingly important role upon the infant's development. The altered status of the infant and revised expectations of the caregivers determine new interactions, and the transactional process continues.

Within this context, early education can be implemented by working directly with the child, or indirectly by counseling the family or instructing the parents in alternative interactional styles. The comparative value of various approaches to infant education then becomes a matter of cost-effectiveness. The rationale for the approaches derives from the assumptions concerning the functioning and adaptability of family systems and of infants.

IMPLICATIONS FOR PREVENTION AND REMEDIATION

Intervention presumes the malleability of the child, the caregiver, the family, and the environment. It is an optimistic enterprise. However, whether and to what extent development of specific abilities can be modified by educational practices is an empirical and not a philosophical question, and educators have often been guilty of overstating their prowess and being naive to the enormity of the task implied in prevention and remediation programs.

The task of educators using the remediation model is relatively clear if not easily accomplished. The rate of the infant's development must be altered so that, at least for the period of intervention, it proceeds at a faster course than it did before. The explicit goal of intervention might be to return the child to a more typical rate of growth or to have the developmentally delayed child catch up to the typical child.

Four factors are particularly important when setting goals for accelerating an infant's development: 1) the length of the time the delay has existed, 2) the severity of the delay, 3) the duration of the treatment interval, and 4) the power of the intervention procedure. The last factor is determined primarily by the state of knowledge concerning causal factors regulating development in any given domain and the knowledge or ability that can be applied to provide compensatory or enhancing experiences. Time is also an important factor. It cannot be assumed that providing a missed earlier experience will be sufficient to allay an already developed deficit.

The logic, if not the practice, of prevention is simpler than for remediation. The goal is to identify the high-risk children who, without intervention, have a high probability of a significant developmental delay, then to ensure that they get sufficient exposure to crucial experiences to provide at least the minimal amount of stimulation necessary for normal growth and development.

CONCEPTS OF CHILD STATUS

The Changing View of Childhood

Less than 200 years ago children were viewed by society as family chattel, pieces of property. By 1850, progress had been made away from this view, and child labor laws were enacted in the United States to prevent further exploitation of youngsters in factories and mines. Some further evidence that changes were taking place in the concept of the child is that the Society for the Prevention of Cruelty to Children, in New York City, was advocating at the turn of the century for legislation that would protect children from physical abuse by parents and other adults. As the rights of the child to good care gained acceptance, the complexities of the child's growth and development became a field for research in medicine, psychology, and nutrition.

There were other milestones in the changing concept of the child. Free public education became mandatory in all the states. And the rights of minority children to integrated school experiences were upheld by the Supreme Court in 1954. The documentation in the mid-1960s of the emotional trauma inherent in hospitalizing young children revolutionized their care in hospitals and recognition grew of the social and emotional components of health. Also in the 1960s, recognition of the battered child syndrome resulted in widespread legislation prohibiting the physical and psychological abuse of children. Changing concepts of the child and his or her rights led to recognition, too, of the child with special needs. And, in 1975, the Education for All Handicapped Children Act specified the legal rights for a large population of handicapped children.

The health care system recognized the specificity of children's health needs as early as 1900, with the development of the pediatric specialty. Public health measures, improved infant nutrition, the introduction of antibiotics, the elimination of metabolic disorders, and the success of immunization eventually made it possible to direct these pediatric efforts to well-child care and preventive medicine. Also, clinic networks for the care of crippled children were initiated, and Medicaid funding brought children of poverty access to health care.

The first report of an association of a chromosomal abnormality with a clinical syndrome in 1959 (Jacobs et al.), initiated the area of cytogenetics and an increased focus on the prenatal period of development. The recognition of neonatology as a subspecialty of pediatrics followed in the 1960s. During the ensuing period, 25 percent of the research published in pediatric journals was related to the field of neonatology. The resulting intensification of care for newborns resulted in a remarkably increased survival rate, with the increased survival of handicapped infants also contributing to this improvement.

Dramatic changes have occurred in the medical care of critically ill neonates. Biological concerns have necessarily led to recognition of the critical importance of the mother/infant interaction (Klaus and Kennel, 1970) and the variability of newborn adaptive behavior and responses (Brazelton, 1973). The focus on patterns of infant development from birth to before birth has led to increasing awareness of the complexities of early development. Similarly, the national decentralization of care for developmentally disabled children has led to increased community awareness and responsibility for the medical and educational needs of children. Primary care physicians report that 17 percent of their practice is related to the behavioral and developmental aspects of pediatrics.

Society's focus on the inherent rights of the child are reflected in the practices of the legal, educational, and health care systems. Intervention in the care of the developmentally disabled child has become an interdisciplinary effort.

Concept of Risk

With increased attention to the development of children has come a concern for those infants who seem less likely than others to make progress and achieve their full potential. There are many terms in the literature and in practice that refer to this risk status. For example, an infant may be called: *at-risk, suspect, high-priority, vulnerable,* or at *developmental risk.* For this book, however, risk is a comparative and relative term used to express the likelihood of a current or future developmental hazard or handicap that, at present, is uncertain. It is thus an actuarial or probabilistic concept.

Tjossem (1976) distinguished three types of risk factors, which are not mutually exclusive: established risk, environmental risk, and biological risk.

1. *Established risk*   This term refers to the infant whose early appearing and aberrant development is related to diagnosed medical disorders of known etiology and which have relatively well known expectancies for developmental outcome within specified ranges of developmental delay.
2. *Environmental risk*   When the life experiences of a biologically sound infant are limited to the extent that, without corrective intervention, they impart a high probability for delayed development, the infant is at environmental risk. These life experiences may include maternal and family care, health care, opportunities for expression of adaptive behaviors, and patterns of physical and social stimulation.
3. *Biological risk*   This term specifies the infant who presents a history of prenatal, perinatal, neonatal, and early development events suggestive of biological insult to the developing central nervous system and which, either singly or collectively, increase the probability of later appearing aberrant development.

Another way to view risk is in terms of its onset during three major developmental periods. These periods are: 1) prenatal (from conception to birth), 2) perinatal (from onset of labor and delivery to fourth week of extrauterine life), and 3) postnatal (subsequent time periods). (See Table 1.) For the concept of risk to be useful to the intervenor, several conditions must be met. First, in order for a criterion state to be predicted with precision it must be operationalized with as much specificity as possible. Thus, rather than specifying "adequate" adjustment to school as a criterion, it would be more useful to specify academic achievement above a given percentile rank on a widely used and standardized achievement test.

Second, the intervenor should have program options that are differentially chosen and based, at least in part, on the risk information. In short, diagnosis without treatment is of limited value.

Implicit in the general concept of risk, and especially in the concept of environmental risk, is the issue of social values. In effect, when an infant's environment is labeled as having high risks for problem development, aspersion is being cast upon the primary caregivers. The aspersion may be deserved, as with parents who neglect or abuse their children, or it may be the result of a more pervasive set of circumstances that force the parents into inadequate resolution between their own rights and responsibilities and those of their children. Therefore, professionals working in this area must be aware that their decisions and actions are based upon value systems that can and should be discussed by the larger community.

Table 1.   Indicators of risk classified by three major time periods

Prenatal	Perinatal	Postnatal
Mutant genes	Disorders of labor and delivery	Acute illness
Radiation		Chronic disease
Toxic chemicals	Neonatal medications	Accidents/ poisoning
Harmful drugs	Prematurity	Malnutrition
Metabolic disorders	Cardiopulmonary problems	Late onset CNS disorders
Nutritional deprivation	Congenital malformations	Syndromes
Maternal infection	Metabolic disorders	Poverty
	Infections	Sensory impairment
		Environmental toxins
		Family dysfunction
		Iatrogenic illness
		Sociocultural disadvantages

The Concept of Handicap

According to Biklen and Bogdan (1977, p. 4), the word *handicap* comes from the eighteenth century and the practice of beggars who held "cap in hand" to solicit charity. These persons were viewed with fear and hostility, and their handicapping conditions were usually gross mental, physical, and sensory deficits quite visible to others. Images of idiocy and fecundity were pervasive, especially for the mentally deficient. Mild, moderate, hidden, or high-risk conditions were virtually unheard of and not dealt with.

The 19th and 20th centuries saw the development of efforts such as the establishment of institutions to provide humane care and training to the mentally and physically disabled. There were also individual efforts by people such as Maria Montessori with the asylum in Rome; Itard with the "wild boy of Aveyron" in Paris; Anne Sullivan, who worked with Helen Keller to overcome her blindness and deafness; and Alexander Graham Bell, who worked with the deaf. They all helped pave the way for the development of special education, its legislation, its advocacy, its litigation, and the simultaneous evolution of different ways of categorizing handicaps.

The evolution of various classification schemes can be traced to several sources. For example, the work of early pioneers (such as Bell) as advocates for a particular type of condition led to the formation of organizations (e.g., Convention of American Instructors of the Deaf), which in turn led to the development of legislation and funding for specific handicaps.

Another source of classification systems is the creation of profiles that identify the strengths and weaknesses of individuals in order to pinpoint the etiology of a condition, set expectations, and select the best intervention.

Four classification systems are discussed briefly. The first is that of Kirk (1972). He clusters children by five groups of impairments:

1. Communication disorders
2. Mental deviations
3. Sensory handicaps
4. Neurological and orthopedic conditions
5. Behavior disorders

Quay (1973) proposed a three-category system:

1. Process dysfunctions
2. Experience defects
3. Experience deficits

A more recent effort at classification is that of PL 94-142, the Education for All Handicapped Children Act of 1975. The act, seeking to ensure a free and appropriate public education to meet the unique needs of children, protect their rights, and ensure effectiveness, establishes eleven categories:

1. Deaf
2. Deaf/blind
3. Hard of hearing
4. Mentally retarded
5. Multihandicapped
6. Orthopedically impaired
7. Other health impaired
8. Seriously emotionally disturbed
9. Specific learning disabled
10. Speech impaired
11. Visually handicapped

Finally, there is the recent movement toward a noncategorical approach. It uses terminology such as *exceptional children, children with special needs, infants with disabilities,* or concentrates on degrees of severity (mild, moderate, severe), especially with young children, because their impairments may be less clear.

Although there appears to be a need for classification, regardless of the approach selected or used, practitioners must be careful to avoid using any terms that promote negative self-imagery or dehumanize children and their families. Furthermore, myths concerning high-risk or handicapped infants must not be perpetuated unintentionally.

SOME EFFORTS IN PREVENTION AND REMEDIATION

This last section of the chapter explores six areas in which progress is being nourished for finding and educating the high-risk and handicapped infant: medical technology and practice, research, practice demonstrations, policy making changes, training, and encouraging expertise and advocacy.

Some Policy Changes

Within the last decade, a number of key policy changes have occurred with respect to finding and educating handicapped and high-risk infants. Examples of some efforts are shared from state and federal levels.

Federal Changes   There are two notable changes. One is the landmark piece of legislation, PL 94-142, which mandates all states to conduct child identification efforts starting at birth. Parent involvement is stressed in the law, which also has provisions for such efforts as pre-school incentive grants. A second federal change is the emergence of developmental review through the Early and Periodic Screening, Diagnosis, Treatment (EPSDT) programs of the U.S. Department of Health and Human Services. This recommended new procedure suggests a three-stage process that evaluates young children on biological, psychological, environmental, and family characteristics. (More information about this trend can be found in Chapter 5.)

State Changes   States have been instituting mandatory special education starting at birth. Currently, 14 states have legislation from ages birth to 3 years. While still in the minority, these states are providing leadership for many others. Another change in several states, such as North Carolina, is recognition that tracking programs are valuable tools for ensuring that all high-risk infants receive regular health supervision within the first year of life.

Medical Advances

The emergence of a variety of new techniques and practices has been in-strumental in working with the high-risk or handicapped infant. For exam-ple, there is amniocentesis, sonography, fetal and neonatal monitoring, echocardiography, peripheral alimentation, phototherapy, computerized axial tomography (CAT) scans, and respirators. Neonatal intensive care units have been developed that have access to the latest available technology and expertise, including the specialist in neonatology.

Research

There are numerous research efforts across the country that are seeking to advance the information base of knowledge and practice for working with infants and families. Examples are the four Early Childhood Research Institutes funded by the U.S. Special Education Programs (SEP) at UCLA, the University of Kansas, the University of North Carolina at Chapel Hill, and the Educational Testing Service in Princeton, N.J. These programs are currently in the last year of a 5-year contract with the government. (Refer to May and Meyer, 1980, for more information about each.)

However, there is one major issue that has captured the attention of early childhood special educators—efficacy. Researchers and public policy makers want to know if educational interventions delivered during infancy can prevent or significantly remediate handicapping conditions.

A recent review of programs designed to prevent developmental re-tardation in high-risk but biologically intact infants has been completed by Ramey, Sparling, Bryant, and Wasik (in press). They located 18 pub-lished reports of programs that used day care, parent groups, home visitations or a combination of these procedures to alter the development of high-risk infants. Each type of program has reported significant intellectual differences between educationally treated and nontreated groups and there have been some reports of significant positive effects on linguistic, social, and later academic achievement. Studies that have reported direct comparisons of various treatment conditions have generally not shown very large differences associated with variations in service delivery formats but much empirical work remains to be done on this issue. The working conclusion that we are now using is that for socially defined high-risk infants, who usually come from the lower socioeconomic strata, early childhood special educational services can take many different forms and have a significant and positive impact on early development. The major unresolved issue is how professionals can identify with greater precision those infants who truly need early childhood special education services and who will benefit from the types of early intervention programs developed thus far.

The efficacy of early educational intervention with organically impaired infants is more difficult to summarize succinctly. In many ways adequate evaluations of educational programs are more difficult to achieve with organically impaired children than with socially defined high-risk children. Organically impaired infants differ from one another in as many ways as socially defined high-risk children differ from one another—including cognitive skills, temperament, and sensory acuity. In addition, however, the specific organic handicaps add additional variability to an already quite varied population. One implication of this tremendous variability is the implied difficulty in establishing scientifically adequate control groups that are truly comparable to groups of handicapped infants in any given treatment program. Without initial comparability of treated and nontreated samples of infants it is very difficult and frequently impossible to meet the standards required for scientific evidence within traditional research and evaluation designs. In addition, there are profound ethical issues involved in balancing the need for additional knowledge about treatment processes for handicapped infants, in general, and in providing what professional consensus indicates is the best treatment process for a given infant at a given time. Thus, research logistical issues and ethical issues make efficacy research with handicapped infants particularly difficult. Nevertheless, efficacy research must be conducted if professionals are to have confidence that various educational treatment processes are in fact therapeutic or, at least, not harmful. At present, however, no definitive review of the empirical literature has been conducted concerning efficacy of early childhood special education for infants with various organically handicapping conditions. That scholarly task remains to be accomplished.

The best available single source concerning efficacy information is contained in the *1980/81 Overview and Directory of the Handicapped Children's Early Education Program* edited by Daniel Assael and Gary Harrison (1981). That document contains on page 194 a listing of SEP projects that have passed review by the Joint Dissemination and Review Panel (JDRP) of the U.S. Department of Education. To pass this review requires the presentation of efficacy data. Interested readers can gain additional information by contacting SEP concerning the JDRP process.

Demonstrations

Many different kinds of demonstration programs have been developed and implemented. Two examples of nationally focused ones are highlighted.

 The Handicapped Children's Early Education Program (HCEEP) Operating under the auspices of the SEP in the U.S. Education Department, the HCEEP has provided extensive leadership nationally in the development and operation of locally based models for demonstration. Over the last decade, the number of infant-oriented projects has grown steadily. These programs are located in hospitals, private and public institutions, and public schools. All have 3 years of federal funding during which time they are to develop, implement, and evaluate their models. Simultaneously, the programs have the mission of finding local funding in order to maintain or expand their programs. For an update of these and related programs, refer to the *1980/81 HCEEP Overview and Directory* (Assael and Harrison, 1981).

 Robert Wood Johnson Foundation Regional Perinatal Care Program The Robert Wood Johnson Foundation of Princeton, New Jersey, is sponsoring an experiment of eight related projects across the nation. Its purpose is to determine whether the application of new technologies in perinatal intensive care can be done in a high quality and cost-effective manner.

Training

Numerous training efforts are going on in the country. Three diverse examples are described below.

 Inservice Training The American Academy of Pediatrics of Evanston, Illinois, has a project to improve physician interpersonal and professional attitudes about handicapped children and increase physician interactions with the educational system. The curriculum is to be completed in late 1980 with training taking place in 1981 and 1982.

 Residents' Curriculum The Nisonger Center at the Ohio State University is currently developing a unique training curriculum in developmental pediatrics with several modules or units. The training experiences are to be used with residents, and will be completed by late 1980, with field-testing and dissemination occurring during 1981/82.

The Bush Institutes for Child and Family Policy   Four programs (Yale, Michigan, UCLA, and University of North Carolina at Chapel Hill) supported by the Bush Foundation of St. Paul, Minnesota, have the mission of preparing social scientists to analyze public policies that affect children and families. Ultimately, these programs aim to create new and better alliances between the public policy maker and the academician/human service administrator.

Expertise/Advocacy Pool

A major effort on behalf of prevention and intervention efforts during the last decade has been the emergence of a growing infant expertise and advocacy personnel pool. For example, there is the Division of Early Childhood, a part of the Council for Exceptional Children in Reston, Virginia. There are also expanding clusters of parents and service providers who, as members of private groups such as United Cerebral Palsy, the March of Dimes, the National Association of Retarded Citizens, and the National Autistic Society, are making changes happen for infants and young children.

Next, there is a relatively young, small group that has been organized in the HCEEP network. It is called INTERACT—a national committee for very young children with special needs and their families—housed at the Pre-Start Project, Loyola University Strich School of Medicine in Maywood, Illinois. The group is finalizing a position paper that documents the need for comprehensive services for young special children and calls for an initiative to formulate a national policy that ensures these services.

Another group worth mentioning is the National Center for Clinical Infant Programs of Glen Echo, Maryland. It was formed by leaders in the fields of mental health, pediatrics, child development, and philanthropy to facilitate information-sharing, stimulate new research, encourage training, and foster public awareness.

Lastly, there are many local and statewide groups of professionals, parents, and advocates. One of these is the United Services for Effective Parenting (USEP) of Ohio, which supports the development and continual existence of birth to age 3 educational programs in the state. Another example is the Texas for Tots, a consortium of diverse programs and personnel who are serving exceptional infants, from birth to 2 years.

CONCLUSION

This introductory chapter aimed at sharing a general but diverse array of material as it pertains to finding and educating high-risk and handicapped infants. In concluding, the authors feel it appropriate to close with a quote from Alice Hayden (1979). Her thoughts and feelings not only capture ours, but we believe the spirit of this entire volume.

> "Some people believe that the problems of the birth to age 3 group are only in the health and medical realms. Indeed, many of these children desperately need health and medical care early, but they and their families also need early educational intervention. While nonhandicapped young children may make acceptable progress without early educational interventions, handicapped or at risk children do not. To deny them the attention that might increase their chances for improved functioning is not only wasteful, it is ethically indefensible" (p. 510).

REFERENCES

Assael, D., and Harrison, G. *1980/81 HCEEP overview and directory.* Seattle: TADS and WESTAR (University of Washington), 1981.

Biklen, D., and Bogdan, R. Media portrayals of disabled people: A study in stereotypes. *Interracial Books for Children,* 1977, *8,* 4-9.

Brazelton, T.B. Neonatal Behavioral Assessment Scale. *Clinics in Developmental Medicine,* 1973, 50.

Denhoff, E. *Infant stimulation or enrichment programs and the developmental disabilities: Pediatric role and responsibilities.* A paper for the Committee on Children with Handicaps, American Academy of Pediatrics, 1979.

Education of Handicapped Children, Rules and Regulations. *Federal Register,* August 23, 1977.

Hayden, A. Handicapped children, birth to age 3. *Exceptional Children,* 1979, *45,* 510-516.

Jacobs, P. A., Baikie, A. G., Brown, W. Mc, and Strong, J. A. The somatic chromosomes in mongolism. *Lancet,* 1959, *1,* 710.

Kirk, S. *Educating exceptional children* (2nd ed.) Boston: Houghton-Mifflin, 1972.

Klaus, M., and Kennel, J. Mothers separated from their newborn infants. *Pediatric Clinics of North America,* 1970, *17,* 1015.

May, M., and Meyer, R. *Handicapped children's early education program: 1979/80 Overview and directory.* Seattle: TADS and WESTAR (University of Washington), 1980.

Parmelee, A. H., Jr. Planning intervention for infants at high risk identified by developmental evaluation. In P. Mittler (Ed.), *Research to practice in mental retardation, Care and intervention,* (Vol. 1.) Baltimore: University Park Press, 1977.

Quay, H. Special education: Assumptions, techniques, and evaluation criteria. *Exceptional Children,* 1973, *40,* 165-70.

Ramey, C. T., and McKinney, J. D. The education of learning disabled children suspected of minimal brain dysfunction. In P. Black, (Ed.), *Brain dysfunction in children: Etiology, diagnosis, and management,* pp. 203-220. New York: Raven Press, 1981.

Ramey, C. T., Sparling, J. J., Bryant, D., and Wasik, B. Primary prevention of developmental retardation during infancy. *Journal of Prevention and Human Services,* in press.

Ramey, C. T., Zeskind, P. S., and Hunter, R. S.   Biomedical and psychosocial interventions for preterm infants. In S. L. Friedman and M. Sigman (Eds,), *Preterm birth and psychological development,* pp. 395-415. New York: Academic Press, 1981.

Sameroff, A. J., and Chandler, M. J.   Reproductive risk and the continuum of caretaking causalty. In F. D. Horowitz (Ed.), *Review of child development research* (Vol. 4.) Chicago: University of Chicago Press, 1975.

Sarason, S., Carroll, C., Maton, K., Cohen, S., and Lorentz, E.   *Human services resource network.* San Francisco: Jossey-Bass, 1977.

Tjossem, T. Early intervention: Issues and approaches. In T. Tjossem (Ed.), *Intervention strategies for high-risk and handicapped children.* Baltimore: University Park Press, 1976.

2

The Epidemiology of High-Risk and Handicapped Infants

Alice H. Hayden and G. R. Beck

"When a baby is conceived it is the beginning of an incredibly complex and delicate process. From the very moment of conception, cells are dividing and differentiating until nine months later a complete small human being is born. Most babies are born whole and healthy, but tragically not all of them come into the world with their full genetic potential" (Smith, 1979, p. 37).

When planning services for high-risk and handicapped infants, it helps to have a broad understanding of the problem. Epidemiology provides this perspective by describing the occurrence, distribution, and determinants of the conditions that threaten the health and development of the very young.

ALICE H. HAYDEN is founder and former director (1969-1980) of the Model Preschool Center for Handicapped Children, Experimental Education Unit, Child Development and Mental Retardation Center, and professor emeritus of education in the College of Education at the University of Washington in Seattle.

G. R. BECK is assistant professor of family medicine in the School of Medicine at the University of Washington in Seattle.

This chapter is most concerned with occurrence and distribution. Its purpose is to give an overall picture of the *kinds* of disorders likely to be found in an infant population requiring special services and to estimate the *numbers* of children who are likely to require such services.

Yet we are also concerned about causes. Our imperfect understanding of causes inevitably affects the incidence of conditions (the rate of new cases), and their prevalence (the total number of children who have them). It is, indeed, sobering to consider how many "unknown" causes contribute to the population of handicapped and at-risk infants.

We will restrict most of our discussion to incidence, because these figures are more accessible: most records are based on reports of incidence. However, we must stress that incidence figures often represent the tip of the iceberg. Many infants are not brought to the attention of screening programs. Others may not be identified if their condition is subclinical. And still others share deficiencies that do not become apparent until school age.

THE SCOPE OF THIS STUDY

The epidemiology of the infant who will be at risk for less than complete independence in our society is a study that must penetrate into every aspect of the lives of the study population. It is an overwhelming task. However, this chapter, in an effort to limit our goals, surveys an extensive literature from the viewpoint of educators who want to plan services.

Understanding "Risks"

When we talk about the epidemiology of "high-risk" children we need to limit our topic so that it is manageable. A child can be at risk for severe handicapping conditions by being a passenger in a car driven carelessly or because of any of a thousand other "accidental" factors. This chapter focuses on children who are at risk because of known or suspected biological insults or those less well defined but acknowledged risk factors associated with environmental deprivation. Stedman (1979), though, has pinpointed one of the great difficulties in discussing the epidemiology of children who are at risk because of socioeconomic environmental factors.

> "Poverty is not an explanatory variable. It provides information useful for predicting behavior, but in itself it is far too general to provide an explanation for the behavior. Rather...it is more likely that poverty is correlated with other variables, such as maternal child-rearing practices, that are more helpful in explaining the predicted developmental outcome" (p. 4).

Categorizing Handicapping Conditions

There are estimated to be over 500 isolated anomalies associated with mental retardation (Bergsma, 1973), over 4,000 separate causes of severe handicapping conditions (Safer et al., 1979), and over 220 recognizable patterns of malformation (Smith, 1976). Some of these conditions are more impairing than others. Some occur so rarely that any given educator, physician, or other service provider is unlikely to see more than a very small percentage of them in a lifelong career. Faced with this enormous array of possible conditions and causes, this discussion is limited to two large categories of handicapping conditions determined by the time of onset: prenatal (occurring before birth) and perinatal (occurring around the time of birth), and to discussions of cerebral palsy and mental retardation, which may have origins in both the prenatal and perinatal periods.

Examined in detail within each category are a few specific conditions that give an appreciation of the difficulties found by investigators. Also included is a reference list that, it is hoped, will be of use to the reader in pursuing information of a more specific nature.

THE ELUSIVENESS OF STATISTICS

Not so long ago, every self-respecting author of a text in special education included figures on the incidence or prevalence of handicapping conditions, at least in the school-age population. Interestingly, however, most such figures were clearly labeled as estimates with appropriate cautions provided (see, for instance, Dunn, 1963; Kirk, 1962; Magary and Eichorn, 1964). The cautions are equally appropriate today.

Many authors have relied upon the estimates provided in the *Proposed Program for National Action to Combat Mental Retardation* prepared by the President's Panel on Mental Retardation (1962). This report estimated that about 12 percent of the school-age population required special assistance to ameliorate handicapping conditions. The breakdown according to disabilities was:

Visually handicapped	0.2%
Crippled	1.5%
Special health problems	1.5%
Deaf and hard of hearing	2.0%
Speech handicapped	2.0%
Socially maladjusted	2.0%
Mentally retarded	3.0%
Total	12.2%

The estimates do begin to tell us the numbers of children for whom we must plan services. As Dybwad and LaCrosse (1963) indicate, though, the estimates do not provide the additional information needed to actually plan the services. How many of these children have multiple handicaps? What is the severity of their disabilities? And what are the emotional and social effects of their handicaps?

Figures are even harder to come by for the infant population than they are for school-age children. To date, the United States does not have a national registry of children who are at risk or handicapped, a situation that seriously complicates the task for this chapter and the complex task of any child-find efforts. Although one can look at a statement saying that syndrome A occurs with a 1:100,000 frequency, that statement does not tell us where the one child is located or anything at all about his or her needs for special services. Further, a child may have four different problems, and if each is listed separately, we do not have an accurate statement about the number of children (instead we have the number of "conditions" requiring services). Because of the lack of a national registry, it is sometimes necessary to look at incidence and prevalence figures from other nations in order to estimate the likely number of affected children in the United States.

Fortunately, some nationwide efforts are being made to gather reliable prospective information about the outcomes of pregnancy, efforts which eventually should yield accurate statistics about certain kinds of handicapping conditions. The Collaborative Perinatal Project, sponsored by the National Institute of Neurological and Communicative Disorders and Stroke of the National Institutes of Health, was undertaken by a consortium of investigators from 12 universities who collected data from 1959 to 1965. According to Niswander and Drage (1977):

> "The primary objective of the CPP was to provide leads to the etiologies of neurological and mental abnormalities of childhood through studies of the conditions and events of pregnancy, labor and delivery . . . . Follow-up examinations were completed in 1974 as the last child born in 1966 was examined at 8 years of age" (p. 43).

Over the past few years, more than 300 papers or books have been published on the CPP data and analyses continue in 10 primary and 10 secondary areas of interest.

Individual Variation   Incidence and prevalence figures do not generally provide information on the variability of the impairing conditions, or the variation within a given population. If no two normal children are alike, that is also the case with handicapped children. Some children have full expression of a particular syndrome or condition. Others are less severely involved. Some cases could even be considered "subclinical."

Reporting Differences   Sometimes it is necessary to talk about a range of incidence figures for a given condition rather than a specific figure. The literature contains wide variations in incidence figures for some conditions reported by different investigators or drawn from different populations. For example, incidence figures for cerebral palsy range from 1.63:1,000 births, reported by Hagberg (1978) on Swedish births from 1975 to 1977, to 2.51:1,000 reported by Davie (1972) in his 1958 British study. The incidence of anencephaly varies widely according to nationality. The British Isles have an extremely high rate although it is extremely rare in other countries. The range of incidence figures we found for Down's syndrome are described later in this chapter. Some of the differences may be traced to environmental or genetic variations in populations; other variations may be traced to the way conditions are defined and the criteria used to diagnose them.

Diverse Data   Some data are available from countries with national registries. There are also studies of specific countries or geographic areas and studies of specific hospitals and groups of individuals. Some of these studies are based on information on birth certificates; some are based on examination of the infant, including some studies which follow their population for varying lengths of time. The countries with national health care systems and birth registries give us the best look at a population in terms of the incidence and prognoses for particular conditions. For a country like the United States, where incomplete studies are reported, the information from other countries can be used to expand on what data we do have. Examples can be found in the Scandinavian life tables for Down's syndrome individuals for use in planning programs for school-age children and community-based care for adults with this syndrome. Some data from other countries represent populations that have incidences of certain syndromes different from those reported in our own population. When this occurs, direct application of their data to our own population is risky. However, proportional information can be used to determine the incidence of complications for a particular syndrome, or to develop life table information.

Estimates for Different Populations   Nationwide estimates of the number of persons who will require certain kinds of special services also vary from country to country, no doubt for reasons that relate as much to the organization and availability of services, the social services philosophy of the country, public health issues, and other complex factors, as to the actual number of handicapped people. For instance, *The Report of the Committee of Enquiry into the Education of Handicapped Children and Young People* published in Great Britain in 1978 (Warnocks) stated that one in every five British school children would need special services at some point in his or her schooling. In contrast, the U.S. Congressional

Report, *Service Delivery Assessment - Education for the Handicapped* (1979), states

> When PL 94-142 was enacted in 1975, it was estimated that about 12% of school-aged children were handicapped: however, federal child counts for the 1977-78 school year indicated that only 7.3% of school-aged children were being served by special education programs.

The report addresses many of the administrative and other problems associated with identifying children needing service and with service delivery. Nevertheless, the interesting issue is the difference in estimates of need.

When limiting our discussion to children younger than the usual school age, the difficulties of obtaining firm figures are even more pronounced; many sources list incidence figures for children without breaking these out into age groups (Hayden, 1979). And many handicaps are not detected until a child reaches school age. Census-based prevalence estimates for mental retardation, based upon responses to the 1976 Survey of Income and Education, are much lower for preschoolers (0.22 percent judged to be retarded) than for children of school age (0.58 percent of the 14 to 17 year olds judged to be retarded) (Jones, 1979, p. 200).

Moreover, regional or geographic differences in incidence figures within a single country must also be considered. The Robert Wood Johnson Foundation recently announced its Rural Infant Care Program designed to reduce infant mortality and disabilities in rural areas. The Foundation's brochure (1979) suggests that one reason for the continuingly disgraceful United States rate for infant mortality (overall, 17.7 per 1,000 live births) is the "relatively high infant death rates among nonwhites . . . and low-income whites, particularly those living in isolated rural communities." Black children have an infant mortality rate almost twice that of white children, and nonwhite children have death rates for disease and birth defects almost 25 percent higher than those for white children (Children's Defense Fund, 1979). These rates become more alarming when we consider that the birth rates among nonwhites are higher than the national rate. According to the *Statistical Abstract of the United States* (1978, p. 59), the birth rate (per 1,000 population) for whites in 1976 was 13.8, while for nonwhites it was 21.1.

Differential availability of resources may also have an impact: lack of treatment may lead to more impairing effects of handicapping conditions; it is also the case that lack of appropriate diagnostic services may be reflected in inaccurate incidence figures. In some communities, conditions that might be identified as risk factors during the prenatal and perinatal periods are not recognized because of the lack of systematic examination, careful observation, and referrals necessary for accurate diagnosis. The recent interest in home childbirth may also affect these problems.

Changes over Time   Incidence and prevalence figures are also affected by changes in technology, demographic trends, and social factors. The impact of antenatal diagnostic procedures (amniocentesis, ultrasound, and other fetal monitoring devices), the availability of legal abortions, delays in childbearing, and reduction in family size will no doubt influence figures in ways that are still uncertain. For instance, improved technology has enabled clinicians to reduce mortality in premature infants but not necessarily to reduce the impairing conditions prematurity causes. Stein and Susser (1971) pointed out that the advances in medicine that increased the longevity of Down's syndrome persons have not ameliorated or eliminated the mental retardation resulting from this anomaly. They considered Down's syndrome an "excellent epidemiological index" insofar as it is a paradigm for those anomalies resulting in mental retardation in which reduced incidence will not compensate for increased prevalence owing to greater longevity (Hayden and Haring, 1976).

Uses of Statistics   Sources of information vary, as do the purposes information serves: birth records, reports of longitudinal studies, prospective versus retrospective data, reports of topical conferences on given conditions, classic texts in pediatrics and other fields, and statistics gathered by government agencies (e.g., the Center for Disease Control, United States Public Health Service, and the National Center for Health Statistics) all yield information regarding the incidence and prevalence of diseases and handicapping conditions. The information is also used for different purposes: for spotting trends and correlating them with given social or other factors, for public health planning and study, and for informing those who will care for handicapped people about the extent of the need for services.

We cannot overstate the major caveat: statistics do not tell us anything about the educational and medical needs of *individual* children who will be referred to programs. Nor do they tell any given program director the exact number of such children who will be referred, or the particular family or social circumstances surrounding the child's handicap, although in general terms plausible correlational statements can sometimes be derived from statistical information. At the end of this chapter, estimates of need, which have been derived from incidence data, are discussed.

The Data Sources   Information is presented here on selected anomalies from the United States Public Health Service (USPHS) and Center for Disease Control (CDC) birth record information. The Center for Disease Control (1979) surveyed 40 states and projected rates for the other states. Although birth records are our most valuable sources of information about handicapping conditions, they fail to describe certain conditions that may not show up until later in life. A source we have found that avoids this problem is the British Columbia Health Surveillance Registry, maintained by the Division of Vital Statistics of the Ministry of Health. The registry was begun in 1950, using birth forms and reports from public health units, special treatment centers, voluntary health agencies, and private physicians. Since 1964, additional sources have been added, permitting the accumulation of more complete incidence rates; for example, the overall ascertained incidence rates for congenital central nervous system anomalies have increased by 15 percent for live births between 1964 and 1972, the period during which the registry added vital and hospital records to their sources. The registry reports good return rates on follow-up surveys (97 percent of forms returned, and 81 percent completed), which are initiated when individuals are 7 and 14 years of age. The registry has focused on children's diseases since its inception.

The Birth Rate   When we attempt to talk about the numbers of children at risk, the obvious information to begin with is the number of children born each year. From our current information, we can estimate a total of 3.3 million live births based on U.S. Bureau of Census data from September 1976 to September 1977 (monthly Vital Statistics, National Center for Health Statistics). This represents a number for a population where fertility, birth rate, and maternal age and parity (number of children previously born) are changing rapidly. Numerous factors affect the total number of births, and clearly factors that influence the broader categories must be considered separately.

THE HANDICAPPING CONDITIONS AND THEIR ONSET

Some of the handicapping and risk-laden conditions that affect infants have their origins in the prenatal period, with a complex interplay of genetic and nongenetic factors. Others have their onset around the time of birth, in the perinatal period. Still others either have combined risk factors from both periods or have still unknown risk factors. Table 1 lists major handicapping and high-risk conditions of infants by their time of onset.

The multitude of central nervous system (CNS) abnormalities that affect infants, and syndromes with multiple primary defects, are associated with prenatal onset. Associated with the perinatal period are prematurity, infection, trauma, and hemolytic (blood tissue) disease. Cerebral palsy and mental retardation have many risk factors that may be in either or both onset periods.

The following sections examine in detail infants who are at risk for these major handicapping conditions.

Table 1.   Major handicapping and risk conditions
(including mental retardation[a]) by onset period of risk factors

Prenatal onset	Perinatal onset	Unknown onset or combination of risk factors
Central nervous system abnormalities	Prematurity (with or without complications)	Cerebral palsy
Syndromes	Infection	
	Trauma	
	Hemolytic disease	

[a] Mental retardation can accompany any or all of the conditions in the table. See Table 5 for a breakdown of the incidence of mental retardation by onset period of risk factors.

Prenatal Onset

Table 2 estimates the number of cases per year for defects of the CNS and the syndromes that have their origins in the prenatal period. In calculating the incidence figures for Down's syndrome, we have used the more conservative incidence of 1:1,000 (Antenatal Diagnosis, 1979, pp. 1-48). Other U.S. estimates indicate that it occurs more frequently: 1:660 (Smith, 1977) and 1:650 (Hartl, 1977).

Table 2.   Incidence of handicapping conditions
with prenatal onset (estimated 9,306 cases per year)

Handicapping conditions	Incidence per 100,000 births
Primary abnormalities of the CNS—2,700 cases estimated	
Anencephaly	21
Spina bifida	42
Congenital hydrocephalus	16
Others	11
Total CNS	90:100,000
Syndromes—6,606 cases estimated	
Down's[a]	38
Autosomal	4
X-linked	1
Other specific syndromes	1
Multiple congenital anomalies	25
Total syndromes	69

Reprinted from Congenital Anomalies and Birth Injuries Among Live Births: United States, 1973/74. Vital and Health Statistics: Series 21, U.S. Department of Health, Education and Welfare, Public Health Service, Office of the Assistant Secretary for Health, DHEW Publication No. (PHS) 79-1909.

[a] This represents a very low estimate; the actual number of Down's cases per year is closer to 3,303 or about 1:1,000; and these cases probably represent one-half the total number of births in the syndromes category.

There is considerable variation in the incidence figures on Down's syndrome reported for different periods of time in different countries. Greater public awareness of the occurrence of Down's syndrome, increased genetic counseling, and prenatal detection and abortions may account for reduced incidence figures in the United States.

Central Nervous System (CNS) Abnormalities   The prenatal onset subcategories in Table 2 for primary CNS abnormalities and syndromes are derived from entries on live birth certificates for 1973. Rates were based on a 100 percent sample of live births in selected states and on a 50 percent sample in all other states (*Congenital Anomalies and Birth Injuries Among Live Births,* 1978).

Most CNS abnormalities are readily recognized at birth or shortly thereafter. Anencephaly is the partial or complete absence of the cranial vault. Affected infants have a degenerative or very rudimentary brain. Most of these infants are aborted or survive only a few hours after birth. Spina bifida results when the neural raches fail to close. Elwood (1976) estimates that only about 20 percent of all cases of CNS malformations are missed at birth, and Trimble and Baird (1978a) estimate that 20 percent are not identified during the first year. Ellwood estimates that all spina bifida cases are detected through birth and death records; however, the frequencies of anencephaly, hydrocephaly, and other CNS anomalies may be underestimated by about 14 percent, 39 percent, and 43 percent, respectively.

The British Columbia Registry (Trimble and Baird, 1978a) provides incidence figures for congenital anomalies of the central nervous system during the period of 1964 to 1970. The British Columbia figures for specific anomalies are

Anencephaly	0.64
Spina bifida	0.84
Hydrocephaly	1.04
Microcephaly	0.03
Other and multiple anomalies	0.52
	3.07 (per 1,000 total births)

The British Columbia rates for anencephaly and spina bifida are low, about one-half the British rate. Davie et al. (1972) found the incidence of anencephaly to be 1.8:1,000 total births in his British study. He reported that only 17 percent of children born with known malformations of the brain and spinal cord survived to age 7.

Smith (1977) estimates that defects of neural groove closure are the most common single defects occurring in the U.S. population, having an incidence of 0.5 to 1.5:1,000. These *single primary defects* may cause:

Anencephaly
Meningomyelocele
Hydrocephalus
Cleft lip
Cleft palate
Cardiac septal defects
Dislocation of the hip
Clubfoot
Pyloric stenosis

This list includes about half of the babies who are identified as having a serious defect in early life, according to Smith.

Smith et al. (1980) have recently studied the effects of hyperthermia on the developing fetus. High body temperatures during pregnancy have been suspected of causing damage to the rapidly growing fetus. Smith's group reported findings that indicate maternal temperatures above 102 or 103 degrees at 3 to 4 months of pregnancy may affect brain development. Maternal hyperthermia may be responsible for as many as 10 percent of neural tube defects. In some cases hyperthermia was caused by prolonged sauna and hot tub bathing.

Saxen, Klemetti, and Haro (1974), using data from the Finnish Register of Congenital Malformations, identified several risk factors associated with CNS defects: maternal age over 40, low birth weight (50 percent of CNS-defect babies were born premature or immature), history of influenza during first or second trimesters of pregnancy (although this finding contradicts the rest of the literature on the subject), single marital status, previous abortions and stillbirths, previous births of defective children, and consumption of certain drugs during pregnancy. Using data from the British Columbia Registry, McBride (1979) found that the risk for anencephaly and spina bifida among siblings or affected individuals was 2.4 percent, 15 times the normal incidence for these disorders. The risks of recurrence after one malformation in a family was 2.1 percent, and after two affected siblings was 4.8 percent. Saxen et al. caution that their estimate for the overall frequency of malformations at birth of 1.27 percent is probably low (by about 30 percent to 40 percent). Underreporting may be due to differences in definitions, variations in sources of data, and in length of reporting time.

It is also of interest here to compare the evidence of neural tube defects in Great Britain and the Scandinavian countries. As we mentioned earlier, the incidence of anencephaly is extremely high in Great Britain. Davie et al. (1972) observed that 3 percent to 4 percent of total births in his British cohort had serious defects—0.6 percent of total births had malformations of the brain and spinal cord, and two-thirds of these had spina bifida and hydrocephaly. The Finnish Register (1963-1972) reports an incidence rate of 0.2:1,000 live births for anencephaly, 0.4 for spina bifida, and 0.3 for hydrocephaly (Saxen et al., 1974). The total Finnish rate for congenital malformations was 12.7:1,000 (p. 301).

Syndromes In the second subcategory of prenatal onset, syndromes, the information comes from birth certificate information and may be less accurate. Smith (1977) estimated that 1:150 babies had multiple defects, some of them forming recognizable patterns, such as Down's syndrome. Smith (1976) described over 200 such recognizable patterns of malformations, some of which had known etiology. He estimated that most of these recognizable patterns of malformation or syndromes had a frequency less than 1:3,000. The exceptions were Down's syndrome (1:660), the XXY syndrome (1:500), and the fetal alcohol syndrome, which is supposed to occur more frequently than 1:3,000 in populations with a high incidence of alcoholism.

For the most common syndrome, Down's syndrome, we can examine multiple sources for the best estimate of the incidence at birth. Trimble and Baird (1978b), using British Columbia Registry data, estimated the incidence of Down's to be 1.46:1,000 live births; Lowry et al. (1976) 1.28:1,000; Smith (1973) 1:640, Smith (1977) 1:660; Davie (1966) 2.0:1,000. Most cases of Down's syndrome are caused by an extra chromosome 21. Trimble and Baird (1978b) compared their rate to those reported in six other studies of trisomy 21. Their overall reported rate was 1.25:1,000. If one were to include mosaicism and translocation, other chromosomal abnormalities that are estimated to contribute about 5 percent of Down's cases, Trimble's average of rates would fall in line with British Columbia figures. Advanced maternal age has been identified as a risk factor for the birth of a Down's infant. Trimble and Baird (1978a, 1978b) and others (Hook and Lindsjo, 1978) observed that the risk of having a child with Down's syndrome increases with maternal age: in the 35 to 39 age group, the risk was 1:326; for women aged 39 the risk was 1:132. About one-half of Down's infants have been born to mothers over 35.

However, changes in the maternal age distribution have caused the birth rate of Down's infants among mothers *under* 35 to increase. Lowry et al. (1976) reported that 80 percent of Down's infants (1972/73) were born to women under 35. Meanwhile, others have noted that the overall incidence rate for Down's syndrome has not decreased (Connolly, 1977). These demographic changes suggest that genetic counseling should be extended to younger mothers as well as those over 30 years of age. Many chromosomal abnormalities have been identified. The trisomy 18 syndrome, for example, is caused by an extra chromosome 19. It occurs with an incidence of about 0.3:1,000 births. Other chromosomal abnormalities involve a rearrangement of chromosomes, a breakage of chromosomes, or a deficiency in the total number of chromosomes. Many of these syndromes seriously threaten the infant's chances of survival; only about 10 percent of infants with trisomy 18 syndrome survive the first year (Smith, 1976). Other syndromes involve the sex chromosomes, including the XXY, and the XXXY syndromes, some of which are more common than trisomy 18. The XXY syndrome as well as the XYY syndrome occur in 1:1,000 male births; the XXX syndrome occurs in 1:950 female births (Hook, 1978). These syndromes are sometimes characterized by insufficient hormone production. Early diagnosis makes it possible to initiate hormone therapy when appropriate (Smith, 1976).

Perinatal Onset

The perinatal onset category includes all of the problems that can complicate the birth of an infant. The most common of these problems is low birth weight associated with prematurity and its attendant complications. The premature infant is at greatest risk of suffering CNS damage from all causes, e.g., hypoxemia, infection, and hemorrhage. Although better intensive medical care for premature infants has decreased mortality it has also decreased the morbidity of the survivors (Hagberg et al., 1975). Many studies have documented this and both Hagberg (1978) and Bennett et al. (1979) have shown a correlation between perinatal complications and subsequent cerebral palsy. Most important, however, no study has shown an increase in severe mental retardation secondary to increased survival of very premature infants.

Unknown Onset or Combination of Factors

A recent study by Bennett et al. (1979) has also demonstrated the interaction of prenatal and perinatal factors in the etiology of certain conditions. After following 240 preterm infants over a period of 2 years, they found that 18 infants had been diagnosed as having spastic diplegia, a type of cerebral palsy, at or before 1 year (conceptual age). Bennett concluded that many of these infants would not have survived before modern neonatal intensive care developed. As more of these high-risk infants are surviving, the incidence of spastic diplegia has been increasing. Prenatal factors, such as maternal bleeding and toxemia, as well as perinatal factors such as low birthweight, and low 1-minute Apgar scores were associated with subsequent problems.

Cerebral Palsy   Table 3 shows incidence estimates for the types of cerebral palsy. Using the rates described in Hagberg (1978), which average about 2:1,000, we have projected that approximately 6,000 infants with cerebral palsy are born annually.

It is difficult to relate specific perinatal events to morbidity. The perinatal period is usually defined as extending from 20 weeks of gestation

Table 3.   Incidence of cerebral palsy
(estimated total cases = 6,000; approximately 2:1,000)

Type	Number of cases	Causes	
Spastic			
spastic	2,100; 420 with MR	Prenatal onset factors	210
		Perinatal onset factors	168
		Postnatal onset factors	42
			420
tetraplegia	300; all with MR/ seizures	Mixed prenatal and perinatal onset factors	
diplegia	2,400; 720 with MR	Perinatal onset factors (Low birthweight)	
Ataxic			
diplegia			
congenital	600; with 300 MR		
Dyskinetic			
choreo- atketonic	150 of normal intelligence		
dystonic	450 with severe motor impairment		

up to and including the 28th day of life (Hobel, 1978). Many events that occur at or about the time of birth may influence outcome. These include deprivation of oxygen, diminished blood supply, birth trauma, and low birthweight. The etiology of cerebral palsy illustrates how difficult it may be to separate prenatal and perinatal factors. The authors of the *Antenatal Diagnosis* (1979) report consider this problem.

"Concern about injury to the fetus during labor and delivery must begin with recognition and measurement of the relative contribution of intrapartum (labor and delivery) events to fetal and neonatal death (perinatal mortality), and damage (perinatal morbidity). The interrelationship of multiple antepartum, intrapartum, and postpartum factors in producing perinatal mortality and morbidity serves to confound attempts to study the problem. Genetic and prenatal influences, such as maternal nutrition or illness, may modify the fetal response to stress encountered during labor, delivery, and neonatal life. The only clear end point in the evaluation of the effect of intrapartum events is the death of the fetus, neonate, or child. Any outcome less extreme is necessarily less precise. Analysis of the effect of intrapartum events upon subsequent morbidity becomes more difficult as the severity of that morbidity decreases, and time span from delivery to analysis increases" (p. 111-112).

Coleman (1981) has also described the difficulty of separating prenatal and perinatal effects.

> "Infants who are classified cerebral palsied may in fact be infants who are at risk prior to the birth process due to intrauterine infections, genetic insults and other etiologies. When these "at risk" babies then enter into the stressful situation of the birth process, they are more likely than the usual newborn to decompensate under the stress and present with evidence of hypoxia. However, decreasing their stress and thus decreasing the amount of hypoxia suffered by such newborns may not alter their clinical course if it is already fixed by congenital brain syndromes with prenatal etiologies" (p. 374).

These compounding factors should be kept in mind when reviewing studies of the origins of cerebral palsy. Drillien's (1978) estimate is most frequently used: that about half of all cases are attributed to perinatal causes. Low birthweight is strongly associated with cerebral palsy. Nearly one-third of all cerebral palsy victims weighed less than 2,500 grams at birth, compared to 19 percent in control populations (*Antenatal Diagnosis,* 1979). And, although low birthweight is already associated with both prenatal and perinatal hypoxia (lack of oxygen), data from the Collaborative Perinatal Study indicate that intrapartum hypoxia (diminished oxygen supply near the time of delivery), contributes independently to the incidence of cerebral palsy (*Antenatal Diagnosis,* 1979, p. 111-113).

Intracranial hemorrhage in the infant is also associated with cerebral palsy. These hemorrhages are often seen in premature infants. And, indeed, prematurity rather than low birthweight is believed to determine the incidence of one type of cerebral palsy, spastic diplegia (Volpe, 1975). Yet, as Coleman (1981) points out, much remains to be understood about the etiology of prematurity.

Mental Retardation

Stein and Susser (1978) estimate that at least 40 percent of all individuals in the U.S. with an IQ less than 50 have either a chromosomal disorder, a single gene disease, or a severe developmental syndrome. Scandinavian literature on severe mental retardation (SMR), shows perinatal factors accounting for only 10 percent of cases; the majority of factors are from the prenatal onset category. Hagberg (1978) also reports a predominance of prenatal factors. Chromosomal aberrations accounted for 36 percent of severe mental retardation cases, with perinatal factors involved to a minor extent. Hagberg found a 3.3 percent incidence of severe mental retardation in 1 year olds. He points out that the Swedish experience in reducing infant mortality (presumably better neonatal intensive care, particularly for the premature) has not caused a parallel increase in perinatal severe mental retardation. However, a follow-up study of 158 very low birth rate infants found that 47 percent of children had serious disabilities and 37 percent had significant handicaps, which included: IQs of 70 to 84, minor motor incoordination, well-controlled epilepsy, serious visual problems, or reading retardation of more than 18 months on the Neale Analysis of Reading Ability Scale (1966).

Incidence data drawn from U.S. Public Health Service information describe a similar breakdown of causes. The total incidence for SMR is from 3 to 5:1,000. These cases may be described according to onset. The rates in Table 4 summarize data reported by three epidemiologic studies of severe mental retardation, by Drillien (1978), McDonald (1973), and Gustavson et al. (1977), as described in Hagberg (1978).

Given our projection for total births of 3.3 million, we have extrapolated the incidence figures in Table 5 using the rates provided by Hagberg (1978).

Looking back at the projected incidence figures for cerebral palsy in Table 3, it can be seen that 1,740 of the estimated 6,000 infants born annually with cerebral palsy are also mentally retarded. If we add these infants to those we estimated to be at risk for severe mental retardation in Table 5, we arrive at the incidence estimate of 16,740—the expected number of children born each year with severe mental retardation. This estimate does not capture the many borderline cases of retardation caused by other factors, however.

We must stress that these are projections for incidence, based on three very similar profiles of a Swedish, Canadian, and British population. We can look at some "harder" data in Table 6, which examines the prevalence rates recorded by the British Columbia Registry in 1977.

Table 4.   Origins of severe mental retardation

Risk factors	%
Prenatal	73
Genetic (one-third Down's)	43
Acquired	10
Unknown	20
Perinatal	10
asphyxia and/or intracranial hemorrhage	90
premature	33
Postnatal	5
Unknown	12
	Total 100

Table 5. Incidence of severe mental retardation by onset period of risk factors (total cases = 15,000; annual incidence of 5:1,000)

Risk factors		Number of cases
Prenatal factors		10,950
Genetic	6,450 cases;	
Acquired	1,500 cases;	
Syndrome	3,000 cases;	
Perinatal factors		1,500
Postnatal factors		750
Unknown		1,800
	Total cases	15,000

Prevalence estimates such as those in Table 6 are often based on the subjective evaluation of the mental retardation of another (in the case of the census estimates this is done by another family member). For this reason they are expected to be lower than the actual prevalence rate. This is discussed by Jones (1979) in his examination of 1976 U.S. Census estimates for mental retardation. The average rate of perceived retardation was only 0.43 percent, although the rates varied widely for different age groups and races (p. 199).

In all the studies reported to date, approximately half of the mentally handicapped populations have neither prenatal nor perinatal risk factors identified, although 80 percent to 90 percent of cases of severe mental retardation can probably be predicted by prenatal and perinatal risk factors, and these children can be identified at birth or shortly thereafter. However, as milder degrees of impairment begin to interest early-intervention-oriented researchers, risk factors must be coupled with accurate assessment and follow-up through the preschool years. The National Institute of Child Health and Human Development has sponsored

Table 6. Age-specific prevalence of mental retardation, British Columbia, 1977, ages 0 to 4, 9,123 children

Degree of mental retardation	Cases
Borderline	3
Mild	9
Moderate	152
Severe	15
Profound	3
Unspecified	78
Total	260
Age-specific prevalence	2.8%

a task force to summarize risk factors to predict instances of morbidity and mortality related to mental retardation. The task force recommended the use of fetal monitoring devices for high-risk mothers to detect changes indicating fetal distress.

Onset During Childhood

Of course many other handicapping conditions have an onset during childhood. These conditions are caused by trauma, infection, and other known and unknown causes. Many children, for example, experience hearing loss as a result of serious otitis media. Other handicaps result from childhood accidents, episodes of child abuse or neglect, and poor childhood nutrition. Jackson (1979) reports that accidents are the most common cause of death after the age of 1 year; however, death rates fail to account for the many more subtle disabilities that may result from accidents. These problems may not be identified until long after the child experiences an injury. Certain childhood diseases, such as acute poliomyelitis and rheumatic fever, have secondary complications which may be handicapping. For these reasons, estimates of incidence at birth do not include all of the children who may come to need special services later.

ESTIMATES OF NEED

We might compare several estimates of need for special services. As our figures indicate, about 16,740 infants are born each year with severe mental retardation. The former Bureau of Education for the Handicapped, U.S. Office of Education, estimates that 3 percent of the 49 million school-age children have some form of learning disability (Comptroller General of the United States, 1979). Davie et al. (1972) estimate that 3 percent to 4 percent of total births in their cohort had serious congenital defects (of that number, two in five died before age 7); over 5 percent of the children in ordinary schools were receiving special help due to educational or mental "backwardness"; and head teachers estimated that an additional 8 percent needed help but did not receive it. Hetznecker and Forman (1977) estimate that about 10 percent of the elementary school population has learning disabilities. The Canadian Commission on Emotional and Learning Disorders in Children (CELDIC) Report (Lazure, 1970) predicts that one out of eight children will have an emotional or learning disorder. The U.S. report, *Antenatal Diagnosis* (1979) indicates that 100,000 to 150,000 infants born annually, or from 3 percent to 5 percent of about 3 million annual births, have either a significant congenital malformation, a chromosomal abnormality, or a clearly defined genetic disorder (p. I-1). The British Columbia Registry reports the average annual incidence rate of congenital anomalies are not detected until the child is older. Table 7 contains 1966 to 1977 incidence rates for major categories of congenital anomalies, as reported in the British Columbia Registry (1978).

Table 7. Incidence rates per 10,000 live births in British Columbia of cases with selected anomalies, 1966 to 1977

Diagnostic category	Rate per 10,000
Nervous system (includes still births)	32.0
Anencephalus and spina bifida (ASB)	14.3
Congenital hydrocephalus	10.2
Eye	14.6
Congenital cataract	3.9
Ear, face, and neck	16.0
Accessory auricle	7.2
Cardiovascular system	78.4
Ventricular septal defect	27.1
Patent ductus arteriosus	18.2
Respiratory system	6.4
Cleft palate and cleft lip	21.0
Cleft palate	8.5
Cleft lip	4.6
Cleft palate with cleft lip	7.9
Digestive system (excluding oral clefts)	52.3
Pyloric stenosis	30.8
Atresia and stenosis of rectum and anal canal	4.4
Genitourinary system	81.7
Undescended testicle	31.1
Hypospadias	22.7
Obstructive defects of urinary tract	7.6
Atresia and stenosis of urethra and bladder neck	9.0
Musculoskeletal system	147.8
Clubfoot	58.9
Polydactyly	10.0
Reduction deformity	5.5
Congenital dislocation of hip	38.4
Skin, hair, and nails	7.8
Congenital syndromes affecting multiple systems	19.1
Down's syndrome	11.5

Reprinted from Health Surveillance Registry Annual Report, 1978. Appendix 1 Ascertained cases of selected anomalies in British Columbia annual birth cohorts. British Columbia Registry, Division of Vital Statistics, Ministry of Health, Province of British Columbia, 1979.

Many learning disabilities caused by these anomalies are not identified until the child has reached school age. The British Columbia Registry data illustrate this problem; incidence rates are influenced by case-finding rates after birth, especially for defects not readily identified until screening and assessment are conducted. For example, hearing loss is not accurately reflected in incidence figures for preschool children.

The 12 percent estimate of school age children who are handicapped translates into about 5.5 million children who require special services. When we include children in the 3 to 5 and 18 to 21 age ranges, this estimate of need increases to 7 to 8 million children in need (Office of Education, U.S. Department of Health, Education, and Welfare, 1979). As of April/May, 1978 "children professionally diagnosed as handicapped accounted for 13.4 percent of total enrollment in full year [Head Start] programs" (Head Start Bureau, 1979, p. 14). The percentage of children enrolled in Head Start who are professionally diagnosed as handicapped varies across the country: in 1978, it was 7.48 percent in the District of Columbia, 9.50 percent in Hawaii, 11.73 percent in Wisconsin, and 23.36 percent in North Dakota. It seems that the most effective state screening and diagnostic programs are those that rely upon the efforts of Head Start assessments, which identify specific needs. Ongoing assessment and parental involvement are also recommended (Head Start Programs, 1979, p. 25-26).

Acquiring Appropriate Information   It is altogether unrealistic to expect educators or physicians to know about every possible indicator of developmental delay or dysfunction. At the same time, failure to recognize impairing conditions can have appalling consequences for the child who is at risk. Our resolution to this dilemma—understanding that one cannot know everything but that one needs to know "enough"—is to suggest that practitioners, including educators, learn everything they possibly can about the children in their care. Once again, this involves careful observation of the child over time, acquainting oneself with the professional literature and the services of colleagues from different disciplines, and maintaining a spirit of inquiry about the child's progress and the program developed for him or her.

Some children's handicapping conditions can be diagnosed before or immediately after birth. Down's syndrome, for instance, can be detected through antenatal diagnosis (amniocentesis), which identifies the extra chromosome in the fetal cells. In addition, this syndrome is usually recognized at birth because of certain physical features characteristic of the Down's syndrome newborn, and the diagnosis can be confirmed by chromosome studies. Forty inborn metabolic disorders can now be successfully detected in utero (*Antenatal Diagnosis,* 1979, p. I-69). But many handicapping conditions and risk factors do not have such clear indicators so early in a child's life.

Relying on Parents   Many more subtle handicapping conditions are first noticed by parents who suspect that something is not right about their child. They may not be able to pinpoint their concerns exactly, or they may actually make wrong "diagnoses." The critical point, however, is that their concerns must be heeded. Their children need referral for specialized diagnoses and placement in programs where they can be followed by trained staff who have worked with large numbers of infants and children. For example, a recent report (Shah and Wong, 1979) discusses the recurrent failure to identify hearing impairment in young children, with strong evidence that clinicians in many cases dismissed the parents' findings concerning their children and falsely reassured the parents that nothing was wrong.

Inclusiveness and Overreferral   No single assessment instrument can definitively yield the educational information needed in identifying or diagnosing an infant who will require special services. Accordingly, our bias is for an inclusive referral policy that can tolerate false positives, those individuals without the disorder who are incorrectly labeled as having the disorder, and that would encourage pediatricians or other clinicians to refer *all* children suspected of being at risk, because of biological, genetic or environmental factors, to programs where the infants' progress can be monitored closely over time. Willemsen (1979) emphasizes the importance of identifying factors associated with psychological or learning handicaps: to alert parents and other caregivers to possible problems that can sometimes be averted through special programs.

Willemsen describes the uses and potential abuses of the terms *at risk* and *perinatal stress* in discussing infants with histories that contain factors related to psychological or educational handicaps. She cautions parents and professionals to avoid being influenced by the label to expect certain behaviors. Ongoing observation of the at-risk infant allows us to thoroughly delineate educational and medical needs and to design an appropriate intervention program, including all necessary ancillary services (Hayden, 1979b).

THE RISK FACTORS

For many diseases, incidence and prevalence rates are lacking, and the complex interplay of genetic and nongenetic factors cannot yet be described. Where registries have collected data on groups of individuals over time, valuable information has been obtained. The Lowry et al. (1976) study of Down's syndrome found that although the proportion of women over 35 years of age giving birth had declined, the crude incidence of Down's syndrome remained relatively constant over a 20-year period. Other recent studies have shown that paternal age is also related to incidence of Down's syndrome. A re-examination of two previous case-control studies (Sigler et al., 1965; Cohen et al., 1977) of Down's syndrome children by Abroms and Bennett (1979) suggests that the high correlation of maternal and paternal age in these earlier studies masked the independent effects of paternal age. Recent reports of cytological staining techniques, which make it possible to determine which parent contributed the extra number 21 chromosome, indicate that 20 to 25 percent of Down's cases are of paternal origin (Abroms and Bennett, 1979; Magenis et al., 1977; Mattei et al., 1979).

The British Columbia data indicate increased risks among siblings for anencephaly and spina bifida. As mentioned earlier, Saxen et al. (1974) describe various risk factors. James Miller, genetic consultant for congenital defects to the British Columbia Health Surveillance Registry, discusses trends in the use of newborn risk registers during the past 10 years (Miller, 1977). Problems of ascertainment caused many of these registers to be abandoned. He describes the potential for a register to help describe the gene/environment interaction in many common diseases, uncovering time trends and risk factors. At present, most countries do not classify or count the number of cases in any systematic fashion. However, a register that draws upon multiple sources, such as the British Columbia registry, and that allows for follow-up surveillance, could yield valuable information on incidence and prevalence, as well as identify factors for use in preventing certain genetically determined disorders.

Others have tried to identify environmental variables that influence child development, with the hope that demographic risk factors can be used to predict special educational needs. Ramey et al. (1978) found that information available on birth certificates, such as education of mother and month prenatal care began, could be used to predict the educational and psychological status of first graders. A 1977 report by the Comptroller General to the Congress stated that an estimated 75 percent of the incidence of mental retardation can be attributed to adverse environmental conditions during early childhood (Comptroller General of the United States, 1979, p. 23). The task remains to determine which demographic variables are merely correlated to other less obvious variables and which are in fact causally related to educational status (Stedman, 1979).

Other environmental and demographic risk factors for childhood disabilities are being identified. Two hundred twenty children born to women denied legal abortions in Czechoslovakia have been studied to determine the effects of "unwantedness" on child development (Matejcek, Dytrych, and Schuller, 1979). The findings show a higher incidence of illness and hospitalization, and less satisfactory school performance by 9 years of age than in matched controls. A subsequent follow-up at age 14 showed significantly more referrals for serious behavioral disorders.

Demographic changes suggest that new risk factors may be identified. During the last two decades the proportion of births to women under 20 has risen to 17 percent of total births. In 1977, 42,000 births were recorded to women under 16 (David and Baldwin, 1979). Many of these infants are at risk for the consequences of inadequate prenatal care. It is possible that further studies will indicate the relationship of variables like marital status and maternal age, education, and employment, to child development. It is especially important to study these relationships because more children are being reared by single parents, many of whom are young.

PREVENTION

Once risk factors are identified, we can take steps to monitor births and prevent the occurrence of many disabilities. Amniocentesis, sonar scanning, fetography, and other physical methods are available to detect certain abnormalities for mothers identified to be at risk. Unfortunately, some of these procedures carry their own risks. The risks believed to be associated with amniocentesis and sonar scanning are minimal. Other diagnostic techniques at this time may carry a greater risk. For example, the miscarriage rate for fetoscopy by an experienced practitioner is from 3 percent to 5 percent (*Antenatal Diagnosis,* 1979, p. I-114). The level of alpha fetoprotein in serum can be determined by screening blood samples of women in the second trimester of pregnancy. These AFP studies are used to detect defects in the central nervous system and other developmental abnormalities. Most neural tube defects occur during the first trimester. Using AFP tests during pregnancy, about 80 percent of the approximately 5,000 neural tube defects that occur annually in the U.S. can be detected. Intrapartum events, estimated to account for 20 percent of stillbirths and 10 percent of severe mental retardation may also be monitored to detect and prevent fetal distress.

Hundreds of metabolic disorders have been identified. Hypothyroidism, phenylketonuria (PKU), and maple syrup urine disease, which have estimated frequencies of 1:3,800, 1:15,000 and 1:400,000 respectively, are three of the more common disorders (Infant Metabolic Diagnostic Laboratory, 1979). Screening tests have been developed to detect many of these disorders in newborns. Many of these disorders can now be detected in utero. When these disorders are detected at or shortly after birth, the appropriate therapy can be initiated to prevent serious abnormalities such as mental retardation, hepatic disease, vascular problems, ocular abnormalities, and psychosis. For example, infants who are screened for PKU and found to have phenylalanine in their blood or urine are placed on a low phenylalanine diet.

Active immunization against many infectious diseases is often taken for granted, yet the levels of immunization vary across the nation. Although immunization against diphtheria, tetanus and pertussis, polio, measles, mumps, and rubella is recommended by 1 year of age, U.S. immunization surveys indicate that many children between the ages of 1 and 4 living in urban poverty areas do not receive these immunizations. For example, about 13.7 million children (30.1 percent) 13 years old and under had not received a measles immunization in 1976, and about 18 million students did not have adequate protection against polio, rubella, mumps, diphtheria, whooping cough, and tetanus (Comptroller General of the United States, 1979, p. 24).

Certain environmental factors have been associated with the occurrence of birth defects. These risk factors include exposure to certain drugs, x-rays, viruses, such as herpes and rubella, and parasitic infections such as toxoplasmosis. As additional environmental hazards are identified, it is important that pregnant women be informed in order to avoid exposure to potential teratogens.

Infants who are born prematurely (having a gestational age less than 37 weeks) experience an increased risk for many diseases that affect newborns and that may cause long-term disorders. Prematurity has an incidence of 8 percent, increasing to 16 percent in low socioeconomic areas (Guthrie et al., 1977). These premature infants are more susceptible to bacterial infections. For example, the incidence rate of infections is 1:1,000 for live full-term births and 1:250 for live premature births. Premature infants are more prone to respiratory distress syndrome (RDS). Complications of RDS include: pulmonary complications such as pneumonia and interstitial emphysema, complications of endotracheal intubation, side effects from oxygen therapy, and metabolic disturbances (Dabiri, 1979). Sostek et al. (1979) report that premature infants who had been ill with prolonged respiratory distress had significantly lower developmental scores, and about 50 percent had neurological abnormalities. It has been estimated that "very small premature babies are 10 times more likely to be mentally retarded than normal weight babies" (Comptroller General of the United States, 1979, p. 24). As the survival rates for these infants improve because of advances in neonatal intensive care, it is important to identify factors that place these infants at risk for subsequent handicaps and to suggest interventions to improve long term development.

CONCLUSION

Readers will realize by now that incidence figures are by nature conservative. The wide range of data sources cited here indicates the problems posed by vague and overlapping definitions of disabilities, variations in reporting systems, and gaps in descriptive data for many populations. Incidence figures probably remain the educator's most useful resource to estimate needed service for at-risk infants and their families. However, professionals have long recognized that the availability of services or the lack thereof also impacts on reporting procedures. The need for clearer definitions of handicapping conditions, and for uniform data collection and recording systems should stimulate coordination and cooperation among agencies and the different disciplines in order to increase current knowledge and understanding of factors influencing learning and development. All professionals would benefit from the development of consistent and comparable reporting mechanisms.

The epidemiology of handicapping conditions, like the epidemiology of disease, includes the study of correlates, as well as determinants, of developmental disabilities. Risks continue to be discovered, some related to natural histories, and others to socioeconomic and environmental variables. When risk factors are clearly identified, primary prevention is possible. This includes prenatal care, genetic counseling for high-risk parents, and nutrition programs for infants and mothers. The need for these preventive programs has been demonstrated. For example, the *Early Childhood and Family Development Programs* report (Comptroller General of the United States, 1979) states that about 34,700 women who gave birth in 1975 did not receive prenatal care; although about 20.1 percent of babies born to these women were classified as low birthweight infants, only about 7.4 percent of all births were low weight (p. 23). Secondary prevention and screening efforts should be directed at vulnerable high-risk groups, such as low birthweight infants. Finally, tertiary prevention or rehabilitation is needed to develop the abilities of children who have handicaps.

It is not enough, however, to end our efforts after we obtain accurate incidence or prevalence figures, or establish uniform reporting systems. Parents and educators must ensure that all those children identified to be at risk receive services. The passage of PL 94-142 requires educators and those responsible for public education to consider many important questions related to the provision of education and related services to handicapped children and youth. A timely research study by Charlene Behrns in Washington State, however, suggests:

"There are a substantial number of persons ages 3-5 and 18-21 who are not involved in special programs, even when the most conservative estimates are used . . . . The count of pupils with handicapping conditions in the public schools in the State of Washington appears to be correlated to the available funds, legislative controls and the reporting requirements peculiar to fiscal channels" (Behrns, 1980, p. i).

Unfortunately, this is not an isolated problem. The December 12, 1979 *Report on Education Research* describes a U.S. Office of Education report stating that "about half the states are serving 8 percent or more of their school-age population as handicapped, (while) many states are below this figure." The Advisory Committee on Child Development in 1976 defined "high risk" children as "all those who were in families below the poverty line by government definition (3.1 million) plus those in families with annual incomes between $5,000 and $7,000 where the mother works (600,000). There were therefore 3.7 million high risk children under age six" (Comptroller General of the United States, 1979, p. 19). Yet according to this report, "the only major Federal program providing comprehensive child development services to high risk families is the Head Start Program, which served about 402,000 children in fiscal year 1978" (p. 41). It was estimated that Head Start served only about 15 percent of the eligible population in fiscal year 1978 (p. 41).

While our problems are complex, they are not, although compounded, necessarily new. Many of them were recognized by professionals who participated in the 1930 White House Conference on Child Health and Protection. The four sections of the conference—medical service, public health service and administration, education and training, and handicapped children—were composed of specialists working in different fields. But, with few exceptions, significantly similar threads were woven into the patterns of the reports presented. The report of the 1930 White House Conference was heralded as a blueprint for ensuring the future of exceptional children. The history of the American public's concern for young children needing special services is described in *The Story of the White House Conferences on Children and Youth* (1967). We need to examine what progress has been made in implementing some of the recommendations of the sharing, caring professionals who understood and sought to resolve some of the problems that were so evident.

We have long recognized that in the United States many changes in society affected the health, the care, and the education of young children. Some of the problems were well stated by Aldrich and Wedgwood in 1970:

"Change is a process of response to a variety of forces many of which are not readily seen as having an impact on the health of children and youth. Similarly, the changes that can be visualized are often not nearly so significant as the forces behind them which give a premonition of further change. It is believed that the rapid rate of change and the nature of the professionals, government officials, and the general public over the collective failure to create a national health system for children and youth that works effectively, efficiently, and acceptably. A better understanding of these forces may make it possible to anticipate the future, and it may lead to a systematic health care program with adequate feedback and adaptability to accommodate the health needs of children and youth" (p. 110-111).

In "Exploration 1993: The effects of future trends on services to the handicapped," Safer et al. (1979) cite three economic trends that are expected to affect handicapped persons in the future: the continued growth of an information/service economy; changing employment patterns, including an increase in the average age of the work force and growing underemployment; and a reduction in the economic growth rate. The authors warn that

> "The projected decline in the rate of economic growth will mean a decreased number of federal, state, and local dollars available for new or existing services and programs . . . . Critical initiatives in extending equal rights to the handicapped, such as PL 94-142 or Section 504 of the Vocational Rehabilitation Act of 1973, have come from the federal government and have been supported in large part because of financial incentives (federal dollars to cover a percentage of excess costs) or sanctions (the withholding of HEW funds). Decreased levels of federal funds could make the incentives seem less attractive and the sanctions less damaging, and thus could seriously slow this movement" (p. 8-9).

Edwin Martin, former head of the U.S. Office of Education's Bureau of Education for the Handicapped, emphasizes that it will be difficult to make early education for all handicapped children a reality: "[It will be] a difficult theme in a tight budget year, so don't expect immediate leaps." However, he believes that we must

> "set a goal of education from birth for all handicapped children by the end of the 1980s and rally public support for the goal . . . . The Education for All Handicapped Children Act should be expanded so each handicapped child can receive special education and related services from birth" (*Report on Preschool Education,* December 18, 1979, p. 8).

Support to serve the handicapped must be thoroughly demonstrated as a cost-efficient approach to prevent later problems that may be reflected in increased illnesses, disabilities, mental health problems, school failure or lack of success, and possible unemployment. The public must be made to recognize the need for such services, and gathering reliable information about the scope of the problem is a necessary first step.

The communication of basic information and viable solutions to specified problems is a second step. It is our responsibility as professionals to set priorities in order to accomplish these goals. Looking back to the 1930 White House Conference we can see that there are no easy or final victories. We must continue to focus attention on the steps that should be taken to implement our recommendations. We can ill afford to have the problems of children unresolved while adults air their seemingly minor differences. This results in delays in early intervention that actually reduce eventual costs and problems, besides improving the quality of life for many handicapped children and their families.

REFERENCES

Abroms, K., and Bennett, J. *Paternal chromosomal aberrations and Down's syndrome.* Paper presented at the Fifth International Congress of the International Association for the Scientific Study of Mental Deficiency, Jerusalem, 1979.

Aldrich, R. A., and Wedgwood, R. J. Examination of the changes in the United States which affect the health of children and youth. *Educational Horizons,* Summer 1970, *48,* 110-116.

Antenatal Diagnosis. Report of a Consensus Development Conference sponsored by the National Institute of Child Health and Human Development assisted by the Office for Medical Applications of Research and the Fogarty International Center, March 5-7, 1979. Bethesda, Md.: National Institutes of Health, 1979, NIH Publication No. 79-1973.

Behrns, C. *An analysis of the discrepancy between the projected number of handicapped students eligible for PL 94-142 services and the actual number being served in the public schools in the state of Washington.* Unpublished doctoral dissertation, University of Washington, 1980.

Bennett, F. C., Chandler, L. S., Robinson, N. M., and Sells, C. J. Spastic diplegia: Perplexing "disease of prematurity." *Child Development and Mental Retardation Center Newsletter,* University of Washington, Seattle, Washington, December 3, 1979.

Bergsma, D. *Birth defects: An atlas and compendium.* Baltimore: Williams & Wilkins, 1973.

British Columbia Registry, Division of Vital Statistics, Ministry of Health, Province of British Columbia. Health surveillance registry annual report, 1977. *Chronic disabilities, congenital anomalies, genetic defects.* British Columbia: Author, 1979.

British Columbia Registry, Division of Vital Statistics, Ministry of Health, Province of British Columbia. *Ascertained cases of selected congenital anomalies in British Columbia annual birth cohorts.* Health Surveillance Registry Annual Report, 1978, Appendix I. British Columbia: Author, 1979.

British Columbia Registry, Division of Vital Statistics, Ministry of Health, Province of British Columbia. Health surveillance registry annual report, 1978. Appendix II: *Annual incidence of B.C.-born cases with congenital anomalies, 1966-1977.* British Columbia: Author, 1979.

Center for Disease Control. *Congenital malformations surveillance report.* July 1977-June 1978 (issued March, 1979). DHEW Publication No. (CDC) 79-8362.

Children's Defense Fund. *Children's Defense Fund Reports* 2 October 1979, *1.*

Cohen, B.A., Lilienfeld, A. M., Kramer, S., and Hyman, L. C. Parental factors in Down's Syndrome: Results of the second Baltimore case-control study. In E. B. Hook and I. H. Porter (eds.), *Population cytogenics.* New York: Academic Press, 1977.

Coleman, M. Congenital brain syndromes. In M. Coleman (ed.), *Neonatal neurology.* Baltimore: University Park Press, 1981.

Committee of Enquiry into the Education of Handicapped Children and Young People. *Special educational needs: Report of the committee of enquiry into the education of handicapped children and young people.* London: Her Majesty's Stationery Office, 1978.

Comptroller General of the United States. *Early childhood and family develop-ment programs improve the quality of life for low-income families.* Report to the Congress by the Comptroller General of the United States. Washington, D.C.: United States General Accounting Office (HRD-79-40), February 6, 1979.

Congenital Anomalies and Birth Injuries Among Live Births: United States 1973-74. U.S. Department of Health, Education, and Welfare, Public Health Service, National Center for Health Statistics, 1978.

Connolly, J. A. Down's syndrome incidence: Practical and theoretical consid-erations. *Journal of the Irish Medical Association,* 1977.

Dabiri, C. Respiratory distress syndrome. In T. M. Field (ed.), *Infants born at risk: Behavior and development.* New York: Spectrum Publications, 1979.

David, H. P., and Baldwin, W. P. Childbearing and child development. *Amer-ican Psychologist,* (October 1979), *34,* 866-871.

Davie, R., Butler, N., and Goldstein, H. *From birth to seven.* London: Longman's (in association with the National Children's Bureau), 1972.

Drillien, C. M. Etiology of severe handicapping conditions in early childhood. In *Major mental handicap: Methods and costs of prevention.* Ciba Foundation Symposium 59 (new series). Amsterdam: Elsevier/Excerpta Medica/North Holland, 1978.

Dunn, L. M., (Ed.). *Exceptional children in the school.* New York: Holt, Rine-hart & Winston, 1963.

Dybwad, G., and LaCrosse, E. ABC 123: Early childhood education is essential to handicapped children. Reprinted from the *Journal of Nursery Education,* January, 1963, by the National Association for Retarded Children, 1969.

Elwood, J. M. Anencephaly and spina bifida in North America. In S. Kelly, E. B. Hook, D. T. Janerich, and I. H. Porter (Eds.), *Birth defects, risks, and consequences.* New York: Academic Press, 1976.

Gustavson, K. H., Hagberg, B., Hagberg, G., and Sars, K. Severe mental retardation in a Swedish county. II. Etiologic and pathogenic aspects of children 1959-1970. *Neuropädiatrie,* 1977, *8,* 293-304.

Guthrie, R. D., Prueitt, J. L., Murphy, J. H., Hodson, W. A., Wennberg, R. P., and Woodrum, D. E. The newborn. In D. W. Smith, (Ed.), *Introduction to clinical pediatrics.* Philadelphia: W. B. Saunders, 1977.

Hagberg, B. The epidemiological panorama of major neuropaediatric handi-caps in Sweden. In J. Apley (Ed.), *Clinics in developmental medicine.* Philadelphia: J. P. Lippincott, 1978.

Hagberg, B., Hagberg, G., and Olow, I. The changing panorama of cerebral palsy in Sweden 1954-1970. *Acta Paediatrica Scandinavia,* 1975. *64,* 187-192.

Hartl, D. L. *Our uncertain heritage: Genetics and human diversity.* Philadelphia: J. B. Lippincott, 1977.

Hayden, A. H. The effects of educational intervention on cognitive develop-ment. In *Proceedings of the symposium on developmental disabilities in the preschool child: Early identification, assessment, and intervention strategies.* Cosponsored by the College of Medicine and Dentistry of New Jersey, Rutgers Medical School; Institute for the Study of Exceptional Children, Educational Testing Service; and the Institute for Pediatric Service, Johnson and Johnson Baby Products Co., September 6, 1979. Chicago, 1979a.

Hayden, A. H. Effectiveness of early intervention. In *Proceedings of the con-ference on prevention of developmental disabilities.* June 19, 1979. Columbus,

Ohio: Nisonger Center, 1979b.

Hayden, A. H.   Handicapped children, birth to age 3. *Exceptional Children,* 1979c, *45,* 510-517.

Hayden, A. H., and Haring, N. G.   Early intervention for high risk infants and young children: Programs for Down's syndrome children. In T. Tjossem (Ed.), *Intervention strategies for high risk infants and young children.* Baltimore: University Park Press, 1976.

Head Start Bureau.   *The status of handicapped children in head start programs.* Sixth annual report of the U.S. Department of Health, Education, and Welfare to the Congress of the United States on services provided to handicapped children in Project Head Start. Washington, D.C.: U.S. Department of Health, Education and Welfare, Human Development Services, Administration for Children, Youth, and Families, Head Start Bureau, February, 1979.

Hetznecker, W., and Forman, M. A.   Developmental issues and psychosocial problems in childhood. In D. W. Smith (Ed.), *Introduction to clinical pediatrics.* Philadelphia: W. B. Saunders, 1977.

Hobel, C. J.   ABCs of perinatal medicine. In *Major mental handicap: Methods and costs of prevention.* Ciba Foundation Symposium 59 (new series) Amsterdam: Elsevier/Excerpta Medica/North Holland, 1978.

Hook, E.   Spontaneous deaths of fetuses with chromosomal abnormalities diagnosed prenatally. *New England Journal of Medicine,* 1978, *299,* 1036-1038.

Hook, E., and Lindso, A.   Down's syndrome in live births by single year maternal age interval in a Swedish study: Comparison with results from a New York State study. *American Journal of Human Genetics,* 1978, *30,* 19-27.

Infant Metabolic Diagnostic Laboratory.   *Infant screening* (Vol. 1). Washington, D.C.: Author, 1979.

Jackson, R. H.   Accidents in childhood. *Developmental Medicine and Child Neurology,* 1979, *21,* 534-536.

Jones, L. A.   Census-based prevalence estimates for mental retardation. *Mental Retardation,* August 1979, *17,* 199-201.

Kirk, S. A.   *Educating exceptional children.* Boston: Houghton-Mifflin, 1962.

Kitchen, W. H., Rickards, A., Ryan, M. M., McDougal, A. B., Billson, F. A., Keir, E. H., and Naylor, F. D.   A longitudinal study of very low-birthweight infants. II. Results of controlled trial of intensive care and incidence of handicaps. *Developmental Medicine and Child Neurology,* October 1979, *21,* 589-682.

Lazure, D. (Ed.).   *The CELDIC report: One million children.* Toronto: Crainford, 1970.

Lipsitt, L. P.   Critical conditions in infancy: A psychological perspective. *American Psychologist,* October 1979, *34,* 973-980.

Lowry, R. B., Jones, D. C., Renwick, D. H. G., and Trimble, B. K.   Down's syndrome in British Columbia, 1952-73: Incidence and mean maternal age. *Teratology,* 1976, *14,* 29-34.

Magary, J. F., and Eichorn, J. R. (Eds.).   *The exceptional child.* New York: Holt, Rinehart & Winston, 1964.

Magenis, R. E., Overton, J. M., Chamberlin, J., Brady, T., and Lovrien, E.   Parental origin of the extra chromosome in Down's syndrome. *Human Genetics,* 1977, *37,* 7-16.

Matejcek, Z., Dytrych, Z., and Schuller, V.   The Prague study of children born from unwanted pregnancies. *International Journal of Mental Health,* 1979, *7,* 63-74.

Mattei, J. F., Mattei, M. G., Aymes, S., and Giraud, F.   Origin of the extra-chromosome in trisomy 21. *Human Genetics,* 1979, *46,* 107-110.

McBride, M. L.   Sibling risks of anencephaly and spina bifida in British Columbia. *American Journal of Medical Genetics,* 1979, *3,* 377-387.

McDonald, A. D.   Severely retarded children in Quebec: Prevalence, causes and care. *American Journal of Mental Deficiency,* 1973, *78,* 205-215.

Medical Research Council.   An assessment of the hazards of amniocentesis. *British Journal of Obstetrics and Gynecology,* Supplement 2 1978, *85,* 1-41.

Miller, J. R.   The use of registers in morbidity studies in human populations present and future. In E. Inouye and H. Nishimura, (Eds.), *Gene-environment interaction in common diseases.* Tokyo, Japan: University of Tokyo Press, 1977.

Neale, M. D.   *Neale analysis of reading ability scale.* London: MacMillan Education Ltd., 1966.

Niswander, J. R., and Drage, J. S.   Environment and reproduction: The American study. Proceedings of the VIII World Congress of Gynecology and Obstetrics held in Mexico City, October 17-22, 1976. In L. Castalazo-Ayala and C. MacGregor (Eds.), *Excerpta Medica International Congress Series No. 412: Gynecology and Obstetrics.* New York: Elsevier/North Holland, 1977.

Office of Education, U.S Department of Health, Education and Welfare. *Progress toward a free appropriate public education.* A report to Congress on the implementation of Public Law 94-142: The Education for All Handicapped Children Act. Washington, D.C.: Author, 1979.

Office of Education, U.S. Department of Health, Education and Welfare. OE predicts 3.9 million handicapped in school by 1981. *Report on Education Research,* 1979, *11;25,* 9.

Office of Education, U.S. Department of Health, Education and Welfare. 222 million and counting: Facts about the 1980 census. *Report on Education Research,* 1979, *11;26.*

Office of Education, U.S. Department of Health, Education, and Welfare. Martin advises early education for all handicapped children. *Report on Preschool Education,* 1979, *11;25,* 8.

The President's Panel on Mental Retardation.   *Proposed program for national action to combat mental retardation.* Washington, D.C.: Superintendent of Documents, U.S. Government Printing Office, October, 1962.

Ramey, C., Stedman, D., Borders-Patterson, A., and Mengel, W.   Predicting school failure from information available at birth. *American Journal on Mental Deficiency* 1978, *82,* 525-534.

The Robert Wood Johnson Foundation.   Rural infant care program (brochure). Princeton, N.J.: Authors, 1979.

Safer, N., Burnette, J., and Hobbs, B.   Exploration 1993: The effects of future trends on services to the handicapped. *Focus on Exceptional Children,* 1979, *11,* 297-306.

Saxen, L., Klemetti, A., and Haro, A. S.   A matched-pair register for studies of selected congenital defects. *American Journal of Epidemiology,* 1974, *100,* 297-306.

Service Delivery Assessment: Education for the handicapped. Congressional Report from the Inspector General's Office, 1979.

Sigler, A. T., Lilienfeld, A. M., Cohen, B. H., and Westlake, J.E.   Parental age in Down's syndrome (Mongolism). *Journal of Pediatrics,* 1965, *67,* 631-642.

Shah, C. P., and Wong, D.   Failures in early detection of hearing impairment in preschool children. *Journal of the Division of Early Childhood,* 1979, *1,* 33-40.

Smith, D. W.   Recognizable patterns of human malformation: Genetic, embryologic, and clinical aspects. *Major problems in clinical pediatrics* (Vol. 8). Philadelphia: W. B. Saunders, 1976.

Smith, D. W.   *Introduction to clinical pediatrics.* Philadelphia: W. B. Saunders, 1977.

Smith, D. W.   *Mothering your unborn baby.* Philadelphia: W. B. Saunders, 1979.

Smith, D. W., Clarren, S., and Harvey, M. S.   Advances made in dysmorphology research. *Child Development and Mental Retardation Center Newsletter,* 1980, *5:*3.

Smith, D. W., and Simons, E. R.   Rational diagnostic evaluation of the child with mental deficiency. *American Journal of Diseases of Children,* 1975, *129,* 1285-1290.

Smith, D. W., and Wilson, A. A.   *The child with Down's syndrome.* Philadelphia: W. B. Saunders, 1973.

Soboloff, J. R.   Developmental enrichment programs (guest editorial). *Developmental Medicine and Child Neurology,* 1979, *21,* 423-424.

Sostek, A. M., Quinn, P. O., and Davitt, M. K.   Behavior, development and neurological status of premature and full-term infants with varying medical complications. In T. M. Field (Ed.), *Infants born at risk: Behavior and development.* New York: Spectrum Publications, 1979.

Statistical Abstracts of the United States 1978. Washington, D.C.: U.S. Department of Commerce, Bureau of the Census, 1978.

Stedman, D. J.   Effects of educational intervention programs on the cognitive development of young children. In *Proceedings of the symposium on developmental disabilities in the preschool child: Early identification, assessment, and intervention strategies.* Co-sponsored by the College of Medicine and Dentistry of New Jersey, Rutgers Medical School; Institute for the Study of Exceptional Children, Educational Testing Service; and the Institute for Pediatric Service, Johnson and Johnson Baby Products Co., September 6-8, 1979.

Stein, Z. A., and Susser, M. W.   Changes over time in the incidence and prevalence of mental retardation. In J. Hellmuth (Ed.), *The exceptional infant* (Vol. 2). New York: Brunner/Mazel, 1971.

Stein, Z., and Susser, M.   Epidemiologic and genetic issues in mental retardation. In N. Morton (Ed.), *Genetic epidemiology.* New York: Academic Press, 1978.

The Story of the White House Conferences on Children and Youth. Washington, D.C.: U.S. Department of Health, Education and Welfare, Social and Rehabilitation Service, Children's Bureau, 1967.

Trimble, B. K., and Baird, P. A.   Congenital anomalies of the central nervous system: Incidence in British Columbia, 1952-1972. *Teratology,* 1978a, *17,* 43-50.

Trimble, B. K., and Baird, P. A.   Maternal age and Down's syndrome: Age-specific incidence rates by single-year intervals. *American Journal of Medical Genetics,* 1978b, *2,* 1-5.

Volpe, J. J.   Perinatal hypoxic-ischemic brain injury. In *Biologic and clinical aspects of brain development.* Mead Johnson symposium on Perinatal and Developmental Medicine (Vol. 6). Evansville, Indiana: Mead Johnson and Co., 1975.

Willemsen, E.   *Understanding infancy.* San Francisco: W. H. Freeman, 1979.

3

Environments of High-Risk and Handicapped Infants

Elouise Jackson

The environment has a great impact on the growth and development of the young child during the first 3 years of life. Research and experience have led to the recognition of two factors: 1) The infant is an active being who elicits and regulates stimulation and has an effect on his or her environment (Yarrow, 1979). Probably at no other time in the child's life will so much be learned so fast as during infancy. 2) The influential effect that the environment has on the infant's development is astonishing. And Yarrow, Rubenstein, and Pederson (1975) found that particular environmental characteristics have their own unique effects on the infant's development. For example, the effect on the infant of the number of adults who interact with him or her may be quite different from the effect of the quality of the interactions. Keeping these two factors in mind,

ELOUISE JACKSON is coordinator of the graduate training program in Early Childhood Special Education at Hampton Institute, Hampton, Virginia.

this chapter examines the nature of the environments of those special infants who are handicapped and/or at high risk for developmental delays.

Because the nature of environmental impacts for high-risk infants differs so greatly in origin and complexity from that for handicapped infants, the chapter discusses each type of impact separately.

First it describes environments of infants at risk for developmental delay or mild retardation. Here, the content is limited to discussion of two key factors in the child's environment, those being the myths of inadequate childrearing practices and social and economic conditions. The impact of various social and economic factors upon the environments of infants and their families is examined, and recommendations are made for future research and social change.

The section of the chapter dealing with the environments of handicapped infants looks at the family in the context of its response to the handicapped infant and also examines the effects of the institutional environment on the infant's growth and development. For both infant settings recommendations are made.

THE HOME ENVIRONMENTS OF INFANTS AT RISK

Used here, the term *infants at risk* refers to those youngsters who because of environmental factors may be prone to developmental delay, mild retardation, or other handicapping conditions. The focus is on infants from low-income families because past and present research efforts have concentrated on these children.

Over the past two and a half decades there has been increased emphasis in research on examining different family environments in an attempt to understand more clearly their natures and the differences in childrearing practices from one to another. The most recent findings indicate that observed differences are related to the degree to which the caretaker directly participates in activities with the child, encourages the child's participation in a variety of activities, provides space and materials for the child, and extends the child's learning through cueing in on the child's thoughts and perspectives (Ramey, Mills, Campbell, and O'Brien, 1975; Watts, Halfar, and Chan, 1974).

Other studies of home environments have concentrated on the effects of different childrearing practices on cognitive development. In these studies, researchers generally have compared cultural and ethnic minority groups to the white population, with the measure of effectiveness of childrearing practices the value system of the white American middle class. Although the studies have indicated that there are differences in childrearing practices, they have a major flaw: they rest on the assumption that "differences" in childrearing practices of poor and minority groups are "detriments" and lead to deficits in children's intellectual skills, an assumption that itself is not supported by research (Dukes, 1976; Dill, 1976). Granger and Young (1976) argue that causal links between specific parenting behaviors and optimum development are undetermined.

Dukes reviewed research on childrearing practices and cognitive development. She reported that efforts to substantiate cognitive differences among infants of various socioeconomic groups (Bayley, 1965; Golden and Birns, 1968; Knobloch and Pasamanick, 1960) upheld no differences during the first 2 years of life, once factors such as birth complications, poor nutrition, and health conditions were ruled out—factors that go beyond childrearing practices to the family's overall position in society.

Although data have not borne out an association between infant care practices, values of the parents, and the cognitive development of children, the assumption that such an association exists resulted in the present day myth regarding the inadequacy of the childrearing practices of poor and minority group parents. This myth has had far reaching effects on black parents especially, since most studies have involved black families.

With respect to the impact of the myth of inadequate childrearing practices on poor and minority families, several outcomes can be cited. First, the myth has resulted in a misplaced focus on the child and family as elements which foster pathogenic retardation. Second, because of assumptions made concerning low-income families, these families are, more often than not, viewed and treated as the inferior element of the American society. And third, in response to assumptions made about these families, various dynamics of the American social stratification system work to keep an inordinate number of these families at the bottom of the economic ladder, thus limiting their chances for a better life.

Another area of concern is related to the impact of certain social and economic factors on the environments of infants at risk and their families. When examining the qualitative level of environment, consideration must be given to the prevailing system of social stratification. This entails looking critically at the nature of existing organizations, institutions, and functions. Within the American society, observations of the home environments of infants at risk must consider the differentiation of economic resources, occupational prestige, educational opportunity, and political power (Dill, 1976). Within this complex microcosm, poor families and those of ethnic minority origin struggle to survive at the lower rungs of society. It is this group of people who are more likely to suffer. Yet, instead of children's experiences being defined in relation to their cultural setting, desirable norms of childrearing and child behavior are imposed by the dominant society.

The imposition of such norms might appear constructive if the valued behavior could be easily attained. But, the fact is that although what is "good, appropriate, and desirable" is defined, for many families these goals can apparently only be reached with drastic economic and educational status changes. This is not to say that economic privations imply an impoverished culture. Indeed, low-income parents often realize educational goals for themselves and their children. Nonetheless, certain groups of parents and children often do not have the freedom to change their life circumstances, even with the hope and desire to do so (Dill, 1976).

Aside from low birthweight, delivery complications, prematurity, and other occurrences, principal factors that do impair children's functioning are poverty, oppression, and racism (Mack, 1979; Myers, 1979), conditions that have been overlooked consistently in all too many research efforts. These conditions have particular relevance for black people in America because black families have been the focus of most comparative research studies on childrearing practices—studies that have generated the myth of low socioeconomic status inadequacies in childrearing practices.

The current findings on poverty, oppression, and racism in America have particular implications for blacks. Jordan (1980) reported that during the 1970s black people suffered from poverty, unemployment, inadequate services, and the rest of the litany of social ills. At the same time they were plagued by the myth of black progress. The myth is reflected in job, income, education, and housing situations. Jordan indicated that the black unemployment rate is higher than when the *Brown v. Board of Education* decision was passed in 1954 ruling separate but equal facilities unconstitutional. Furthermore, blacks are still twice as likely as whites to be in low-paying, low-skilled jobs. A third of black families are under the government's poverty levels, three times the number of whites at this level, and the majority of blacks earn less than the government says is necessary for a minimum adequate living standard.

In the area of education, more children are attending racially isolated schools today than in 1964. Even though more blacks are attending college, the majority are enrolled in 2-year community colleges, whereas the majority of whites are in 4-year schools and universities that place them in career ladders denied to blacks.

There has been some progress in the area of housing. Jordan reported that some blacks are even living in suburbs where the majority of the residents are white. But one out of five black families lives in housing declared physically deficient by the government.

These facts alone would indicate why advocating the childrearing practices of white middle-class parents is unrealistic for poor and minority group families. The approach of past research efforts has resulted in the current thinking about inadequate childrearing practices. This has in turn given way to the belief in inherent pathogenic retardation as a product of the child and his or her parents. In light of current research findings and the prevailing system of social stratification, new directions must be taken in order to study more accurately and objectively factors in the environments of infants at risk that are affecting their development.

Recommendations for Research and Social Change

Directions for Future Research   The myths concerning the effectiveness of childrearing practices of poor and minority group parents stem to a great extent from the neglect of an approach crucial to research, that is, cross-cultural research. With this methodological approach, factors related to childrearing practices can be examined more objectively. Dukes (1976) discusses five of these factors, which she terms *ecological variables of socialization.*

Duke's first ecological variable is household composition. She states that the number of socializing agents in a family contributes to different childrearing techniques and that the amount and quality of interactions may differ substantially. Although it has been postulated that the lack of one or both parents causes serious cognitive and affective deficits in the child and that multiple mothering is detrimental as well, several investigators (Murdock, 1957; Munroe and Munroe, 1975; Whiting, Child, and Lambert, 1966) have shown, in cross-cultural studies, that only about one-fourth of the world's cultures utilize the nuclear family model.

A second variable of socialization open to cross-cultural research is role status. What makes a person influential in a family and in the life of a child may and does vary across cultural groups. The role status of the persons a child interacts with most will affect the child's cognitive and social behavior.

A third socialization variable is community setting. Of particular interest here is the density of the neighborhood and the type of households. These factors determine the mobility of the child, the available resources, and the child's leisure activities. Contingent upon each of these factors is the type and quality of learning experiences to which the child is exposed. The childrearing techniques used by the parents most likely will be consistent with the demands of the community setting so that the child is equipped with the behaviors necessary for adapting to the environment. Thus, the childrearing practices of middle-income parents would have to be quite different from those of low-income parents.

A fourth variable of socialization is climate and geographic location. The family activities affected by this variable include the type of activities the family can engage in, the type of clothing worn, the health and physical well-being of the community residents and the adaptive survival techniques utilized. Each of these environmental factors affects the socialization values and methods used by parents in childrearing.

A fifth variable of socialization that affects childrearing practices is the economic base of a given group. Along with family income, other important aspects of one's economic base are maternal resources available within the home, community goods and services available, occupational demands, the spacing of children, and medical and nutritional resources. The degree to which each of these factors affects the family will determine the methods of childrearing practices used.

After reviewing each of these variables, Dukes concluded that researchers have relied completely upon biased measures (e.g., middle-class value systems) in their assertions that "deficits" characterize the low-income family structure. There appears to have been disregard for differences in conditions and circumstances surrounding the lifestyle of the children. Dill (1976) draws similar conclusions after considering these and related socialization variables.

Initiating more research based on a holistic view of what takes place within the environments of infants can provide information that begins to account for differences in developmental outcomes. The involvement of more professionals who represent the various cultures and groups in question can also strengthen the nature of the information gathered.

Recommendations for Social Change   Jordan's (1980) review of current circumstances regarding job, income, education, and housing for blacks in America provides a picture of the environment for minority and racial groups in America. For the infant at risk for developmental delay, or mild retardation, working to combat those societal elements that affect the family negatively (i.e., racism and poverty), and thus the infant's immediate environment, would enhance the opportunity for increased developmental potential.

Some progress has been made to combat these negative societal elements, but there is still much to be done. Barriers that prevent minorities from having accessibility, opportunity, power, and respect have to be overcome. Second, in labor, education, housing, and other basic areas, minorities must have opportunities for productive, meaningful participation. Finally, the task at hand is to rescue those families and children whose present circumstances condemn them to an uncertain fate. "What matters is not to know the world but to change it" (Fanon, 1969, p. 54).

THE ENVIRONMENTS OF HANDICAPPED INFANTS

For the handicapped infant there are two major environments: the family and the institution. Within the family milieu, this section of the chapter examines parent and family reactions to the birth of a handicapped child and patterns of interactions among family members. It also discusses the decision of placement outside the home and makes recommendations for examining the family environment. Later, the effects of institutionalization on the development of handicapped infants is discussed and recommendations made for modifying the institutional environment.

The Family Context

The reader is reminded that little has been done in studying the reactions of minority parents and families to the birth of a handicapped child. Studies describing parental reactions can be traced directly to studies of Anglo-American parents; much of the data was obtained from observing, examining, and reporting on the activities of nonminority parents (Marion, 1980). Thus, care should be taken in generalizing the following information to all groups of people.

Parent and Family Reactions to a Handicapped Child   The course of parenthood is a developmental process. It is influenced by the characteristics of the child; first by the child's appearance, then by his or her responses. The process takes time to develop, with parents gradually falling in love with their infant. The enjoyment of this process may be greatly altered by the presence of a handicapped child.

Solnit and Provence (1979) state that prospective parents go through a psychological process in which they examine and reexamine their fantasies about the unborn child. With the birth of the child and the first interactions of the child with the parents, the cycle is complete. At this time, the parents normally complete working through the discrepancies between their fantasies and the realities of the child. However, with the birth of a handicapped infant, parents frequently respond with depressive reactions, defensiveness, and resentment.

MacKeith (1973) suggests six types of feelings that parents may experience and which may be accompanied by various behavior patterns. Table 1, a synopsis of MacKeith's work, summarizes these feelings and behavior patterns.

Other compensatory responses that parents may experience are reported by Coda and Lubin (1973). They state that parents may experience responses of denial or of overacceptance—reactions that may prevent the parents from recognizing their own capabilities or the child's potential abilities, which can retard progress.

Several authors have cited various factors that influence the parent or family reaction to a handicapped child (Coda and Lubin, 1973; MacKeith, 1973; Solnit and Stark, 1977). These factors include the culture from which the parents come; the past experiences of the parents and their relatives; the understanding, acceptance, and attitudes of family

Table 1.   Reactions to a handicapped child: parental feelings and behavior patterns

Feelings of parents	Resulting behavior patterns
1. a. Desire to protect the helpless infant b. Revulsion at the abnormal	

2. Feelings of inadequacy at
  a. reproduction
 	
  b. childrearing
	2. a. General anxiety, marital tension and lack of self-confidence in daily activities
	
	  b. Feelings of inadequacy at childrearing may undermine the competence of parents at childrearing

3. Bereavement with its accompanying emotions of
  a. anger
  b. grief
  c. adjustment
	3. a. Anger may present itself as aggression towards the obstetrician or pediatrician
	
	  b. Grief may present itself as depression
	  c. Adjustment usually occurs if given time

4. Shock and surprise at what has happened	4. Shock may lead to disbelief of what has happened, causing the parents to "shop around" for a doctor who will give hope.
5. Guilt of personal responsibility for something that has gone wrong. There may also be overtones of conscience that the event may be morally wrong.	5. Feelings of guilt may cause behavior of depression or even apathetic behavior.
6. Feelings of embarrassment	6. Embarrassment may lead parents to avoid social contacts.

members; parents' values; the child's particular handicap and its severity; and whether the handicap is overt at birth. Given the influence of these factors, a parent or family's reactions may take many forms.

After taking a closer look at parental reactions, Marion (1980) concluded that, indeed, the culture from which a parent comes influences his or her reactions. One study (Marion and McCaslin, 1979) found that minority families did not experience the same strong emotional feelings as those experienced by nonminority parents to the birth of the handicapped child (Marion, 1980). This observation is supported by a study conducted by Luderus (1977). The Marion and McCaslin findings show that frequently parents of culturally diverse handicapped children did not express shock, disbelief, sorrow, and other associated feelings of guilt and depression in relation to the child. Feelings of protection and acceptance were the most common in Mexican-American and black families, suggesting that much research has overlooked the strengths of minority families, the feelings of acceptance and security within them, and the role of religion in their lives.

Although a number of parental and family reactions have been identified, most in the context of nonminority families, there appears to be three life milestones about which feelings and behaviors may intensify. These are 1) the age of public school entry for the child: parents are concerned as to whether or not the child can enter an ordinary school, 2) the point when the young adult should become employed: parents wonder if the person will be independent, and 3) the time when the handicapped adult will have to survive alone: parents are concerned if the person will be able to manage when they are no longer living (MacKeith, 1973).

Patterns of Interactions among Family Members   Family patterns of interaction established before the birth of a handicapped child largely determine the impact of the family on the child, and conversely, the effect of the child on the family. The presence of the handicapped child, though, can result in role distortions. Coda and Lubin (1973) describe four types of role distortions, the first of which is that of an excessively strong mother/child tie. This type of situation may tend toward mother/child separation anxiety. The fact that the child is handicapped may bring about a more intense mother/child relationship than would have otherwise developed.

A second type of role distortion is characterized by a husband and wife being unable to expand their marital roles to meet the needs of the handicapped infant. The resulting situation is one in which the child is viewed as an interference. The child tends to be isolated and withdrawn or may relate to the parents on a superficial level. In some instances, out-of-the-home placement may be sought.

A third distortion pattern that may occur is that of an excessively strong family tie. In this type of situation the child may not be allowed to participate in opportunities that would enhance development. The parents may see these investments as impingement upon the family unit unless the family as a whole can participate. This type of family togetherness usually fosters dependence rather than independence.

The fourth pattern of role distortion is that of an excessive emphasis on independence. The handicapped child may be left to his or her own resources before really ready to manage alone.

The nature of parent and family interactions with the presence of a handicapped child depends, of course, on the type of handicap the child has as well as its severity. Another important influence is whether or not the handicapped child is a second or third child where the older children are normal. Solnit and Stark (1977) state that the impact may be somewhat less if normal children preceded the birth of the handicapped child. The impact is also less if the handicap is not present or detected at birth but is gradually detected during the second or third year of life.

Home or Alternative Placement   For some parents, placing a child outside of the home is a real alternative. But for others, the decision may not even be a consideration. For those who are facing the decision, it is important to work with them slowly, keeping all possible alternatives open. The most appropriate alternative may not be immediately evident, and if possible any action during the early decision stages should be left open-ended (MacKeith, 1973).

MacKeith sees three situations in which long-term placement other than in the home may be best. One is when another placement would provide better care and education than the home. The other is when another person in the home would suffer as a result of the handicapped person's presence. Another instance when outside placement may be appropriate is when lack of communication between family members and the child becomes so severe that it will eventually lead to the exclusion of the child from the family. Also, as Coda and Lubin (1973) suggest, outside placement may be an alternative when local services are not available.

Depending upon the circumstances of the family and the stresses it may face, temporary care outside the home may be the best arrangement. When available in the community or nearby, respite care for brief periods of time may be helpful. Also, for children with severe multiple handicaps, brief periods of hospitalization may be necessary. Today, because of the increased interest in early intervention and a surge in the number of programs, community-based services are more readily available to families. Several such programs are described in Chapter 9.

Recommendations for Examining the Family Context

Information is needed regarding the reactions to handicapped children of parents and families representing a wide diversity of cultural and ethnic backgrounds, including the dominant culture, so as to design and implement programs that are even more appropriate to the populations they serve. To be most useful, research with minority families should take into account their strengths, as well as any weaknesses, and the role of religion in family interaction.

Nature of the Institutional Environment

For some families, and for those handicapped infants who are given up for adoption at birth, institutional placement is the ultimate environment. Insight into the effects of that environment on the development of handicapped infants comes from studies in which institutionalized handicapped and nonhandicapped infants have been observed. Only a few such studies have been conducted however, and research specific to minority populations appears to be lacking.

Characteristic of an institutional environment is its lack of individualization. Infants are congregated into residential groups larger than those typically found in the home; the autonomy of the children is reduced with feeding, diapering, cuddling, and sleeping on a schedule that is almost exclusively externally determined; typically, there are too few adults assigned to care for a large number of infants; little variety in cognitive and affective stimulation is available (Page and Garwood, 1979; Provence and Lipton, 1962; Wolfensberger, 1971). These problems are compounded by lack of a specific maternal figure attuned to the individual child's needs.

Today, there appears to be a decrease in the number of youngsters placed in institutions for care, even among the severely and profoundly handicapped population. This decrease is partly attributable to a reduction in the birth rate, but also to improvement in preventive health services and to legislation and litigation supporting the provision of more appropriate services for the handicapped (Wolfensberger, 1971). However, many infants still are placed in institutions, and attention should be given to improving their environments. The reader is referred to the work of Provence and Lipton, 1962; and Stedman and Eichorn, 1964.

Effects of the Institutional Environment   Infants in institutions are adversely affected by lack of a parent caretaker. The problem is less one of nurturing than it is of the absence of regular stimulation. Upon initial placement in the institution, infants appear to progress developmentally the same as infants in traditional nuclear families. But about the third or fourth month of life, development begins to show delay. Generally, the infants experience little variety in cognitive and affective stimulation, have little opportunity to explore the environment, and experience little personalized interaction with an adult caretaker (Page and Garwood, 1979; Provence and Lipton, 1962).

In a study of institutionalized infants in which their development during the first year of life was compared to that of infants living in a family setting, Provence and Lipton (1962) found striking results. From the onset, the infants selected for both groups were free from congenital handicaps, neurological disorders, and acute or chronic illness. Those included in the study were admitted to the institution under 3 weeks of age. The study found that at the end of the first year of life the institutionalized infants showed a discrepancy between the maturation of the motor system and its use in adapting to the environment. As early as the second month, the infants began to show diminished output of vocalization in response to people; at the end of the first year, the retardation of all forms of communication was striking. The infants also seemed to have low interest in all aspects of the environment, even in themselves. At the end of the first year of life, the basic processes of learning as well as the mastery of developmental tasks were seriously disturbed and distorted in the institutionalized infant.

With the handicapped infant who may initially make minimal, or in some cases, no attempt to extract information from his or her environment, there is almost no potential for development in an institution. The failure of Down's syndrome infants to develop in an institution is exemplified by the research of Stedman and Eichorn (1964). The purpose of their research was not to study institutionalization but rather to explore the course of mental, motor, and physical development of a sample of healthy Down's infants. The 20 selected for the study were free from other severe physical problems. Ten of the infants were wards of a state hospital admitted at from 1 to 4½ months of age, and 10 children resided at home. At the time of the study, all the children ranged from 17 to 37 months of age. (The institutional environment of the infants was somewhat richer than typical institutions for the mentally retarded, as a higher staff/child ratio existed.)

When both groups of children were assessed at about 2 years of age, the home-reared group scored significantly higher on both mental and social scales. The authors pointed out that the hospital group was most retarded in language and in skills for manipulating small objects, apparently because of a lack of opportunities for practicing these behaviors. The mean difference on the motor test favored the home-reared group, but results were not significant.

That prolonged stay in an institution has a detrimental effect on the infant virtually goes without saying. For it is during the infancy period that the child acquires important competencies upon which later learning is dependent. When these basic behaviors and skills are thwarted and distorted from the beginning, prolonged deprivation can only mean extreme regression.

Recommendations for Environmental Change   A change in the environment of an institutionalized infant can mean greater hope for the child's development. Such was the case for the infants in a study conducted by Provence and Lipton (1962). When the institutionalized infants were given the benefit of a stimulating and nurturing environment by means of good maternal care and family life environment, they made dramatic gains. Similar results were also found in the work of Skeels and Dye (1939).

The key to facilitating the development of infants in institutions as well as other environments seems to be distinctive nurturing and stimulating care. If institutional placement has to be an option, the environment should be modified to promote the child's development. As Provence and Lipton (1962) state, this can be done by: 1) increasing the total number of persons available to care directly for the infants, 2) increasing the amount of time devoted to the care of each child; and 3) decreasing the number of different individuals caring for the child.

CONCLUDING REMARKS

This chapter attempted to examine environmental issues related to two groups of infants, those at risk for developmental delay, mild retardation, or handicapping conditions, and those who are handicapped. Major gaps exist in the information base on minority populations. Thus, recommendations for future direction were provided with regard to issues concerning minority populations, as well as environmental issues in general.

The importance of facilitating the development of infants at risk and those who are handicapped remains an area of concern. It is hoped that this chapter will serve to strengthen that concern and focus further advancement in the field.

REFERENCES

Bayley, N.   Comparisons of mental and motor test scores for ages 1-15 months by sex, birth order, race, geographical location and education of parents. *Child Development,* 1965, *36,* 370-411.

Coda, E. J., and Lubin, G. I.   Some special problems and guidance needs of families with handicapped children. In R. Friedman (Ed.), *Family roots of school learning and behavior disorders.* Springfield, Ill.: Charles C Thomas Publisher, 1973.

Dill, J. R.   Toward a developmental theory of the inner-city child. In R. C. Granger and J. C. Young (Eds.), *Demythologizing the inner-city child.* Washington, D.C.: The National Association for the Education of Young Children, 1976.

Dukes, P. J.   The effects of early childrearing practices on the cognitive development of infants. In R. C. Granger and J. C. Young, (Eds.), *Demythologizing the Inner-City Child.* Washington, D.C.: The National Association for the Education of Young Children, 1976.

Fanon, F.   *Toward the African revolution.* (Translated by G. H. Chevalier,) New York: Grove Press, 1969.

Golden, M., and Birns, B.   Social class and cognitive development in infancy. *Merrill-Palmer Quarterly,* 1968, *14,* 139-149.

Granger, R. C., and Young, J. C.   *Demythologizing the inner-city child.* Washington, D.C.: The National Association for the Education of Young Children, 1976.

Jordan, V. E.   The issue of black equality will exert a powerful influence over the next 10 years. *Public Relations Journal,* 1980, *36,* 26-31.

Knobloch, H., and Pasamanick, B.   Environmental factors affecting human development before and after birth. *Pediatrics,* 1960, *26,* 210-218.

Luderus, E.   *Family environment characteristics of Mexican-American families of handicapped and nonhandicapped preschool children.* Unpublished doctoral dissertation, University of Texas, 1977.

Mack, C. C.   Old assumptions and new packages: Racism, educational models, and black children. In D.W. Hewes (Ed.), *Administration: Making programs work for children and families.* Washington, D.C.: National Association for the Education of Young Children, 1979.

MacKeith, R.   Parental reactions and responses to a handicapped child. In F. Richardson (Ed.), *Brain and Intelligence.* Hyattsville, Md.: National Education Press, 1973.

Marion, R. L.   Communicating with parents of culturally diverse exceptional children. *Exceptional Children,* May 1980, *46,* 616-623.

Marion, R. L., and McCaslin, T.   *Parent counseling of minority parents in a genetic setting.* Unpublished manuscript, University of Texas, 1979.

Munroe, R. L., and Munroe, R. H.   *Cross-cultural human development.* Monterey, Calif.: Brooks/Cole Publishing Co., 1975.

Murdock, G. P.   Anthropology as a comparative science. *Behavioral Science,* 1957, *2,* 249-254.

Myers, H. F.   Mental health and the black child: The manufacture of incompetence. *Young Children,* 1979, *34,* 25-31.

Page, D., and Garwood, S. G.   Theoretical issues in social development. In S. G. Garwood, (Ed.), *Educating young handicapped children: A developmental approach.* Germantown, Md.: Aspen Systems Corporation, 1979.

Provence, S., and Lipton, R. C.   *Infants in institutions.* New York: International Universities Press, 1962.

Ramey, C. T., Mills, P., Campbell, F.A., and O'Brien, C.   Infant's home environments: A comparison of high risk families and families from the general population. *American Journal on Mental Deficiency,* 1975, *80,* 40-42.

Skeels, H. M., and Dye, H. B.   A study of the effects of differential stimulation on mentally retarded children. *Convention Proceedings of the American Association on Mental Deficiency,* 1939, *44,* 114-136.

Solnit, A. J., and Provence, S.   Vulnerability and risk in early childhood. In J. O. Osofsky (Ed.), *Handbook of infant development.* New York: Wiley, 1979.

Solnit, A. J., and Stark, M. H.   Mourning and the birth of a defective child. In A. J. Solnit (Ed.), *Physical illness and handicap in childhood.* New Haven, Conn.: Yale University Press, 1977.

Stedman, D. J., and Eichorn, D. A.   Comparison of the growth and development of institutionalized and home-reared mongoloids during infancy and early childhood. *American Journal on Mental Deficiency,* 1964, *69,* 391-401.

Watts, J., Halfar, C., and Chan, I.   Environment, experience and intellectual development of young children in home care. *American Journal of Orthopsychiatry,* 1974, *44,* 773-781.

Whiting, J. W. M., Child, I. L., and Lambert, W. W.   *Field guide for study of socialization.* New York: Wiley, 1966.

Wolfensberger, W.   Will there always be an institution? I. The impact of epidemiological trends. *Mental Retardation,* 1971, *9,* 14-20.

Yarrow, L. J.   Historical perspectives and future directions in infant development. In J. D. Osofsky (Ed.), *Handbook of infant development.* New York: Wiley, 1979.

Yarrow, L. J., Rubenstein, J. L., and Pedersen, F. A.   *Infant and environment.* New York: Wiley, Halsted Press, 1975.

4

Methods for the Identification of High-Risk and Handicapped Infants

Keith G. Scott and Anne E. Hogan

The basic rationale for identifying the infant who is at risk or handicapped is to make intervention programs available so that the child's condition does not significantly interfere with normal progress in school. If a disease state or physical anomaly makes this goal difficult to achieve, the ambition instead is to maximize the child's potential. For either goal, identification is useful only to the extent that it can lead to prescriptive programs of intervention. If such programs are not available, the process is inevitably wasteful, and, because children are labeled (Hobbs, 1975; Scott, 1978), it may be positively harmful. Identification and intervention must be linked: programs that have been developed only to include identification should not be implemented without appropriate referral mechanisms.

KEITH G. SCOTT is professor of pediatrics and psychology and coordinator of research at the Mailman Center for Child Development, the University of Miami, Miami, Florida.

ANNE E. HOGAN is a research assistant at the Mailman Center for Child Development, the University of Miami, Miami, Florida.

IDENTIFICATION OF CHILDREN WITH DIFFERENT DISABILITIES

Identification of handicapped infants may be thought of as presenting three main classes of problems: identifying clear disabilities, identifying hidden handicaps, and identifying high-risk conditions.

Identifying Children with Clear Disabilities

Infants such as those with cranial facial anomalies or gross perceptual or physical disorders are easily identified by any competent medical doctor, psychologist, or educator. A large proportion, perhaps two-thirds of such children, will be identified by the neonatologist in the first days of life. Of the remaining one-third, the majority will come to a pediatrician's attention before their first birthday. On the face of it, there would seem to be no problem of identification for purposes of special education. However, both medical practitioners and parents frequently are unaware of the mandated programs available to such developmentally disabled children, and the children frequently are without appropriate services. Some states are currently instituting birth defect registers in an attempt to ensure that service is available to infants and their parents continuously from a very early age. Without such registers, which have been used in other countries, children in need of services drop out of sight with disturbing regularity. Identifying or locating them remains a problem.

Identifying Children with Hidden Handicaps

Underlying many attempts to identify children with mild handicaps is the model suggesting that infants destined to become, for example, learning disabled have hidden characteristics or ability patterns that will later manifest themselves. Early detection and identification in these cases consists of detecting the latent conditions and instituting compensatory educational programs. Appealing as this model is, in most instances little is known about the developmental origins in infancy of handicapping conditions, and valid measures that will detect these latent traits are not yet available. Indeed, even prediction of intelligence from infant tests such as the Brazelton Neonatal Scale, the Bayley Scale, and others is so poor as to be clinically useless. Professionals cannot at this time reliably identify infants or preschool children who will later have learning disabilities.

Some other hidden handicaps can be detected, however. Sensory handicaps of audition and vision can be assessed reliably in the first few years of life. Appropriate prosthetic devices, such as hearing aids and glasses, can be prescribed or, if necessary, special programs of intervention instituted.

Identifying High-Risk Children

The concept of risk for a handicapping condition has recently received wide attention in the literature related to infancy. The idea is that certain characteristics or experiences in a child's life are precursors of subsequent problems, not in all, but in many cases. Hence, all at-risk individuals should be tracked and perhaps treated as part of a preventive program. The concept is based on medical models for health problems that have manageable factors that place the individual at elevated risk. For example, heart disease is a problem for which two factors, high blood pressure and smoking, have been identified as placing an adult at increased risk. These risk factors can be detected and modified. It may be possible to identify some factors that both place a child at elevated risk for a learning problem and are amenable to intervention.

The Case for Intervention Following Early Identification

The aim of early identification is to detect a condition and treat it as soon as possible. In medicine the policy of treating a disease before it becomes acute is standard practice—in education, early intervention is only now becoming widely adopted. There are two main arguments for intervening early.

The first argument is based on the widely held belief that there are periods early in a child's life when certain things are more readily learned. The first 4 years of life have been called a critical period for language learning and cognitive development (Hunt, 1961). Also, the first few hours of life have been called critically sensitive for mother/infant bonding (Klaus et al., 1972). Clarke and Clarke (1976) offer a detailed review of the hypothesis, and the reader is referred to this source. The evidence for either critical periods or even periods of critical sensitivity is exceedingly weak, however. Thus, the idea that *primary* prevention of handicapping conditions may occur by mounting interventions at certain critical ages or stages must be rejected as unfounded.

The second argument for early identification and intervention is much more straightforward: if the child does not learn a skill at an age-appropriate point in development, then he or she will not only have to acquire the missing skill, but also will have to catch up with age mates who are steadily adding to their knowledge base. That is, the child who has had difficulty learning will have to learn faster than his normal age mates to catch up with the moving target their performance provides. The desirability of preventing significant educational or attainment delays is thus almost self-evident.

Once a child is suffering from a significant delay in attainment, the task of accelerating his or her development is sometimes called *secondary prevention.* It differs from *primary prevention,* where the aim is to prevent the delay from becoming manifest at all.

THE MAJOR METHODS OF IDENTIFICATION

There are three major methods of identification: casefinding and referral, the use of risk registers, and screening. A comprehensive program might use all three methods, or concentrate on just one. Whichever method is used, however, there are at least three stages in the identification process:

1. *Locating*   The initial, and in some cases most difficult stage in identification is to obtain the name and address or telephone number of the child who is potentially in need of services.
2. *Initial screening*   This step involves some initial collection of information about the child to see if he or she is an appropriate candidate for further diagnostic services. This step should eliminate the false positive—the child who actually does not have a problem—as well as the child who for some reason is not eligible for intervention.
3. *Diagnosis and evaluation*   This step involves a more complete workup to confirm initial impressions from screening. It should both confirm the positive identification and provide a prescriptive plan for the child, including placement in an intervention program. Depending upon the relationship between the diagnostic and intervention programs, this stage might also include preparing the child's individual education plan. As its minimum, it should include a psychoeducational and medical component with referrals for social services and sensory evaluations. If costs are to be contained, a process that requires a battery of tests by a team for every child should be avoided.

Case Finding and Referral

There are four primary sources of referrals: primary health care providers, agencies or clinics, social services programs, and the community.

Primary Health Care Referral   This has traditionally been the major method of identifying handicapped infants. The model is basically the same as that used in medical practice where a generalist refers patients to specialists as needed.

Primary health care professionals may be neonatologists, pediatricians, or general medical practitioners. These professionals are so effective in identifying children with severe disabilities, that the majority, in many instances 95 percent, of children with severe or profound mental retardation are identified before they are 1 year old. Since both state and federal programs only recently have encouraged services for children below 3 years of age, however, many medical practitioners are not aware of available services. Personal contact of educational service staff, including visits to hospitals by senior personnel, is essential for a referral pattern to develop.

Children who will later develop mild handicaps represent a different problem. Primary health care professionals are unlikely to detect their developmental delays unless parents call attention to them. The pediatrician's brief contact with a child while conducting routine physicals and immunizations is not enough time to collect significant developmental information. Referrals from primary health care providers are thus generally restricted, usually occurring during infancy for children with severe handicaps.

Agency or Clinic Referral   Most communities have agencies and clinics that are concerned with categorical problems such as drug abuse, or special population problems such as those associated with migrant farm workers. Following systematic contacts with the staff, such clinics can provide a routine method of identification. However, the number of such referrals will be limited because select populations are involved. They also tend to detect children from families whose problems go beyond those caused by having a handicapped child. The family that is "just making it" with a handicapped child may receive little attention—and the child will not be identified. That is, such agencies tend to operate on a crisis intervention model rather than a maintenance model. This is typically due to inadequate funding in the face of massive problems.

Social Service Program Referral   Some communities provide home visits, usually by public health nurses or social workers. The professionals will routinely make one or more calls at the home of a newborn infant during the first few months of life. These community service personnel are a significant resource for identifying infants who may be developmentally delayed and/or in an environment that places them at high social risk because of relative neglect or outright abuse. The use of such referrals in creating registers of social risk has been little explored in the literature.

Community Referral   By far the most successful method of identification is community referral through public contact via the media, advertising, direct mail, telephone surveys, or letters sent home with school-age children. This method of identification produces contacts with the parents of children who are delayed, socially maladjusted, or potentially learning disabled. It relies on the concerned interest of friends and family, and other individuals who have relatively extended contact with the child. Without this type of identification, most programs would locate only a minority of cases (Zehrbach, 1975).

Risk Register

The risk register is based on a model with some generally "invisible" condition that places the infant at highly inflated levels of risk for a handicap. This factor could have three major sources: 1) congenital or family history of specific disorders, such as deafness (genetic risk), 2) events that include complications during pregnancy or delivery that might produce latent or manifest birth defects (neonatal risk), and 3) psychosocial problems, such as environmental deprivation, neglect, or abuse (social risk).

On the basis of such factors, the ambition is to create a "register of risk" and thus, by screening or following a subsection of the population, to detect a major proportion of children who may later have handicapping conditions. Thus, the model defines the risk factor as a latent or invisible handicap in some large percentage of children who are included in a register.

Risk registers, in practice, have proven useful, but they are insufficiently powerful to lead to the identification of most children with handicaps. In the case of neonatal risk, the literature is reviewed in detail elsewhere (Scott and Massi, 1979). In general, as the risk factors become better specified, the proportion of listed children who are likely to have a handicap increases sharply. However, this highly selected at-risk population becomes a smaller segment of the total population and represents only a minority of all handicapped children.

For example, if a risk register is defined by low birth weight (say 1,500 grams), and the presence of neonatal complications such as respiratory distress, perhaps one-third of the infants listed in the register would develop some problem needing special educational intervention. However, the group listed on the register would be less than 1 percent of all births. Such a register would detect only a small proportion of all children who are handicapped.

The risk register is valuable as an indicator of infants and children who need longitudinal follow-up and periodic development evaluations however. Programs of preventive intervention may enroll children who are at risk in the full knowledge that for only some of them will the services be essential in preventing later problems. When this can be done without labeling or categorizing the children, a genuine educational program is created that fits the primary prevention model. If research in the future produces techniques of measurement that allow latent invisible risk factors to become manifest and directly measurable, risk registers will be even more effective.

The Screening Model

The screening model differs from the risk model in that it presumes the symptoms of a handicap can be detected and measured. The essence of screening is to apply relatively quick tests that will sort out those who probably have a handicap from those who do not. The children identified as probably handicapped by the screening test are then referred for a complete diagnosis and evaluation. This is essential to both confirm the results of the screening and to arrive at an appropriate preventive educational plan. Screening is thus a systematic tool in a plan of secondary prevention that aims at identifying handicaps early then promptly intervening to minimize any long-term undesirable consequences.

A general consideration of criteria for pediatric screening is presented by Frankenburg and Camp (1975). In the case of screening for psychoeducational disorders, a number of criteria are of particular importance.

1. The handicapping condition should be well described and specific enough so that a set of characteristics can be presented. Vague categories, such as learning disabled or dyslexic, are rarely adequate.
2. Tests or measures of demonstrated reliability and predictive power must be available. Their lack is a critical flaw in most screening programs.
3. There must be available intervention that is validated by research and demonstration programs.
4. Procedures must be adequate in the follow-up phases of a program so that handicapped children will receive services. This means more than just advising on availability of services. Parents must be made aware of the advantages of the program and encouraged to participate.
5. The use of categorical labels and any other potential stigmatizations should be avoided.
6. The screening and detection must be socially acceptable in the community where they are employed.
7. The programmatic cost of screening must be kept in balance with the cost of service delivery following identification.

COSTS ASSOCIATED WITH THE IDENTIFICATION MODELS

In the detection of a handicapping condition, it is useful to consider the two different kinds of cost. The first is the human cost of making errors of identification. The second is the cost in monetary terms of correctly identifying a child who is or will become handicapped.

The Human Costs: Errors of Identification

At one time, errors of labeling children were not regarded as serious based on the argument that intervention, even if not needed, would do no harm. This position is highly suspect in view of more recent information that the act of classifying or labeling may have consequences in itself (Hobbs, 1975).

The problem of making correct judgments versus errors of identification is traditionally considered in terms of the matrix in Figure 1.

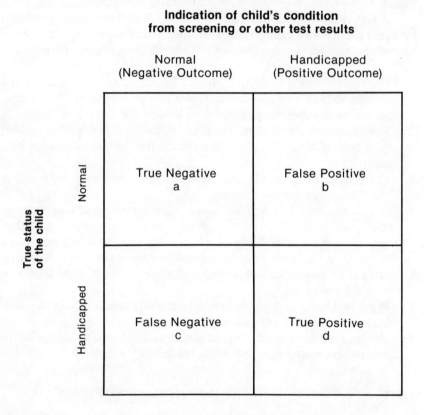

Figure 1.   The relationship between the status of an infant as indicated by a test and the infant's true status. The matrix shows the possibilities for appropriate and inappropriate identification.

Following medical usage, a screening test that indicates a patient may have a disease is said to be a positive test. One indicating the patient does not is called a negative test. Correct identification then are of two kinds:

> *True negative*   The screening or identification procedures indicate that a child is normal, and he or she *is* normal.

> *True positive*   The test indicates correctly that a child is handicapped.

Errors or incorrect identifications are also of two kinds:

> *False positive*   In this case the identification procedure indicates that the child is handicapped when, in fact, he or she is normal.

> *False negative*   The identification procedure indicates that the child is normal when actually he or she is handicapped.

The ideal test or identification is one that has high *sensitivity*. That is, the sensitivity of the procedure is the proportion of truly handicapped infants that are identified—$d/(c + d)$ in Figure 1. The human *cost* of the procedure is the proportion of all decisions that are made in error—$(b + c)/(a + b + c + d)$. As can be seen, there are really two kinds of costs, missing a child who is handicapped and labeling or identifying a normal child as handicapped.

Screening procedures for psychoeducational problems have been rife with both these kinds of errors. There are a number of reasons for this:

1. Infant tests are poor predictors of intellectual status later in early childhood (Lewis and Fox, 1980).
2. Some behaviors commonly thought of as indicators of later learning problems, for example errors of laterality and letter reversals, lead to many false positives as they are temporary in many instances. Neurological soft signs detected in infancy clearly fall into this group.
3. It is easy to lapse into regarding the high-risk infant as almost certain to be handicapped later. In fact, most high-risk infants turn out to have no significant handicaps.
4. Tests and test batteries are often considered in terms of their reliability and validity coefficients rather than in terms of *sensitivity* and *cost,* which are the appropriate statistics.

Finally, the risk model is based on the logic that the children included in a register of risk will in most cases be normal. Because there is no visible direct measure of their potential handicap, and they are not labeled as handicapped, no harm results to them. Thus, at no human cost a substantial number of latently handicapped infants are identified and a program of preventive or primary prevention can be mounted. This model can be successful as long as "being at high risk" is widely understood and does not mean "probably handicapped" or "handicapped in a yet undetermined way." Such misunderstandings of the high-risk infant are becoming alarmingly prevalent.

The Financial Costs (Expense) of Identification

There are a variety of indexes for identification and screening expense. The most commonly used is the cost of administering a test, which is based on the tester's time and the cost of the materials. This is, however, of limited utility. The basic, and critical, index is the cost of making an identification—the cost of a true positive. Thus, a test that costs $10 per administration and detects a disorder in 3 out of 100 children will have a fiscal cost of

$$(\$10 \times 100)/3$$

or $333. If the disorder is rare, like phenylketonuria (one in about 16,000 births), and the cost of administration is $4, the fiscal cost is

$$(\$4 \times 16,000)/1$$

or $64,000. Such expenses are justifiable in terms of the long-term costs of a handicap to society and the alleviation of human suffering. However, identification is basically an expensive business, and its ultimate benefit resides in having low cost in human terms and being linked to effective intervention. Thus, identification, assessment, and intervention are closely linked in both fiscal and programmatic ways (Scott, 1978).

UTILIZING RESOURCES FOR EARLY IDENTIFICATION

There have been few systematic studies of the most effective way to determine a preschool handicapped population. One of the few papers in this area is concerned with 3- to 5-year-old handicapped children (Zehrbach, 1975). There are no similar studies of infant populations. At the outset, it is useful to consider four subgroups of infants on whom available resources must be spent. The incidence (number of new cases) in each group will vary widely depending on the community. The prevalence (total number of cases) data below is for general information only.

Infants from the Normal Nursery
with Family Incomes above the Poverty Level

These are children of healthy parents, normal gestation, uncomplicated delivery, and normal birth weight. Furthermore, they have no detectable physical, metabolic, or neurological deficits. Such children constitute 75 percent to 80 percent of all births. By middle school, about 10 percent of them will have been referred for special school services. They are the largest single group of children who will need broad spectrum services to deal with their problems.

Infants from the Normal Nursery with Families at Social Risk

Children whose families are at social risk for reasons such as poverty, minority-group status, or maternal age make up 10 percent to 15 percent of all births. The prevalence of school-related problems among them is high. Perhaps half to two-thirds of this population function markedly below grade level, for instance. Such groups are said to be a high social risk.

Infants from Intensive Care Units

These infants are typically of low birth weight. They may also be critically ill from infections and suffer from respiratory distress. They are kept hospitalized from 1 week to 4 months and often are deprived of normal maternal contact as a consequence of meeting their medical needs. Programmatically, it is useful to subdivide them into two groups (Scott and Massi, 1979).

Handicapped Infants   These are infants who are clearly physiologically damaged because of birth defects, congenital disorders, severe birth trauma, or other functional defects in the neonatal period. Even at this early stage, their need for special services is clear. The incidence of such handicapped infants is approximately 2:1,000 births.

High-Risk Infants   These infants receive intensive care as neonates but at the time of discharge have no obvious handicaps. They are about 9 percent of births. About twice as many of them will have school problems as those with normal birth experience, but the majority (or about 70 percent) will suffer no more than temporary developmental delays. Some children will be at risk for both medical and social reasons; indeed, since maternal care is poor in minority groups, a disproportionate number of infants who require intensive care will come from them.

As can be seen from the foregoing, handicaps are found in all populations, though they are more frequent in some than others. In focusing on social and medical risk groups, however, it is possible to neglect the most numerous group, children who are at normal risk.

SUMMARY

The primary method of identification is through referrals: medical, social service, and community. The primary health, social service, and community persons who have direct contact with infants and families are the best link to those who may need help. To the extent that a community has good well-baby care programs that provide periodic developmental evaluations, extra screening will prove ineffective. The fiscal cost of an identification is the cost of finding a handicapped child. To the extent that existing services are already effectively locating children, the chance of finding "missed" cases decreases. Thus, the expense of screening is likely to be extremely high when good well-baby care services are in place.

The field of early identification of infants has only recently moved from striving to meet the needs of clearly unserved populations to studying resource utilization in early identification and screening of high-risk and handicapped infants. For now, the practitioner should consider how to effectively contact and locate children in each of the groups and spread resources based on an understanding of local conditions.

ACKNOWLEDGMENT

The preparation of this chapter was supported in part by grant BEH G00-7802091 and the Mailman Foundation.

REFERENCES

Clarke, A. M., and Clarke, A. D. B.   *Early experience: Myth and evidence.* New York: Free Press, 1976.

Frankenburg, W. K., and Camp, B. W.   *Pediatric screening test.* Springfield, Ill.: Charles C Thomas, 1975.

Hobbs, N.   *The futures of children.* San Francisco: Jossey-Bass, 1975.

Hunt, J. McV. *Intelligence and experience.* New York: Ronald Press, 1961.

Klaus, M., Jerauld, R., Kreger, N., McAlpine, W., Steffa, M., and Kennell, J. H.   Maternal attachment: Importance of the first postpartum days. *New England Journal of Medicine,* 1972, *286,* 260.

Lewis, M., and Fox, N.   Predicting cognitive development from assessments in infancy. In B. W. Camp (Ed.), *Advances in Behavioral Pediatrics* (Vol. 1). Greenwich Conn.: JAI Press, 1980.

Scott, K. G.   The rationale and methodological considerations underlying early cognitive and behavioral assessments. In F. D. Minifie and L. L. Lloyd (Eds.), *Communication and cognitive abilities—Early behavioral assessment.* Baltimore: University Park Press, 1978.

Scott, K. G., and Massi, W.   The outcome from and utility of registers of risk. In T. M. Field, A. M. Sostek, S. Goldberg, and H. H. Shuman (Eds.), *Infants born at risk.* New York: Spectrum Publications, 1979.

Zehrbach, R. R.   Determining a preschool handicapped population. *Exceptional Children,* 1975, *42,* 76-83.

GLOSSARY

Critical period   A particular brief time in development at which the organism is especially responsive or sensitive to a type of environmental input.

Diagnosis and evaluation   The process of completing an assessment on children, which will provide a categorization of the child's problem, and should include a plan for remediation.

Handicap   A condition that interferes with normal progress in school.

Identification   A three-step process which discovers children who are in need of intervention, either because they have a handicap, or because their current status (environmental or physical) strongly suggests they will develop a handicap. The three steps are 1) locating, 2) screening, and 3) diagnosis and evaluation.

Incidence   The rate at which new cases of a condition are detected.

Intervention   The process of providing a program of behavioral or educational therapy to ameliorate or prevent a handicapping condition.

Locating   The process of finding children who may benefit from developmental services and thus who would be candidates for screening.

Physical anomaly   A physical irregularity acquired during fetal development, and thus present at birth.

Prescriptive program   A plan of goals, strategies, and timelines written for an individual child that will guide the services and training received. The outline should be based in part on the information gathered in the screening and diagnosis and evaluation processes.

Prevalence   The proportion of a population that has a disorder at any given point or period of time.

Primary prevention   The process of intervention that prevents a handicap from becoming manifest.

Risk factors   Factors, which in the absence of any manifest evidence of a handicap, suggest that a child is more than normally prone to subsequently develop a handicapping condition. Risk factors can include a family history of genetic disease, neonatal history and/or social or environmental conditions.

Risk registers   Records kept that list all children who are at greater than normal risk for a handicapping condition.

Screening   The process of quickly testing children to identify those who appear to suffer from a handicap. Children identified by a screening test subsequently receive a fuller diagnosis and evaluation to confirm the result and prepare an intervention plan where appropriate.

Secondary prevention   The process of intervention with a pre-existing condition or handicap.

A Report on Selected Screening Programs for High-Risk and Handicapped Infants

Pascal L. Trohanis, Ruth A. Meyer, and Sonya Prestridge

Screening is one of the first key steps in early identification and detection of handicapped and at-risk infants, which is so important to successful intervention. For this chapter, it is defined as a brief, first step measurement activity aimed at identifying exceptional infants who may need an in-depth diagnosis and appropriate, comprehensive services. It should be fast, efficient, and economical. The targets of the screening procedures may be either mothers, parents, or infants. The chapter makes available

PASCAL L. TROHANIS is director of the Technical Assistance Development System (TADS) of the Frank Porter Graham Child Development Center, and associate professor of education at the University of North Carolina at Chapel Hill.

RUTH A. MEYER is a writer and editor based in Atlanta, Georgia, and a former publications coordinator for the Technical Assistance Development System (TADS), Frank Porter Graham Child Development Center, University of North Carolina at Chapel Hill.

SONYA PRESTRIDGE is technical assistance coordinator for demonstration projects at the Technical Assistance Development System (TADS), Frank Porter Graham Child Development Center, University of North Carolina at Chapel Hill.

information that can help stimulate, maintain, or improve screening practices. First, it reports the results of a survey of programs that screen mothers, parents, or infants. Second, it provides detailed descriptions of six diverse, exemplary screening programs that responded to the survey. In addition, an annotated listing of all respondents is provided in Appendix A. Finally, based on the survey results, the authors raise some issues of concern regarding the state of the art of present screening practices. (See Appendix C for the screening questionnaire.)

THE SURVEY

Before high-risk infants and those with handicaps can be helped with early intervention, they must be found and referred to appropriate agencies. The six programs described in this chapter are examples of some of the ways programs can successfully screen very young children. They were chosen from respondents to a survey that was conducted in the fall of 1979 for the purpose of locating programs providing various services to high-risk and handicapped infants. (See Table 1 for an overview of the six programs.)

The Survey Design

Packets containing two questionnaires, one for programs screening infants and one for programs intervening with infants, were sent out in October to 142 programs that had been identified as likely providers of either or both types of service. A total of 56 programs (approximately 40 percent) responded, including four that completed only the screening questionnaire, another 12 that completed both the screening and the intervention questionnaires, and 32 that completed only the intervention questionnaire. (For addresses and brief annotations of all the projects that responded, refer to Appendices A and B. Chapter 9, "A Report on Selected Demonstration Programs for Infant Intervention," contains more detailed descriptions of nine of the intervention programs.)

Screening programs for infants are an emerging phenomenon in the United States, and there is no easy way to locate all that are in existence. The projects identified for the survey mailing included Mental Retardation Research Centers, American Association of University Affiliated Programs for the developmentally disabled, current and former demonstration and outreach projects of the Handicapped Children's Early Education Program, and many other projects located through a search of the current literature and recommendations by medical, public health, and educational professionals.

The criteria that were developed for exemplary status are reflected both in the definition of screening for the chapter, which was included on

Table 1.   Selected comparative information about six screening programs

Name and location	Areas of comparison							
	Target audiences for screening	Conditions or handicaps being screened	Screening delivery mode	Geographic service area	Type of fiscal agency	Number of years in operation as of 12/79	Funding source
Infant Stimulation/ Mother Training Program, Cincinnati, OH	Mothers and infants	All	Hospital	Urban	Hospital	5	Federal and state
Newborn High Risk Hearing-Screening Program, Salt Lake City, UT	Infants	Hearing loss and deafness	State wide computer program from birth certificates	State wide	State Department of Health	6	State
High Priority Information Identification and Tracking Program, Raleigh, NC	Infants	Developmental delays and physical problems	County health department	State wide	State Division of Health Service	6 months	State
Child Development Resources Information Program/Outreach Project, Lightfoot, VA	Infants	Developmental delays, vision/hearing losses & speech impairments	Community screening	Rural, multi-county	Private nonprofit agency	5	State, local, contributions and UGF
Project RHISE/Outreach, Children's Development Center, Rockford, IL	Infants	All	Center based and community wide	Urban, multi county	Private nonprofit agency	5	State, local, fees and contributions
At-Risk Parent Child Program, Hillcrest Medical Center, Tulsa, OK	Mothers and infants	Mother bonding difference, relationship difference, family and marital crises, financial crises, infant at risk for abuse or neglect	Hospital	Urban, single county	Hospital	5	Federal, local, and United Way

the questionnaire, and in the individual questions on the form. The criteria include such factors as: clearly defined model and implementation methods, validated screening instruments, established service history of 2 years or more, well-developed interagency coordination, and high participation (screening of 100 children or more). The projects described in-depth in this chapter met most of the exemplary criteria and, in addition, are representative of the many variations the survey indicated exist in the settings in which screening programs operate and the populations they serve.

General Impressions of Survey Results

Only 16 completed screening questionnaires were received from the survey. There may be several reasons why there was such a small number of responses. First, it could be a sampling fault. Although 142 survey forms were sent out to a wide range of projects, they may have been more appropriate for the intervention program survey than the screening one. Second, the design of the questionnaire itself may have been confusing to some of the programs who received it. Third, the definition of screening may have been problematic for some. It has been our experience in working with preschool projects over the years that *screening* often becomes synonymous with *casefinding, assessment,* and *diagnosis.* Therefore in reviewing these general impressions of the data, keep in mind that they represent a very small number of screening programs across the United States.

Some Demographics The majority of responding programs (66 percent) have been in existence 5 to 6 years with 90 percent reporting stable, on-going funding. Almost half the programs are urban ones covering multicounty regions. Finally, 45 percent reported that screening is done in the home, 30 percent reported that they screen in a comprehensive health care setting, and the remaining 25 percent reported that they screen in a combination of the above settings.

Risk Indicators The list below shows the indicators of risk for handicapping conditions identified most frequently by programs that screen mothers or parents in order to identify their high-risk and handicapped infants. All eight of these programs checked "low-income parents" as a prime risk factor.

Older mother
Teenage mother
Addicted/alcoholic mother
Maternal illness or trauma
Genetic factors
Low parental education status

Mentally retarded parents
Exposure to environmental hazards
Parental history of abuse/neglect
Low-income parents

Programs that screen infants directly (8) were asked to report which indicators of risk they emphasized, if applicable. The choices they were offered are presented below. Almost half of the programs reported emphasizing all the indicators listed, while the remaining programs checked various combinations of indicators.

Obstetric complications
Low birthweight
Postnatal illness
Prematurity
Physical anomalies
Neurological problems
Developmental problems
Sensorimotor problems
Environmental hazards
Multiple factors

Instrumentation   The screening instruments that programs reported using were diverse, including as many locally developed instruments as validated, commercially available ones. Some of those mentioned are: The Maternal Risk Score Instrument, the Kent Infant Development Scale, the Education for Multi-handicapped Infants (EMI) Assessment Scale, the Comprehensive Identification Process, and the Denver Developmental Screening Test. It seemed that in some cases projects were using what are actually assessment and diagnostic instruments for screening. For example, the Bayley Scales of Infant Development, Vineland Social Maturity Scale, and Koontz Child Development Program were all identified as screening tools. This variance in instrumentation may be related simply to a definition problem within the field as to what distinguishes screening from such terms as diagnosis, assessment, and evaluation. On the other hand it may represent a lack of understanding of the functional variation in these activities.

Cost Data   The majority of responding programs had no cost data available. This was surprising to the authors because cost data seem so necessary for effective program planning and implementation, as well as for dissemination and replication efforts.

SELECTED EXEMPLARY SCREENING PROGRAMS

The six programs whose descriptions follow were selected in order to present diverse approaches to screening. They include:

1. Urban and rural programs
2. Programs screening for specific conditions and others screening for all impairments
3. Statewide and community efforts
4. Computerized systems
5. Programs that screen parents and programs targeted at infants
6. Hospital-affiliated programs

Infant Stimulation Mother Training Program
College of Medicine/University of Cincinnati
Cincinnati, Ohio

Background and Program Overview

This 5-year-old project is based in the Cincinnati General Hospital, where 90 percent of the patients are medically indigent. The targets of screening are teenage mothers (16 years and younger) and their full-term infants and premature, low birthweight infants and their parents. The purpose of this primary prevention program is to identify infants who are at either social or both social and biological risk so that preventive action may be taken to avoid serious developmental problems.

In 1977, the program developed the Maternal Risk Scope (MRS), an instrument that assesses four social-environmental factors thought to influence maternal care-giving ability: maturity of the mother, degree of planning of the mother, family support systems, and level of income. Fifteen related items were identified and grouped under the four categories and assigned weights.

Information used to compute the MRS for each mother/infant pair is recovered from the history taken during the intake interview at Cincinnati General Hospital. Mothers are also screened during the lying-in period following delivery. Tools used to screen the infants are the Brazelton Neonatal Behavioral Assessment Scale, Hobel Perinatal Risk Score, and Amiel-Tison Neurological Evaluation. Statistical analysis of initial program data was undertaken to validate the usefulness of the MRS instrument. The results were reported at the meeting of the Society for Pediatric Research (May 1978). The MRS demonstrated adequate stability across a 3-year period and its usefullness is being further investigated by the project.

Target Audience for Screening

Mothers and infants
Infant risk indicators

Obstetric complications
Low birthweight
Prematurity
Neurological problems
Developmental problems
Sensorimotor problems
Environmental hazards

Maternal risk indicators

Teenage mother (16 years and under)
Low income
Low educational status
Mental retardation

Conditions, Environmental Insults, Genetic Traits, or Handicaps Being Screened
All conditions and impairments

Implementation Requirements

The MRS instrument is disseminated to interested persons and given out to the participants during a 4-day short course, Infant Enrichment Through Mother Training, offered twice a year at the project site.

Cost Data

None available on screening costs.

Services/Training/Materials Available

A paper is available describing the rationale, procedures, and initial validation of the MRS. A 4-day course is offered twice annually for those interested in replicating the program.

For More Information, Contact

Earladeen Badger, Assistant Professor, Project Director
Infant Stimulation/Mother Training Program
Department of Pediatrics
College of Medicine
University of Cincinnati
231 Bethesda Avenue
Cincinnati, Ohio 45267
(513) 872-5341

Newborn High Risk Hearing Screening
Utah State Department of Health
Salt Lake City, Utah

Background and Program Overview

Statewide high-risk hearing screening is made possible in Utah through the use of a state-funded computer program that locates high-risk infants from a master list of all birth certificates. When the high-risk infant is 6 to 8 months of age, a questionnaire is mailed to the parents in order to determine whether audiological testing is required. Those infants scheduled for audiological evaluation are provided comprehensive testing of both hearing and middle ear function. If a hearing loss is confirmed, the infant is referred for habilitation services.

The program has successfully screened nearly 100 percent of the state's newborn population since 1978, when it was begun as a pilot project.

Target Audience for Screening

Infants

Indicators of Risk

Obstetric complications
Low birthweight
Postnatal illness
Physical anomalies (ENT)
Neurological problems
Multiple factors
Family history (genetic)

Conditions, Environmental Insults,
Genetic Traits, or Handicaps Being Screened

Hearing loss and deafness

Cost Data

A gross estimate of 75 cents per child (40,000 children expected to be screened during 1979-80).

Services/Training/Materials Available

There is an information packet available. Also, the director and other staff consult with interested state systems.

For More Information, Contact

Thomas Mahoney, Director
Newborn High Risk Hearing Screening
Utah State Department of Health
Speech Pathology/Audiology Section
44 Medical Drive
Salt Lake City, Utah 84113
(801) 533-6175

High Priority Infant Identification and Tracking Program
Maternal and Child Health Branch, Division of Health Service
Raleigh, North Carolina

Background and Program Overview

The purpose of this statewide system, begun in July 1979, is to ensure that all high-risk infants born in North Carolina receive regular health supervision within the first year of life. The program is funded by Maternal and Child Health and implemented by county health departments operating under state guidelines. Allocations of funds to the county agencies are based on the number of live births and the percentage of families below the poverty level.

Hospitals regularly transfer to local health departments information on infants identified as high priority. Thereafter, tracking is done at intervals of 3 to 4, 6 to 7, and 13 months. Parents of high priority infants not receiving routine medical care are contacted by a public health nurse and counseled as to the importance of regular medical supervision. Referral of infants with suspected abnormal development to appropriate facilities is at the discretion of the physician or local health department involved.

The High Priority Infant Identification and Tracking Program is now underway in 99 out of the state's 100 counties. Physician's participation has been good—over 75 percent of those providing newborn care are participating in the program. Preliminary figures for infants born since July 1979, and tracked for 6 months (and for whom parental permission was obtained), indicate that 85 percent were receiving care at 3 to 4 months and over 90 percent at 6 to 7 months.

Target Audience for Screening

Infants

Indicators of Risk

Teenage mother (16 years or under)
Gestational age of 36 weeks or less
Birthweight under 5 pounds, 8 ounces (or 2500 grams)
Apgar score of 4 or less at 5 minutes
Hyaline membrane disease (RDS)
Meconium aspiration syndrome
Pneumonia
Infant requiring respirator support
Recurrent apnea
Seizures and/or convulsions
Intracranial hemorrhage
Other birth defects or syndromes
Serious environmental, social or parenting disturbances

Hydrocephalus
Meningocele, meningomyelocele
Meningitis
Hepatitis
Bilirubin greater than 20 mg/dl
Congenital heart disease

Conditions, Environmental Insults,
Genetic Traits, or Handicaps Being Screened
Developmental delays and physical problems

For More Information, Contact
John F. Dunning, Assistant Branch Head* or
Laura Harbinson, Public Health Nurse Consultant†
High Priority Infant Identification and Training
Division of Health Services
P.O. Box 2091
Raleigh, North Carolina 27602
*(919) 733-7791
†(919) 733-2973

Child Development Resources Infant Program Outreach Project Lightfoot, Virginia

Background and Program Overview

This community screening program known as Child Check grew out of the Early Identification Project, which was funded by a grant from the Virginia State Department of Developmental Disabilities from 1973 to 1975. So many infants were identified during the 2 years of the project that a comprehensive identification system was developed with four contact strategies: 1) Child Check (community screening), 2) media public service announcements (newspaper, radio, posters), 3) physician/hospital referrals, and 4) surveys.

Because the community served ranges from very rural to sophisticated urban, Child Check goes into the community every spring to screen infants from birth to 2 years old. Places are identified where large numbers of people frequent, (e.g., theatre lobbies, shopping centers, schools, churches, and social services offices) and at key times of the day and week, (lunch, early evening, on Friday or Saturday) Child Check staffers administer the Prescreening Denver Questionnaire and other appropriate tools for vision, hearing, and speech problems. The Denver questionnaire is scored on the site with parents given results immediately. If the child fails, a recommendation is made for a further, in-depth screening at another date and site using the whole Denver questionnaire.

Current funding sources for the Child Check program are: the state

(60 percent), United Way (20 percent), public contributions (10 percent), and private contributions (10 percent).

Target Audience for Screening
Infants
<u>Indicators of Risk</u>

Obstetric complications
Low birthweight
Postnatal illness
Prematurity
Physical anomalies
Neurological problems
Developmental problems
Sensorimotor problems
Environmental hazards
Multiple factors

Conditions, Environmental Insults, Genetic Traits, or Handicaps Being Screened
Development delays, vision/hearing losses, and speech impairments

Cost Data
The following cost data are based on serving approximately 100 children during 1979:

1. Approximately $2.42 per child without mailing evaluations and results to parents first class.
2. Approximately $3.97 per child *with* mailing evaluations and results to parents first class
3. Cost will vary depending on amount of postage and number of paid staff, because all other costs are minimal.
4. These costs include one speech therapist at $20.00 per day and 20 hours of staff time to coordinate, train, and do follow-up. Once a core of volunteers has been trained, costs are reduced since future training can be done by volunteers with minimum staff supervision.
5. This estimate does not include staff time for follow-up home visits. It does include Denver rescreening.

Services/Training/Materials Available
Child Find: A Manual. Describes the process of locating and identifying children who are handicapped, suspected handicapped, or at-risk. Techniques include community education, use of the media, involving the medical profession, surveys, interagency relations, and community screening.

For More Information, Contact
Barbara Kniest, Executive Director
Child Development Resources Infant Program/Outreach Project
Child Development Resources
P.O. Box 299
Lightfoot, Virginia 23090
(804) 565-0303

Project Rhise/Outreach
Children's Development Center
Rockford, Illinois

Background and Program Overview
Project RHISE was originally funded under the HCEEP to develop a model for service delivery to handicapped and developmentally delayed infants and their parents in an urban, multicounty area. Now in its sixth year, the project focuses on outreach—providing training and technical assistance to those replicating the model or adapting it to meet their service needs.

One component of the RHISE model is screening, which is accomplished three ways. First, children referred to the program are screened to determine their need for an in-depth assessment (before program entry). Some children with clearly demonstrated disabilities bypass the screening process and go directly into in-depth assessment. Second, children in high-risk groups are routinely screened. These include all graduates of the neonatal intensive care unit at the local hospital, all children identified as having high levels of lead in their blood, and children living in economically depressed areas who are considered at risk for developmental delay. Third, mass screening efforts are made three to four times a year using such methods as publicizing free screening at shopping centers and in conjunction with preschool and public school registration.

Funding sources for screening are: the state (45 percent), local agencies (40 percent), fees (11 percent), and private contributions (4 percent).

Target Audience for Screening
Infants
Indicators of Risk

Obstetric complications
Low birthweight
Postnatal illness
Prematurity
Physical anomalies
Neurological problems

Developmental problems
Sensorimotor problems
Environmental hazards
Multiple factors

Conditions, Environmental Insults, Genetic Traits, or Handicaps Being Screened

Screening is for delays in development; many could be due to any of the full range of handicapping conditions: environmental factors, miscellaneous genetic traits, or health impairments.

Evidence of Effectiveness

A statistical summary report can be obtained from Project RHISE which details both children's progress and parents' progress. Screening data from the Denver Developmental Screening Test (DDST) is also available in a written report.

Mass Screening Costs

The cost data from 1979 in Table 1 are based on a model that has the following allowances per child screened:

20 minutes for actual screening
10 minutes for the individual administering the screening to write
the report
10 minutes for the secretary to type and file reports
 5 minutes for the client coordinator to do scheduling, etc.
 4 minutes for the media coordinator to do advertising and
public relations

The recommended initial investment in permanent equipment and materials to do the DDST on a mass screening basis is 16 Denver Kits, 16

Table 1.   Costs for mass screening by Project RHISE[a]

Basic costs by DDST outcome	Costs of screening by administrator			
	Aide ($1.56)	B.S. teacher ($2.85)	M.S. teacher ($3.68)	Volunteer (0)
Pass ($1.57)	$3.13	$4.42	$5.25	$1.57
Fail ($2.21)	$3.77	$5.06	$5.89	$2.21

[a] The basic cost figure includes materials and secretarial, client coordinator, and media coordinator time. It is considered a fixed amount per child screened. It *does not* include either the initial investment in the permanent equipment and materials needed to the DDST or the cost of training volunteers.

Denver Instruction Manuals, 1 Instructor's Manual, and 1 Proficiency Manual. Volunteers can be trained with these materials.

The cost of initial investment in materials is approximately $152.50. The cost of training volunteers, based on a workshop with 15 participants, is approximately $7.10 per volunteer.

The model costs assume that screening is done at the program. If they are done at another site, transportation costs must be added, as well as additional salary for the traveling personnel.

Individual Referral Screening Costs

The cost data from 1979 in Table 2 are based on a model which has the following allowances per child screened:

30 minutes for actual screening

30 minutes for the individual administering the screening to write the report

30 minutes for the secretary to type and file reports

30 minutes for the client coordinator to make contacts, schedule the screening, etc.

Services/Training/Materials Available

Workshop Training Format for the Denver Developmental Screening Test   The format for a 6-hour workshop in the use of the DDST is available for use in training paraprofessionals and volunteers in the community to screen children for potential developmental difficulties.

Table 2.   Costs for individual screening by Project RHISE[a]

| Basic costs by DDST outcome | Cost of screening by administrator | | |
	Aide ($3.11)	B.S. teacher ($5.69)	M.S. teacher ($7.35)
Pass all areas ($6.20)	$ 9.31	$11.69	$13.55
Fail one area ($7.75)	$10.86	$13.44	$15.10
Fail two areas ($9.30)	$12.41	$14.99	$16.65
Fail three areas ($10.85)	$13.96	$16.54	$18.20
Fail four areas ($12.40)	$15.51	$18.09	$19.75

[a] The basic cost figure includes materials and secretarial and client coordinator time. It is a fixed amount per child screened. It does not include the initial investment in permanent equipment and materials needed to do the DDST. The initial investment is $6.25 for each kit and $3.00 for the instruction manual.

For More Information, Contact
Sue Wilke, Training Coordinator
Project RHISE/Outreach
Children's Development Center
750 North Main Street
Rockford, Illinois 61103
(815) 965-6745

At-Risk Parent-Child Program
Hillcrest Medical Center
Tulsa, Oklahoma

Background and Program Overview

The At-Risk Parent-Child Program evolved out of an awareness that a significant number of infants and children either born at Hillcrest or admitted to the pediatric service for common medical problems later were seen abused or neglected. Significant efforts to identify and treat abused children had been established within the hospital, but it appeared that the staff was unable to intervene until after the fact.

A screening procedure for identifying parents at risk for poor parenting was developed. From 26 criteria, four major problem categories were identified: 1) bonding difficulties, 2) relationship difficulties with other adults, 3) family and marital crises, and 4) financial or social crises. Members of the At-Risk team (which includes pediatricians, a public health nurse coordinator, a social worker, a pediatric mental health nurse, and dietitian) and nurses in both the newborn unit and pediatrics assess each child and family in terms of the risk criteria.

The program, set in an urban, single-county area, receives funding from federal sources (48 percent), the United Way (19 percent), and in-kind contributions (32 percent).

Target Audience for Screening
Parents and infants.
Parent Risk Indicators

Teenage mother
Older mother
Addicted/alcoholic mother
Maternal illness or trauma
Genetic factors
Low parental education
Mentally retarded parents
Exposure to environmental hazards
Parental history of abuse/neglect

Infant Risk Indicators

Obstetrics complications
Low birthweight
Postnatal illness
Prematurity
Physical anomalies
Neurological problems
Developmental problems
Sensorimotor problems
Multiple factors

Conditions, Environmental Insults, Genetic Traits, or Handicaps Being Screened

Parents

Bonding difficulties
Relationship difficulties
Family and marital crises
Financial crises

Infants

At-risk abuse or neglect related to assessed criteria

Evidence of Effectiveness

Program will have outcome data and a formal assessment of the program by October, 1982.

For More Information, Contact

Catherine Ayoub, Director
At-Risk Parent-Child Program
Hillcrest Medical Center
1120 S. Utica
Tulsa, OK 74104
(918) 584-1351

CONCLUSION

Screening has been viewed as a first, key measurement activity that enables service providers to detect potential handicapped and high-risk infants. Based upon the results of screening, an infant may need retesting, may need no followup services, or may need an in-depth diagnosis which could lead to the development of appropriate and individualized comprehensive services.

Some Observations

Because of the limitations of the survey conducted in conjunction with the development of this chapter, care must be taken in generalizing from our results. However, the authors wish to offer some observations, which may have importance for planning, expanding, or implementing screening services.

1. The variability of terms being applied to screening activities may be adversely affecting program development and implementation. The survey data suggest that terms such as *screening, assessment, evaluation,* and *diagnosis* are used interchangeably. This lack of precision in terms was inconsistent with the straightforward definition of screening employed for our survey. For example, *screening* by definition is a process that is fast and economical. Yet the responses suggested that the length of screening ranged from 5 minutes to 2 hours and the costs ranged from 75 cents per child to $2,179.23 per mother/infant pair.

2. Apparently related to the variability in screening terms, survey results indicate that diverse measurement instruments are being used. A review of these instruments indicates that some of them are inappropriate for screening as it was defined. For example, the Bayley Scales of Infant Development and Vineland Social Maturity Scale were instruments some programs reported using for screening. Yet, these and other similar devices reported are more appropriate for assessment and diagnosis than for screening. It is clear that appropriate instrumentation, matched to a precise definition of screening, is needed by programs screening children from birth.

3. It was difficult to assess program effectiveness, both in terms of outcomes and implementation processes, because evaluation data seemed nonexistent. Thus, those planning programs must be prepared to work with anecdotal information from others when harder evaluation data cannot be obtained.

4. Cost data were also sparse. For responding programs, data were either nonexistent, quite variable, or difficult to understand. Therefore, new programs must be prepared to develop their own cost projections for screening.

In retrospect, perhaps a broader definition of screening than that used for the chapter is needed to accommodate the apparent diversity of activities known as "screening." In reality, screening seems to be not an isolated phenomenon, but rather one that is an integral part of a systematic approach to serving handicapped and high-risk infants.

Developmental Review: A Future Trend?

There is a new concept in screening that may subdue some of the problems discussed here. It is developmental review, which has a process orientation and moves away from the prevalent cross-sectional view of screening. Rather than focusing on diagnosing a specific condition, the review assesses a range of crucial functions. The result is a profile of strengths and weaknesses. The concept, first proposed to the former Department of HEW in a report by the American Association of Psychiatric Services for Children in 1977, is gaining support across the country and has been recommended as a model to all the states for implementation by January 1, 1981, in the Early and Periodic Screening, Diagnosis, and Treatment Programs (EPSDT).

In a three-stage process the biological, psychological, and family dimensions of each child are reviewed along with environmental, social, and cultural factors. Stage 1 involves a basic pediatric examination that includes an opportunity for the child and family to discuss any problems or to identify strengths. The child's functioning is assessed by means of parent report. Stage 2 is initiated when a parent expresses concern or when stage 1 review suggests a need for further information. It involves direct structured observation of the child's functioning in the areas of gross and fine motor, language, social/emotional development, and adaptive behavior. Stage 3 review is for those children and families whose reviews indicate they need complete evaluations. This level of review is conducted by trained professionals from the appropriate fields and is aimed more specifically at diagnosis and eventual remediation.

Through a grant from the Bureau of Developmental Disabilities, the staff of the Developmental Disability Center, Louisiana State University Medical Center, under the direction of J. Steven York, has been refining the system of developmental review. It is assembling a package for use by paraprofessionals in administering stage 1 and 2 reviews. This package will be available in 1981.

The authors hope that this chapter has provided some insights into the reality of present practices and the technology needed to develop and implement successful programs.

Methods of Assessment for High-Risk and Handicapped Infants

Frances Degen Horowitz

The earliest attempts to evaluate infant development were guided by two interests: to document the developmental status of an infant in relation to other infants of the same age, and to predict later intelligence. The first type of interest is best represented in the work of pediatrician-psychologist Arnold Gesell and his colleagues in what has become known as the Gesell Scales or Schedules of Development (Gesell, 1925; Gesell and Amatruda, 1947). The second approach is evident in the early efforts of such pioneers as Nancy Bayley, creator of the California Infant Scales, (Bayley, 1933; Bayley, 1935) and Psyche Cattell who developed the Infant Intelligence Scale (1940).

During the half century that has passed since these initial attempts, a great deal has been learned about infant behavior and development. It is now known that the normal human infant is born into the world with

FRANCES DEGEN HOROWITZ is a professor in the Department of Human Development and Family Life at The University of Kansas in Lawrence, Kansas.

functioning sensory systems and is capable of interactive behavior (Osofsky, 1979). During the first 2 years of life the infant's development is both rapid and complex, with the growing child displaying increasingly sophisticated behavior, not only in the development of the well documented motor milestones, but also in cognitive, linguistic, and social domains. Our expanded knowledge has led to a growing appreciation for the complexity and plasticity of developmental processes.

It is clear that the early measures of infant development do not reflect the pure unfolding of the infant's natural abilities because they are too strongly influenced by the variety of environmental variables affecting the infant. It is also clear that traditional measures of infant intelligence do not predict later intelligence. And coming into question is whether the standard concept of intelligence is at all applicable for the first 2 years of life (Horowitz and Dunn, 1978; Scarr-Salapatek, 1976).

Because it has become evident that many infants at-risk for abnormal development can benefit from intervention programs that lessen the impact of disabilities and minimize developmental delays (Beller, 1979; Horowitz and Paden, 1973), the problems of finding and educating high-risk infants, to which this volume is dedicated, are intimately related to issues surrounding the assessment of infant development. The nature of available assessment tools, as well as their utility, are of concern to all those who work with high-risk infants. However, before reviewing and discussing current methods of assessing infants it is important to address the question of why infant behavior and development is assessed at all.

WHY ASSESS INFANTS?

Early assessment does not necessarily predict later development. In fact, it is usually the purpose of intervention programs to upset facile predictions. For example, suppose a 9-month-old infant is assessed to have the developmental level of a 6-month-old infant, and no major organic factors or metabolic disorders seem to account for the developmental lag. One view would be that the developmental delay is just a natural expression of the child's developmental capacity. This outlook leads to advising parents that the infant will develop more slowly than normal infants, that nothing can be done to alter the child's natural rate of growth, and that the parents should accept the fact that the infant will not be normal in comparison to other children of the same age. Under such circumstances, evaluation of the infant's behavior and development serves the sole purpose of verifying delayed development—assessment becomes the tool for diagnosis.

However, if it is believed that providing a special program of intervention might increase the rate or quality of the infant's development, then assessment has a use beyond diagnosis. Under these circumstances, an assessment strategy (which may involve several assessment tools) serves three purposes: 1) to identify where the infant is developmentally, 2) to guide the formulation of an intervention program, and 3) to evaluate the effectiveness of subsequent intervention. Assessment thus contributes to finding and educating the high-risk infant and not simply to labeling the child.

The discussion in this chapter assumes that assessment will be undertaken in the service of finding and educating high-risk infants, and not just to diagnose and classify them. Because of this orientation, different assessment tools are evaluated in terms of their utility for identifying high-risk infants, for helping in the formulation of intervention programs, and for evaluating the effects of intervention on the children. The choice of an assessment tool, then, must be based on a careful understanding of the purpose for using it, with different selection criteria appropriate for different purposes.

The assessment instruments reviewed in this chapter were selected only if they met the basic requirement of reliability, which is expected of any standard evaluation procedure. In order to be considered a reliable instrument, a test or observation procedure done by one examiner must produce the same results when it is done by another, independent examiner at approximately the same or some near point in time. Although issues of reliability over time and the relationship of a test to other measures often are discussed as criteria for acceptability of evaluation tools, they are not invoked in this review. Developmental assessments that involve changing organisms present special issues that are beyond the scope of this chapter. Suffice it to say that the assessment tools presented here have all met the criterion for reliability in the restricted sense that two examiners using the tool at proximate times will score an infant's behavior similarly.

INITIAL ASSESSMENT OF RISK

Prenatal Procedures

The moment of birth is not a beginning, but rather a point on the continuum of a developmental journey that began approximately 9 months before. The fetus is not totally protected by the amniotic sac from the influence of environmental variables or from variations in the habits of the mother. Physical complications, maternal age, nutritional status, alcohol consumption, and smoking behavior all influence the health and well-being of the infant during the 9 months before birth.

The knowledge that has been acquired concerning prenatal development, and the detection techniques that have been developed, make it possible to identify some potentially high-risk and handicapped infants before birth and to elect to terminate a pregnancy. This reduces the frequency of new cases of certain developmental disabilities while advances in prenatal and neonatal care practices increase infant survival. At the present time the major tool for such identification is the withdrawal and analysis of amniotic fluid after about the 16th week of pregnancy. However, only conditions that have known genetic or waste-product characteristics for which analytical techniques have been developed can be subjected to amniotic fluid evaluation. The next several decades we will probably see an increased ability to identify high-risk and handicapping conditions prenatally, as well as the development of effective prenatal techniques for the intervention and for prevention of these conditions.

Evaluation at Birth

It is clear that events before birth can increase an infant's risk of subsequent abnormal development. However, since our ability to detect conditions during the prenatal period is limited, especially those that are subtle or mainly affect interactive abilities, in most instances the earliest practical point for identifying high-risk infants is during the first hours and days after birth. One of the oldest techniques for infant assessment is the Apgar rating scale (Apgar, 1953), which evaluates five physiological and reactive characteristics of the infant at 1, 5, and 10 minutes after birth. The five characteristics are heart rate, respiratory effort, reflex irritability, muscle tone, and color. The Apgar is done in the delivery room and is used to identify those infants who need immediate special care if they are to survive or if damaging conditions are to be minimized.

Although the Apgar rating provides a measure of the infant's health status and reaction to the birth event, the Dubowitz Scale (Dubowitz et al., 1970) evaluates the infant's gestational age by scoring several neurological and physical appearance characteristics. Gestational age is an important factor for classifying the infant. When combined with weight and length data, it helps predict mortality and morbidity. (The greater the downward deviation in weight and length for gestational age, the higher the risk level). The Dubowitz can be done within the first 5 days of life. And while medical personnel typically make the gestational age estimate, nonmedical personnel also can be trained to use the Dubowitz scoring system.

Both the Apgar and Dubowitz help in identifying infants at birth whose status may be a cause for concern. Neither is a "developmental" scale to be used over time or to chart developmental progress, but both have had wide acceptance as useful tools in the early observation of the human infant. (See Self and Horowitz, 1979, for further discussion.)

Neonatal Procedures

In a review of instruments available for newborn assessment, Self and Horowitz (1979) listed eight different procedures for evaluating the status of the neonate in the first hours and days of life, and two others which can be used at the end of the neonatal period as the infant reaches 1 month of age. Some 85 different behaviors and characteristics are evaluated by these instruments. Although some procedures, such as the Apgar, sample only a few characteristics, others are more extensive.

Two neonatal assessments are primarily physiological and neurological evaluations. The scale described by Prechtl and Beintema (1964) was designed as an extensive test of the neurological status of the full-term infant. A shorter "screening" version is also available. The Prechtl and Beintema Scale has been shown to discriminate high-risk infants among the full-term population and to predict later neurological status in infants judged to be of concern. Though it is an extensive measure of neurological integrity at the time of birth, the scale is not a developmental evaluation. It does not lend itself to charting the infant's progress over time, and there has been no demonstration yet that the scale can be used to select infants for particular kinds of intervention programs.

The second neonatal assessment that relies heavily upon physiological and neurological characteristics was devised by Parmelee and his colleagues (Parmelee, 1974; Self and Horowitz, 1979). This evaluation is much shorter than the Prechtl and Beintema Scale. When used with infants at 40 weeks conceptual age, the scale discriminates premature from full-term infants. Parmelee has long been interested in using early identification so that appropriate intervention might be undertaken with high-risk infants. He and his colleagues have used the Parmelee Scale in conjunction with other observations that can be organized in a cumulative fashion to arrive at an overall estimate of risk status (Parmelee, Kopp, and Sigman, 1976). Like the Dubowitz and Apgar Evaluations, the Parmelee and the Prechtl and Beintema Scales were designed to provide an evaluation of neurological status; they were not developed to record developmental progress.

There are two neonatal evaluations that are more behavioral in nature. One is the Graham/Rosenblith Scale developed by Rosenblith (1979), and the other is the Neonatal Behavioral Assessment Scale developed by Brazelton and his colleagues (Brazelton, 1973). The Graham/Rosenblith Scale evaluates the infant's motor maturity and tonus (general body tone), and the infant's responsiveness to light, auditory, and moderately irritating tactile stimuli. It takes 20 to 30 minutes to administer and requires specific state or alertness conditions to be present. Used to evaluate a large number of infants associated with the National Collaborative Perinatal Research Project located at Brown University in Providence, Rhode Island, the prognostic value of the Graham/Rosenblith Scale has been tested at 8 months and at 4 years of age. Some relationships have been found, but the scale is primarily a promising research tool, and Rosenblith is cautious in her interpretation and in her claims (Rosenblith, 1979).

The Neonatal Behavioral Assessment Scale (NBAS), commonly known as "the Brazelton," provides the broadest sample of newborn behavior and has attracted the most attention. It consists of a semistructured observation of the infant's responses to inanimate visual, auditory, and tactile stimuli as well as responses to the examiner's face, voice, and body. Each of 27 items is scored on a 19-point scale, and reflective behavior is evaluated as well. The examination was designed for normal, full-term newborns and is not appropriate for premature infants, though it has been used with low birthweight and short-for-date infants (Self and Horowitz, 1979; Sameroff, 1978). The exam requires intensive observation of state changes and of such general characteristics as alertness, cuddliness, and self-quieting ability. During the test, the examiner scores the best behavior observed for the orientation items, as well as for some others.

A supplemented version of the NBAS, the Neonatal Behavioral Assessment Scale with Kansas Supplements (NBAS-K) has recently been published (Horowitz, Sullivan, and Linn, 1978) and evaluated (Lancioni, Horowitz, and Sullivan, 1980). The NBAS-K scores not only the infant's best responses during the examination but also "modal" responses, making it possible to derive a score for the difference between the best and modal behavior. New scales that have been added to the NBAS-K rate the quality of the infant's responsiveness, the amount of persistence required of the examiner to elicit the best behavior, the infant's general irritability, and the examiner's subjective evaluation of how reinforcing the infant is during the test. One study of the reinforcement value scale found that the better the infant's orientation behavior and the lower its general irritability, the more likely the examiner was to rate the infant as being highly reinforcing (Lancioni, Horowitz, and Sullivan, 1980).

The NBAS and NBAS-K have generated a great deal of interest among infant researchers as well as among clinicians. They can be used from the first day of life through about 1 month of age and require 20 to 30 minutes to administer. Pediatricians and nurses have found that the instruments sensitize them to the extensive range of behavior that can be observed in the normal newborn infant, and informal demonstrations of the assessments have been used by hospital personnel to show mothers what their babies can do. However, the utility of the scales for identifying infants at risk has not yet been documented.

There is some evidence that the scales may be useful for discriminating which behavioral characteristics of normal and abnormal infants predispose them to having adverse interactions with caretakers. The reinforcement value scale of the NBAS-K may prove particularly useful in discriminating which infants are less likely to elicit optimal caretaking and parental interaction and, therefore, are predisposed to greater risk for adverse environmental events. But this remains to be demonstrated. There are problems with the NBAS and NBAS-K in relation to stability over the first month of life and in relation to how best to use the scores that may be derived. (See Sameroff, 1978, for an extensive discussion of this.) However, the NBAS and the NBAS-K are currently the most extensive evaluations of neonatal behavior available.

Because the individual items on the NBAS and the NBAS-K are scaled over nine points, in many cases from the poorest to the best performance in a developmental sense, physical and occupational therapists as well as other intervention workers have been interested in using some of these items with severely retarded or disabled children to describe small increments in steps of response-shaping programs. While the normal infant may be expected to show the top performance on items by 1 or 2 months of age, the severely retarded child may take several months of carefully programmed instruction to move from the poorest to the best performance on an item such as tracking a moving visual object. Much of the interest in using the NBAS and NBAS-K for programming small intervention steps has been informal. Clear demonstration of the utility of the scales for this purpose remains to be done.

Summary

Most children in the United States are born in hospitals, making it theoretically possible to evaluate early almost every child. Therefore, the idea of identifying all children at risk for normal development with an assessment during the first few days of life is very attractive. However, if high-risk and handicapping conditions are the result of an interaction of a child with certain aspects of his or her environment, no neonatal assessment by itself will be sufficient for identifying the child.

Several reviews of current knowledge of handicapping and risk conditions lead to the conclusion that neonatal assessment can provide only limited identification of infants who might benefit from intervention programs (Kopp and Parmelee, 1979; Sameroff and Chandler, 1975). The most useful assessments may require measurements of environmental stimulation as well as evaluations of infant behavior (Horowitz, Sullivan, and Linn, 1978). However, although neonatal and infant behavior measures have been developed over the last 50 years, development of comparable measures of environmental stimulation is only just beginning (Linn, 1979). It is possible that present neonatal evaluations will be supplemented or supplanted in the future by evaluations derived from analysis of sensory and learning abilities in the first few days of life. Recent experimental developments, discussed by Lipsitt (1979) and others point out the need for more powerful and sensitive procedures than are now available.

RECORDS OF DEVELOPMENTAL PROGRESS

Though the Gesell Developmental Schedules and the Bayley Scales both can be used for infants as young as 1 month of age and thus are neonatal measures, they are primarily broad spectrum developmental measures for use across the first 2 years of life. In his general review of infant assessment, Yang (1979) discusses these and another available instrument, the Uzgiris-Hunt Piagetian Scales. Table 1 provides the major reference for each of these scales and for the Denver Developmental Screening Test (DDST). Some descriptive characteristics of these assessments are also provided.

A number of other general developmental infant scales are available. Most of them are older than the Bayley and have not been updated or are less well standardized (Horowitz and Dunn, 1978). Many of them were designed as measures of infant intelligence for the specific purpose of predicting later intelligence and are not as useful in the context of assessing high-risk and handicapped infants. They will not be reviewed here.

Table 1.   General developmental infant assessments

Assessment instrument	Major reference	Standardization sample	Age range	Developmental area evaluated
Denver Developmental Screening Test	Frankenburg and Dodds, 1967	Relatively extensive	0-6 years	Fine motor, gross motor, language, personal-social
Bayley Scales	Bayley, 1969	Relatively extensive	1-36 months	Mental, motor, social
Gesell Developmental Schedules	Knobloch and Pasamanick, 1974	Limited	1-36 months	Fine motor, gross motor, adaptive, language
Uzgiris-Hunt Piagetian Scales	Uzgiris and Hunt, 1975	Limited	0-2 years	Sensorimotor

The Denver Developmental Screening Test (DDST)

Of the assessments listed in Table 1, the Denver Developmental Screening Test is probably the most widely used (Frankenburg and Dodds, 1967). Pediatricians and public health nurses often employ the DDST as part of their routine care of infants and young children, and many pediatric referrals for further evaluation are the result of a DDST performance that indicates delayed development. The DDST is quick and inexpensive to administer, and there is good evidence that past 6 months of age it is relatively efficient in identifying children with significant general developmental delays who warrant further evaluation (Frankenburg et al., 1971). The test consists of direct observations or mother reports in the areas of gross and fine motor behavior, language development, and personal-social behavior. The assessments, especially during the first year of life, are relatively global and unlikely to detect subtle cognitive or language difficulties. However, the DDST has wide appeal for clinicians and has probably played a significant role in increasing detection of developmental delay in the United States.

The DDST is best used with seemingly normal children for it does not have any compensatory procedures for evaluating children with specific handicaps (e.g., visual or hearing impairments). Because the DDST was designed as a relatively gross and quick evaluation, it is not useful alone either for selecting children to participate in a high-risk intervention program, for evaluating the outcome of intervention efforts, or for guiding the development of steps in an intervention program. Nor was it meant to serve these purposes.

The Bayley Scales of Infant Development

The Bayley Scales of Infant Development (Bayley, 1969) had their origins in the California Infant Scales of the 1930s and are the result of many years of careful standardization and reliability efforts on the part of Nancy Bayley and her colleagues. (See Yang, 1979, for a review of this history.) It is currently the best and most widely used general instrument to evaluate infant developmental status. A mental and motor index can be obtained, and an interpretive social behavior record can be filled out as an adjunct to the mental and motor assessment portion of the Bayley. Many clinicians and researchers use only the mental and motor scores. Sometimes only the mental index is employed.

The Bayley Scales are uneven in the depth of evaluation in different areas. This unevenness is partly the result of the variability in the depth of our understanding of different areas of development (e.g., receptive language in the first year of life) and partly the fact that some more recent advances in descriptions of infant development occurred after the major work on the scales had been completed (e.g., steps in cognitive development derived from Piagetian work). The Bayley Scales can, in contrast to the DDST, be used to identify infants who might profit from intervention programs. They are often used to provide the pre- and post-treatment measures that evaluate program effectiveness. By paralleling the Bayley items it is possible to choose a progression of target behaviors to be used as the goals of an intervention program, though it is obvious that direct dependence on specific Bayley items in an intervention program would invalidate the utility of the Bayley as a post-treatment measure.

The scores on the Bayley Scale are derived from a chronological age and items-passed index with 100 the mean performance at any given age. The result is a developmental index score, and not an IQ score. But the resemblance to traditional intelligence score values makes it easy to misinterpret the Bayley scores as IQ values. Also, infants with specific disabilities that affect sensory systems or restrict motor activity cannot be easily evaluated with the Bayley. Like the DDST, it is best suited to seemingly normal infants or those exhibiting general developmental delays.

When the Bayley is employed to evaluate pre- and post-treatment differences, there is a problem in determining what magnitude of difference is developmentally meaningful. If a group of developmentally delayed infants that receives a treatment and gains an average of 8 points is compared to a control group that does not, even if this difference is statistically significant, an 8-point difference on a Bayley Score may not be functionally meaningful. The magnitude of functional differences is a question that is relevant to many developmental assessment instruments and is not necessarily an issue specific to the Bayley Scales. It is possible to note overall changes in performance on the Bayley, but the scales do not easily lend themselves to charting a particular infant's specific developmental progress.

The Gesell Developmental Schedules

The Gesell Developmental Schedules, which yield a developmental quotient, were originally published in 1925. Though there have been revisions and a recent updating (Knobloch and Pasamanick, 1974), they have remained in essence the same. There are many similarities between the Gesell Schedules and the Bayley Scales, and they share similar advantages and problems. However, the Bayley Scales are probably more adequately standardized, though the revision by Knobloch and Pasamanick involved a large number of infants from a variety of backgrounds. Overall, Gesell's approach was somewhat more clinical in nature than Bayley's and more geared to diagnosis. Gesell's scales tend to be better known among pediatricians. In interdisciplinary teams, those trained in the behavioral sciences will usually opt for the Bayley as opposed to the Gesell Scales, and they often must defend the choice. The defense is that at this time the Bayley is better standardized and more widely used so that comparisons from one project or program to another are easier. Another advantage of the Bayley Scale over the Gesell Scale is that the Bayley is probably more closely related, conceptually, to the Stanford-Binet Intelligence Test. Because the Stanford-Binet is often the assessment used for preschool children in programs where follow-up is planned into the preschool years, there are advantages in choosing the Bayley Scales for relating the results across time.

The Uzgiris-Hunt Piagetian Scales

The final assessment instrument to be discussed in this section is not actually a general developmental tool, for it focuses on cognitive development. However, the Uzgiris-Hunt ordinal scales of psychological development (Uzgiris and Hunt, 1975) are some of the most recently developed instruments and reflect the broad definition of cognition that is captured in Piaget's description of sensorimotor development. They involve an entirely different approach to infant assessment than the traditional infant developmental scales.

There are six subscales in the Uzgiris-Hunt instrument: I. the development of visual pursuit and the permanence of objects, II. the development of means of obtaining desired environmental events, IIIa. the development of vocal imitation, IIIb. the development of gestural imitation, IV. the development of operational causality, V. the construction of object relations in space, and VI. the development of schemes relating to objects. Each subscale is broken down into items that represent different steps in the progression from the beginning of the sensorimotor period to the end (birth to 2 years) with 7 to 14 steps on each of the scales. The specific items and their displacement on the scales derive directly from Piaget's theory of sensorimotor development in the first 2 years of life and from sample testing by the authors. No overall score is derived from these scales. Rather, the result is a record of highest steps achieved by the infant on each subscale. By comparison of achievement to the norms, one can determine how many months delayed or advanced each infant is.

The final standardization group for the Uzgiris-Hunt was relatively small and unrepresentative of the larger American population, and considerable work needs to be done before the scales take their place among well-standardized tests. However, the scales are particularly relevant to our purposes. First, they have the most depth in cognitive development of any evaluation instrument available; second, they describe very small steps in cognitive development in a manner that might be particularly useful when programming intervention programs for high-risk or handicapped infants. On the debit side, learning to administer the scales appears to be difficult. Assessments can take a long time and sometimes require more than one session. And achieving reliability in scoring is a challenge.

The scales may not be particularly useful at the present time for identifying at-risk infants because of the standardization problems, but they may be the best set of guides to cognitive achievement available. In this regard they can be useful in identifying target cognitive behaviors for which programmatic intervention might be designed. Through repeated testing, they also may make it possible to chart the developmental progress of individual infants. Though caution must be used in interpreting results until confidence in the normative standardization base of the Uzgiris-Hunt is established, cognitive achievement is often a major area of concern with high-risk and handicapped infants, and the scales have important promise for those who wish to assess cognitive growth. Despite the problems cited, they can provide valuable information about the development of individual infants.

EVALUATIONS OF SPECIFIC COMPETENCE AREAS

Although a general evaluation of developmental status is used as a first line of assessment, an individual working with infants often needs more specific evaluations of competence. This is particularly true if one wishes to evaluate or rule out handicaps in special areas. Such assessments usually require a specialist, and it is beyond the scope of this chapter to review these special assessment techniques. However, the reader may find some references helpful. Hammer (1978) provides a good review of assessment and intervention with visually impaired infants. Haith (1979) discusses some of the mechanisms possibly underlying the relationship between visual processing and cognitive development in high-risk infants. In the area of audition, there are several excellent reviews of the hearing assessment techniques available for use with infants (Cox and Lloyd, 1976; Lowell and Lowell, 1978; Vernon, 1976; and Wilson, 1978). Below 6 months of age accurate assessment of hearing loss requires the use of sophisticated equipment. However, given the importance of hearing for the development of language, a good assessment is essential for any infant suspected of hearing impairment. In this area, brain stem audiometry now seems to be the most useful technique.

Language, like cognition, is considered a key competence area for early development and has been the subject of a great deal of research in recent years. Productive language does not usually appear until the second year of life, and many of the most useful measures for evaluating language acquisition in young children are more suited to the period beyond 2 years of age than to the prime years of infancy. Although it is suspected that important milestones of language development may be occurring during the first year, only limited and gross means of assessing such acquisition is possible at the present time. As with hearing, there have been a number of recent comprehensive reviews of available language assessment tools (Lloyd, 1976; Miller, 1978; Ruder, 1978; Siegel and Broen, 1976; Spradlin, Karlan, and Wetherby, 1976).

CHECKLISTS, PROFILES, AND PROGRESS CHARTS

Those who work with identified handicapped and high-risk infants must not only design special programs for the children, they must also try to document developmental progress in targeted areas and evaluate the effectiveness of their interventions. The general developmental scales reviewed here are only minimally helpful with these tasks, and more specific evaluation tools for hearing, vision, and language have limited usefulness for initial identification and the measurement of language progress. The lack of traditional, well-standardized, widely used tools for evaluating infants, programming intervention, and documenting progress has led to the development of a large number of checklists, profiles, progress charts, and a variety of "home-made" systems to meet these needs. Some of these are becoming standardized and have a certain popularity across intervention projects; others are in use only in one place and by only their authors or inventors. As programs develop or expand, the need to know about the existence of these instruments increases.

A variety of materials are available that provide inventories of assessment instruments along with descriptive information. They are often aimed at individuals who work with retarded children, yet imbedded in them are descriptions of a variety of assessments that are useful for other infants as well. The *Assessment and Management of Developmental Changes in Children* by Erickson (1976) covers many of the assessments that have been reviewed in this chapter but also includes some that have not. For example, Erickson describes the Developmental Profile developed by Alpern and Boll (1972). Similarly, Krajicek and Tearney in their book *Detection of Developmental Problems in Children* (1977) provide a useful overview of assessment techniques in a variety of areas.

A particularly helpful bibliography-inventory of assessment instruments has been put together by Cross and Johnston (1977). Twenty-one different assessments applicable to infants are included. They range from the standard Bayley Scales to more recently devised instruments such as the Koontz Child Development Program (Koontz, 1974) and the Learning Accomplishment Profiles (Griffin, Sanford, and Wilson, 1975). These last two assessments are typical of those techniques that are as much pro-gramming guides as they are assessments. They provide sequenced tasks and training activities designed to facilitate developmental progress in at-risk and handicapped infants. Also described in Cross and Johnston is the Portage Guide to Early Education (Bluma et al., 1976) an attractively packaged combination tool with 580 developmentally sequenced be-haviors for developmental progression from birth to 6 years of age. Cards describe activities designed to teach particular behaviors, while a checklist is provided as an assessment to show what the child has ac-complished and what is yet to be accomplished. All of these instruments facilitate charting of developmental progress of individual infants.

Several paperbound references provide further compilations of for-mal and informal assessment tools. The former Coordinating Office for Regional Resource Centers at the University of Kentucky has issued a compendium of descriptions of individual tests for infants and preschool children (CORRC, 1976). Mayeda, Pelzer, and Van Zuylen (1978) in association with the University of California at Los Angeles have issued an inventory of individual "performance measures of skill and adaptive competencies in the developmentally disabled." Many of the instruments included are applicable to infants. The Technical Assistance Develop-ment System (TADS) at the University of North Carolina at Chapel Hill has published a proceedings document, *Perspectives on Measurement* (Black, 1979) that includes discussions on both standardized and non-standardized instruments for screening, diagnosis, and assessment of handicapped infants and preschoolers. The Western States Technical Assistance Resource (WESTAR) has issued a set of papers, *Infant Assessment: Issues and Applications,* edited by Darby and May (1979), which includes many thoughtful discussions of infant assessment. Fi-nally, Johnson and Kopp (1979) have made available a descriptive bibli-ography of screening and assessment measures for infants.

Some of the instruments in these references have been well evaluated for reliability, standardized on relevant populations, and investigated for their utility. Others were devised for specific projects and have not been widely employed. By judicious choice, helpful information and perspec-tives can be gleaned from these inventories.

CONCLUSIONS

The assessment tools available for the evaluation of at-risk and handi-capped infants vary greatly. A selection of the best known and most stan-dardized ones have been reviewed here. And references have been pro-vided to sources for more information. Before any assessment instrument is considered or chosen, however, the question must be asked, Why are we assessing the infant? As our sophistication about development increases, assessments for the purpose of predicting later developmental status decreases. Rather, assessments are being used to describe current developmental status and to determine whether and what kinds of programs might be beneficial to an infant whose current developmental status is a cause of some concern.

Some infants exhibit delayed development initially yet subsequently develop normally without any purposeful intervention. Conversely, there are infants who are normal at the time of assessment who subsequently exhibit developmental problems and delays. We do not know whether, in the first instance, there are some self-righting mechanisms that function to return the child to a normal developmental vector or whether the particular natural environment for that child happened to be especially functional for changing the developmental course. We do not know whether, in the second instance, the assessments were not sufficient or subtle enough to identify developmental problems or whether after the point of assessment problems developed that were not previously present.

Any serious consideration of the assessment of high-risk and handicapped infants reveals that our portion of ignorance and uncertainty is much larger than our portion of knowledge. Continued basic and applied research will eventually tip the comparison in the direction of knowledge. In the meantime, however, infants are born into this world who need help. They cannot be put on hold until our knowledge is sufficient to fully inform our efforts. Assessments made with a healthy respect for what we do not know, and discretely aided by good doses of common sense and folk knowledge, can provide important insights about the needs of these children, which in turn can help us facilitate their development.

REFERENCES

Alpern, G. D., and Boll, T. J. *Developmental profile*. Aspen, Col.: Psychological Development Publications, 1972.

Apgar, V. A proposal for a new method of evaluation of the newborn infant. *Current Researches in Anesthesia and Analgesia,* 1953, *32,* 260-267.

Bayley N. Mental growth during the first three years. *Genetic Psychology Monographs,* 1933, *14,* 1-92.

Bayley, N. The development of motor abilities during the first three years. *Monographs of the Society for Research in Child Development,* 1935, *1,* (Serial No. 1).

Bayley, N. *Bayley scales of infant development*. New York: Psychological Corporation, 1969.

Beller, E. K. Early intervention progams. In J. D. Osofsky (ed.), *The Handbook of infant development*. New York: Wiley, 1979.

Black, T. (Ed.), *Perspectives on measurement: A collection of readings for educators of young handicapped children*. Chapel Hill, N.C.: Technical Assistance Development System, 1979.

Bluma, S., Shearer, M., Frohman, A., and Hilliard, J.   *Portage guide to early education.* Portage, Wisc.: Portage Project, 1976.

Brazelton, T. B.   *Neonatal behavior assessment scale.* London: Heinemann, 1973.

Cattell, P.   *The measurement of intelligence of infants and young children.* New York: Psychological Corporation, 1940.

CORRC (Coordinating Office for Regional Resource Centers). *Preschool test matrix.* Lexington, Ky.: University of Kentucky, 1976.

Cox, B. P., and Lloyd, L.   Audiologic considerations. In L. L. Lloyd, (Ed.), *Communication assessment and intervention strategies.* Baltimore: University Park Press, 1976.

Cross, L., and Johnston, S.   The bibliography. In L. Cross and K. Goin, (Eds.), *Identifying handicapped children: A guide to casefinding, screening, diagnosis, assessment, and evaluation.* New York: Walker and Co., 1977.

Darby, B., and May, M. J.   *Infant assessment: Issues and applications.* Seattle: Western States Technical Assistance Resource, 1979.

Dubowitz, L. M. S., Dubowitz, V., and Goldberg, C.   Clinical assessment of gestational age in the newborn infant. *Journal of Pediatrics,* 1970, *77, 1.*

Erickson, M.   *Assessment and management of developmental changes in children.* St. Louis, Mo.: C. V. Mosby Co., 1976.

Frankenburg, W. K., Camp, B. W., and VanNatta, P.A.   Validity of the Denver Developmental Screening Test. *Child Development,* 1971, *42,* 475-485.

Frankenburg, W. K., and Dodds, J. B.   The Denver Developmental Screening Test. *Journal of Pediatrics,* 1967, *71,* 181-191.

Gesell, A.   *The mental growth of the preschool child.* New York: Macmillan, 1925.

Gesell, A., and Amatruda, C. S.   *Developmental diagnosis.* New York: Paul B. Holder, 1947.

Griffin, P. M., Sanford, A. R., and Wilson, D. C.   *Learning Accomplishment Profile.* Winston-Salem, N.C.: Kaplan School Supply, 1975.

Haith, M.   Visual cognition in early infancy. In R. B. Kearsley and I. E. Sigel (Eds.), *Infants at risk: Assessment of cognitive functioning.* Hillsdale, N.J.: Lawrence Erlbaum, 1979.

Hammer, E. K.   Interaction of assessment and intervention for visually impaired infants and preschool children. In F. D. Minifie and L. L. Lloyd, (Eds.), *Communicative and cognitive abilities: Early behavioral assessment.* Baltimore: University Park Press, 1978.

Horowitz, F. D., and Dunn, M.   Infant intelligence testing. In F. D. Minifie and L. L. Lloyd (Eds.), *Communicative and cognitive abilities: Early behavioral assessments.* Baltimore: University Park Press, 1978.

Horowitz, F. D., and Paden, L. Y.   The effectiveness of environmental intervention programs. In B. M. Caldwell and H. N. Riccuiti (Eds.), *Review of child development research* (Vol. 3.). Chicago: University of Chicago Press, 1973.

Horowitz, F. D., Sullivan, J. W., and Linn, P.   Stability and instability in the newborn infant: The quest for elusive threads. In A. Sameroff (Ed.), *Organization and stability of newborn behavior: A commentary on the Brazelton Neonatal Behavioral Assessment Scale. Monographs of the Society for Research in Child Development,* 1978, *43,* 29-45.

Johnson, K., and Kopp, C. B.   *A bibliography of screening and assessment measures for infants.* Los Angeles: UCLA, Department of Psychology, 1979.

Knobloch, H., and Pasamanick, B. *Gesell and Amatruda's developmental diagnosis: The evaluation and management of normal and abnormal neuropsychologic development in infancy and early childhood.* (3rd Ed.), New York: Harper and Row, 1974.

Koontz, C. *Koontz Child Development Program: Training activities for the first 48 months.* Los Angeles: Western Psychological Services, 1974.

Kopp, C., and Parmelee, A. H. Prenatal and perinatal influences on infant behavior. In J. D. Osofsky (Ed.), *Handbook of infant behavior and development.* New York: Wiley, 1979.

Krajicek, M. J., and Tearney, A. J. (Eds.), *Detection of developmental problems in children.* Baltimore: University Park Press, 1977.

Lancioni, G., Horowitz, F. D., and Sullivan, J. NBAS-K: I. A study of its stability and structure over the first month of life. *Infant Behavior and Development,* 1980, *3,* 361-366.

Lancioni, G., Horowtiz, F. D., and Sullivan, J. NBAS-K: II. Reinforcement value of the infant's behavior. *Infant Behavior and Development,* in press.

Linn, P. *Assessment of the infant environments: A review of the literature.* Unpublished paper, the Department of Human Development, the University of Kansas, 1979.

Lipsitt, L. P. The newborn as informant. In R. B. Kearsley and I. Sigel (Eds.), *Infants at risk: Assessment of cognitive functioning.* Hillsdale, N.J.: Lawrence Erlbaum Associates, 1979.

Lloyd, L. L. (Ed.), *Communication assessment and intervention strategies.* Baltimore: University Park Press, 1976.

Lowell, E. L., and Lowell, M. O. Interaction of assessment and intervention: Hearing impairment. In F. D. Minifie and L. L. Lloyd (Eds.), *Communicative and cognitive abilities: Early behavioral assessment.* Baltimore: University Park Press, 1978.

Mayeda, T., Pelzer, I., and Van Zuylen, J. E. *Performance measures of skill and adaptive competencies in the developmentally disabled.* Los Angeles: Neuropsychiatric Institute, UCLA, 1978.

Miller, J. F. Assessing children's language behavior: A developmental process approach. In R. L. Schiefelbusch (Ed.), *Bases of language intervention.* Baltimore: University Park Press, 1978.

Osofsky, J. D. *Handbook of infant development:* New York: Wiley, 1979.

Parmelee, A. H. *Newborn neurological examination.* Unpublished manuscript, Los Angeles, Department of Pediatrics, UCLA, 1974.

Parmelee, A. H., Kopp, C. B., and Sigman M. Selection of developmental assessment techniques for infants at risk. *Merrill-Palmer Quarterly,* 1976, *22,* 177-199.

Prechtl, H., and Beintema, D. *The neurological examination of the full term newborn infant.* London: Heinemann, 1964.

Rosenblith, J. F. The Graham/Rosenblith Behavioral Examination for Newborns: Prognostic value and procedural issues. In J. D. Osofsky (Ed.), *Handbook of infant development.* New York: Wiley, 1979.

Ruder, K. Planning and programming for language intervention. In R. L. Schiefelbusch (Ed.), *Bases of language intervention.* Baltimore: University Park Press, 1978.

Sameroff, A. J. (Ed.). Organization and stability of newborn behavior: A commentary on the Brazelton Neonatal Behavioral Assessment Scale. *Monographs of the Society for Research in Child Development,* 1978, *43.*

Sameroff, A., and Chandler, M.   Reproductive risk and the continuum of care-taking causality. In F. D. Horowitz (Ed.), *Review of child development research,* (Vol. 4). Chicago, Ill.: University of Chicago Press, 1975.

Scarr-Salapatek, S.   An evolutionary perspective on infant intelligence species patterns and individual variations. In M. Lewis (Ed.), *Origins of intelligence.* New York: Plenum Press, 1976.

Self, P. A., and Horowitz, F. D.   Neonatal assessment: An overview. In J. D. Osofsky (Ed.), *Handbook of infant development.* New York: Wiley, 1979.

Siegel, G. M., and Broen, P. A.   Language assessment. In L. L. Lloyd, (Ed.), *Communication assessment and intervention strategies.* Baltimore: University Park Press, 1976.

Spradlin, J. E., Karlan, G. R., and Wetherby, B.   Behavior analysis, behavior modification and developmental disabilities. In L. L. Lloyd (Ed.), *Communication assessment and intervention strategies.* Baltimore: University Park Press, 1976.

Uzgiris, I., and Hunt, J. McV.   *Assessment in infancy.* Urbana, Ill.: University of Illinois Press, 1976.

Vernon, McC.   Psychologic evaluation of hearing-impaired children. In L. L. Lloyd (Ed.), *Communication assessment and intervention strategies.* Baltimore: University Park Press, 1976.

Wilson, W. R.   Behavioral assessment of auditory function in infants. In F. D. Minifie and L. L. Lloyd (Eds.), *Communicative and cognitive abilities: Early behavioral assessment.* Baltimore: University Park Press, 1978.

Yang, R. K.   Early infant assessment: An overview. In J. D. Osofsky (Ed.), *Handbook of infant development.* New York: Wiley, 1979.

7

Program Planning for At-Risk and Handicapped Infants

Diane D. Bricker

Planning and organizing an effective early intervention program requires insight into the needs of infants and their families as well as information about available resources. This chapter tries to provide both by posing a series of key questions about essential planning areas to the reader and then suggesting a variety of strategies for answering them. Such an approach should lead to a more thoughtful analysis of the issues facing program developers.

It is essential that program developers and implementers devote sufficient time to evolving plans for answering the following questions:

1. What group of at-risk or handicapped infants is the program intending to help?
2. How will the target population be identified and referred to the program?

DIANE D. BRICKER is professor of special education and director of the Early Intervention Program, Center on Human Development at the University of Oregon, Eugene, Oregon.

3. What is the rationale for selecting the program's approach and content?
4. What are the major operating principles that guide the program?
5. What is the program's operational model?
6. What is the curricular content of the program?
7. What strategies will be employed to determine intervention objectives?
8. How will the selected intervention objectives be reached?
9. In reaching program goals and individual child objectives, what implementation problems exist?
10. How will program effectiveness be monitored and evaluated?
11. What are the mechanisms that assure a smooth transition of infants from the program?
12. What system has been devised to track previously enrolled children?

The order of the above questions is not arbitrary. It represents a logical progression of issues or concerns to be focused upon during program planning. Responses generated to the initial questions will have a substantial impact on the type of strategies adopted for dealing with subsequent areas (e.g., the program population and objectives surely will affect the choice of curricular content). Developing a comprehensive overview of the areas and issues to be confronted before initiation of the program should enhance the quality of the services offered to the at-risk or handicapped infant and his or her family.

What group of at-risk or handicapped infants is the program intending to help?

Most early intervention programs are developed to provide educational and associated health services to young children who have either specific disabling conditions or some genetic, prenatal or environmental characteristic that place them at risk for developing problems that will interfere with the acquisition of essential skills (e.g., walking, talking, problem solving). In this chapter education is defined in the broadest sense to include any activity that is designed to assist the child in the modification of current behavior or the acquisition of new behavior. Within this population of young children there is considerable variability from infants who are developing within normal limits to those with catastrophic disabilities.

The settings, in which the infants to be served reside, may vary from homes with educated, concerned caregivers to homes with caregivers poorly suited, either educationally or attitudinally, to understand the impact of a handicapping condition and the necessity to make compensatory arrangements for the child. Appropriate concern for the disabled or at-risk infant does not necessarily co-vary with income level; therefore, one should not assume that middle and upper income families are automatically better prepared than families with more modest incomes to provide a therapeutic environment for their disabled or at-risk infants. Many complex variables interact to affect a family's ability to reckon with its handicapped member (Turnbull and Turnbull, 1978).

The age of the target children, as well as their conditions and home settings, should be reflected in the program's structure—the type of program suitable for 3-year-olds would probably not suit infants in their first year of life. Also, the geographic locale of the proposed program could affect the initial choice of the target population to be served. For example, an infant program operating in a large metropolitan area may be able to target a specific group of children, as does the Down's syndrome project at the University of Washington in Seattle (Hayden and Dmitriev, 1975) or the program for severely handicapped infants at the Debbie Institute, Mailman Center for Child Development (Bricker and Dow, 1980) in Miami. Programs located in rural areas or smaller population centers, however, may have to provide services to a much more diverse population of handicapped or at-risk children, such as the Portage Project in rural Wisconsin (Shearer and Shearer, 1976) or the PEECH Program at the University of Illinois (Karnes and Teska, 1975).

In general, when selecting a target population it is important to consider several issues: First, does the community, large or small, have a specific need? It is possible that an early intervention program is already operating (e.g., a United Cerebral Palsy program for motorically handicapped infants), but that there are a number of infants needing educational services who are not eligible for the existing program. Unless extenuating circumstances exist, such information should stimulate creation of a program for those infants not already receiving essential services. Second, assuming a need has been established, what are the specific parameters of the population of children with unmet needs, including ages, handicapping conditions, cultural-ethnic background, and other variables that may be relevant?

How will the target population be identified and referred to the program?

Past experience suggests that those who develop and implement programs often assume that the critical processes of identification and referral occur "naturally." Of course, this is not the case. Infants will not just come in off the street. Time should be spent in specifying how the population will be identified and referred to the program. The greater the liaison between the detection/referring agency and the intervention program, the more likely it is that limited resources will be intelligently used. Identification and referral are time-consuming activities needing the skills of specially trained professionals. Steps must be taken by interventionists to link closely with them. In a small city there may be only one or two agencies that provide such services; in a large metropolitan area there will be a large variety of referring/detection agencies. Program developers are well advised to spend time discussing their program with personnel from these agencies, and then following up the discussions with letters that provide:

1. A detailed description of the target population (e.g., age, disability, other important parameters).
2. An overview of the program's content and structure (e.g., home- or center-based; curricular emphasis).
3. The name of the contact person for referrals.

Maintaining liaison with the referral agencies is also necessary. Personnel and program changes make periodic communication essential if inappropriate referrals are to be kept to a minimum and appropriate referrals at a maximum.

Once a baby has been identified as needing assistance and a proper referral has been made, the program should have a relatively fixed procedure for enrolling the child. A detailed descripton of such a procedure may be found in Bricker and Casuso (1979). The enrollment process should be reciprocal in the sense that it gathers information about the family and infant and likewise offers information to the family about the program.

What is the rationale for selecting the program's approach and content?

A philosophical stance or program rationale, no matter how eclectic, is a necessary foundation for designing a program. It is an underlying theme that provides the essential threads for weaving a cohesive intervention effort. Articulation of a program rationale should provide the program developers and implementers with the following critical guidelines: a) a system for the inclusion and exclusion of programmatic and curricular approaches and content, b) criteria for decision-making when faced with options or choice points, and c) criteria for personnel selection and inservice training.

Every service provider is faced with the dilemma of deciding what to include in an infant's individual educational program. In a broader sense, the same problem exists in terms of deciding what areas of intervention the total program will provide. Inevitably there are too many intervention goals, and a series of intelligent compromises must be made based on the program's rationale. Rationales can range from the most global (e.g., improve the child's general functioning level) to the relatively discrete (e.g., improve the child's head control). If the selected orientation is developmental, then selection of curricular areas tends to encompass multiple domains and to be arranged in sequences according to the best information on normal developmental patterns (Cohen and Gross, 1979; Bricker, Seibert, and Casuso, 1980). If a specialized approach is indicated (e.g., toddlers with only communication problems), then a more focused orientation might be chosen; for example, including activities that deal primarily with communication functions. In planning an intervention program for at-risk and handicapped infants, time should be spent in developing satisfactory responses to the following questions:

1. What will the nature of the intervention be?
2. Why was that particular intervention chosen?
3. How will it be accomplished?

There will be many naturally occurring choices points where the program rationale can guide decision-making. For example, most intervention programs for infants emphasize the importance of parental involvement. Frequently, however, despite a barrage of words about the meaningful roles of parents, the staff retains the major training responsibility. A program might well be confronted with a choice point early on—that is, should the teachers or the parents do the majority of hands-on activities with the infants? If the major rationale for the program is to assist parents in becoming better change agents with their infants, the choice of having the parents direct the majority of the teaching seems appropriate.

Finally, a carefully considered program rationale is crucial to the selection of staff members and their subsequent training. First, the disciplines from which staff members are recruited should reflect the program rationale and goals. If the major focus is on motorically disabled infants, specialists in motor development and manipulation are essential. If the program includes chronically ill, severely health-impaired, and multiply or severely disabled children, medical personnel must be on staff or accessible. Second, the personnel selected should have philosophical positions congenial with the program orientation. For example, if the program has chosen to proceed from a behavioral perspective, a social worker with a psychoanalytic background and mode of operation might prove incompatible. Third, the type of in-service training organized for the staff should reflect the program's emphasis and goals. It is of questionable value to organize special training for the staff focusing on curricular materials developed for the mildly handicapped when the target children are severely impaired.

What are the major operating principles that guide the program?

The selection of guiding operating principles for a program should be contingent upon a number of variables including the essential components of program philosophy, target population, and curricular focus. A few principles are of such overriding importance for serving handicapped and at-risk infants that all program developers should consider their adoption.

1. *Intervene as soon as a problem is reliably detected.* Intervening early with children who have significant development problems assumes that there is continuity in behavioral development and that early responses or processes provide the materials from which later, more complex levels of behavioral organization evolve. Thus, it is efficient and effective to provide a structured intervention program at the point the infant's behavioral repertoire is significantly delayed or there is a substantial reason to believe problems will emerge. For many children, particularly those with genetic or organic problems, the point of detection may be during the first year of life.

2. *Be on the alert for co-occurring behavioral involvement.* The interrelated nature of early behavior strongly suggests that a program should focus its habilitation efforts across a number of behavioral domains. At the very least, the service provider needs to be alert to the possibility that an infant with a delay in one area may have other behavioral deficits that require remediation.

3. *Include the family as a part of the intervention team whenever possible.* It may be unnecessary to emphasize this point since most early intervention programs now report the inclusion of parents (Bricker, Seibert and Scott, in press). However, the nature of that inclusion is important. Having parents attend meetings, sell cookies to raise money, or talk to civic organizations is admirable, but it is not the form of involvement being advocated here. Family members must become at least equal partners with the professional staff in the education of their handicapped infants. For example, with delayed infants, key aspects of parent/child social interactions could be singled out as a focus for educational programming. In effect, the interactional patterns of nondelayed infants and their mothers could be approximated by training parents to intervene during everyday exchanges with their infants.

4. *Develop an intervention program with training that is child-oriented rather than adult imposed.* The teacher and parent input should focus on training activities that are functional for the *child,* with intervention efforts relevant to his or her level of development and motivation system. For example, one approach to training object

permanence would be to place the small child in front of a table and cover objects which are assumed to be reinforcing. However, the same training could also be done using opportunities that occur frequently throughout the child's day. "Natural" displacement of interesting objects could involve placing a napkin over a cracker at snack time or putting a desired object behind a barrier.

Of course, it is not always possible to rely on the occurrence of "natural" events to teach specific concepts. But with a little creativity on the part of parents and interventionists, a number of situations can be structured to enhance both the acquisition and generalization of important responses. Such a child-focused orientation may be less applicable to severely handicapped infants with extremely limited repertoires who may be almost entirely dependent on others to arrange the environment and delivery consequences.

What is the program's operational model?

After deciding on the program's rationale and content areas, the operating model should be structured. Careful consideration of alternatives before implementation may save significant time and effort. Although numerous issues can be discussed under the rubric of program structure, the more important components are location of the intervention, staffing patterns, and hours of operation.

Intervention can be home-based, center-based, or some combination of the two. The choice of setting should take into account population needs and program goals, as well as such factors as funding level, geographic area, and family income level. The goal is to select an operating model most appropriate for the clientele.

The basic operational model will dictate the structure of the daily schedule and the deployment of staff. For example, center-based programs can operate on a full-day, half-day, or alternating-day basis in which staff are generally assigned to specific classrooms. In general, these programs include:

Arrival routine (e.g., bathroom time, talking with parents)
Group activities in which some general task is targeted
Small group or individual training
Snack time
Rearrangement of small group or individual training
Group activity
Closing routine

Conducting intervention in the home setting is, of course, more individualized but tends to follow a standard routine:

Arrival (e.g., greeting child)
Discussion with parents of child's weekly progress
Individual work with child
Assessment of progress
Demonstration of new activity to be conducted by parents
Departure

Some programs are able to use a combined center and home approach in which the parents and infant are seen in the home setting and have the opportunity to visit the center on a systematic basis as well. It may be that this combination model is generally the most effective because it provides the staff information about the home, maximizes home-center coordination, provides respite for the family, exposes the child to peers, enhances generalization of responses across environments, and allows for more efficient deployment of specialists.

What is the curricular content of the program?

The adoption of a program rationale provides the foundation for the selection of curricular content to be included in the program. The majority of intervention programs described in the literature cover a broad spectrum of curricular domains that appear to be essential for the balanced growth and development of the young child (Meier and Malone, 1979). Inclusion of the following domains should be carefully considered in light of the program's rationale:

1. *Communication*   This covers the sending and receiving of gestural, vocal, or gestural-vocal signals or symbols for the purposes of requesting, demanding, answering, greeting, or protesting (Bricker and Carlson, 1981).
2. *Sensorimotor*   This includes the acquisition of problem-solving behaviors relating to causality, means-ends, action schemes, object permanence, imitation, and spatial relations (Uzgiris, 1976).
3. *Preoperational*   This involves more complex problem-solving behaviors and levels of cognitive organization such as those in classification, conservation, and seriation (Flavell, 1977).
4. *Gross motor*   This area refers to motoric activities and coordination using the large muscles necessary for balance and movement through space (Finnie, 1975; Ford, 1975).
5. *Fine motor*   This area refers to those activities dependent upon the muscles used for precise movement and manipulation (Cohen and Gross, 1979).
6. *Socioemotional*   This includes a constellation of diverse facial, gestural, postural, vocal, and intonational responses used for interacting with the social environment (Sroufe, 1979).

7. *Self-help* This refers to a broad set of generalized responses leading to independent functioning across environments (Cohen and Gross, 1979).

The interrelated nature of early development argues for attention to each of the areas described above. For example, the classification of an infant's cooing response as vocal is arbitrary at best. In fact, the baby's vocalization may be social (e.g., to make contact with the caregiver), cognitive (e.g., the infant has discriminated a social being from the inanimate world), motor (e.g., the vocal cords have vibrated, mouth and tongue movements occurred), or communicative (e.g., "World pay attention to me!"). Most probably the infant's cooing has aspects of all these domains (Saarni, 1978; Bricker and Carlson, 1981).

What strategies will be employed to determine intervention objectives?

Once the rationale is selected and curricular domains chosen, attention should be directed toward the establishment of a sound procedure for determining intervention objectives for individual children. Although there are numerous mechanisms for doing this, below is a suggested step-by-step procedure:

Step one: A comprehensive history should be gathered for each child.
A compilation of information should include:
Social and medical information relevant to educational intervention (e.g., child has lived in several foster homes; description of seizure activity).
Any medical or physiological conditions that may affect educational intervention (e.g., hearing impairment, nutritional deficiencies).
Information on present environmental circumstances that may affect intervention (e.g., family having an economic crisis).

Step two: The child's baseline or entry behavior in critical intervention domains should be assessed.
The program staff may have the resources to administer a standardized instrument, such as the Bayley Scales of Infant Development, but should do so with the understanding that the information generated will not be particularly useful in selecting intervention objectives except at the general level. More useful in establishing specific behavioral goals are instruments providing more discrete information (e.g., Uniform Performance Assessment System, White, Edgar, and Haring, 1978). Such assessment tools yield specific information about the presence or absence of skills in a particular domain.

Step three: If the child's past history and current behavioral repertoire indicate the need, support personnel should be consulted.

For example, a 9-month old infant who is unable to move his hand to his mouth because of apparent spasticity must be examined by a physical or occupational therapist. The evaluation of such specialists is critical to the selection of appropriate intervention objectives.

Step four: Following evaluation, a meeting should be held with the direct intervention staff, relevant specialists, and the parents or primary caregivers.

Based on an analysis of the assembled information by all parties, an individual education plan can be developed including both long- and short-term objectives.

Following a procedure as outlined above should ensure the participation of all important members of the intervention team. Such participation and comprehensive information-gathering should, in turn, assist in choosing those areas of intervention most likely to produce subsequent developmental progress in the infant.

How will the selected intervention objectives be reached?

This question focuses on the selection of instructional strategies once intervention objectives have been determined. One effective strategy is a behavioral approach. Instruction may be viewed as a three-part sequence which relies on the establishment of contingencies or relationships between antecedent events, response goals or behaviors, and consequent events. This instructional sequence is illustrated below.

Antecedent ——————⟶ Behavior ——————⟶ Consequence

in which:

A ___(precedes)___   B ___(followed by)___   C_____

Each long-term training target should be divided into component steps or short-term targets. Each of these steps can then be specified according to this format. In programming for the targets, the service provider may manipulate the antecedent or consequent events that occur in tandem with the behavior or the precurser behaviors. The systematic presentation of antecedent events is, in reality, the curriculum. The curriculum should specify the arrangement of the environment as well as the form of the target response. Careful definition of antecedents, target behaviors, and consequences is essential for establishing agreement about the presence or absence of a response and under what circumstances it does or does not occur. A fairly typical procedure for operationalizing the antecedent-behavior-consequence sequence is suggested below:

1. Write a description of the behavior to be acquired or modified (e.g., labeling a ball).
2. Develop and write a set of antecedent events to precede the targeted behavior (e.g., teacher holding up the ball asking what it is).
3. Write a description of the events to follow the targeted behavior (e.g., consequences).
4. Write a ratio statement that sets the ratio between the response and the arranged events.
5. Write a description of any child behavior that has been targeted for deceleration in the context of the antecedent events.
6. Write a description of events to follow the child's performance of behaviors to be decelerated.

Williams and York (1978) have defined these strategies and discussed their use in detail.

Service providers need to give careful consideration to the training tasks selected for facilitating development of target objectives. Goals should not be establishing one-to-one correspondence between stimuli and responses. Rather, selected tasks should ensure that children acquire general strategies or concepts that can be used across different settings, people, and objects. Learning the label "coat" only for the toddler's own jacket is not nearly as useful as being able to appropriately label all coatlike garments regardless of size, color, texture, or location.

Selecting instructional tasks with multiple goals is also important in order to maximize the training effect. For example, it is often appropriate to superimpose language activities on the training of other skills. Using thoughtfully chosen words, the service provider can label an activity or a child's action, or encourage the child to do so. Playground activities may be ideal for encouraging the older infant to communicate what he or she wants to do (e.g., to swing or slide).

Instructional tasks selected also should be functionally reinforcing for the child whenever possible. That is, some aspect of the training activity should be designed to be inherently interesting. In some cases, this might be accomplished simply by placing interesting toys on low tables for a young child who needs practice in pulling to a standing position. In other situations, development of functional reinforcers may require a major act of creative insight by the teacher.

Regardless of which instructional approach is employed, it should have a substantial impact on the infant's rate of progress. Therefore, efforts should be made to ensure that teachers, clinicians, and parents are using the most effective instructional strategies available.

**In reaching program goals and individual child
objectives, what implementation problems exist?**

Implementation problems may appear relatively insignificant when compared to such issues as program rationale and curricular content. Unfortunately, the reality is often that smooth and effective functioning of a program is substantially hampered because inadequate attention has been given to developing policies and procedures for handling mundane, everyday problems. Some of the areas that most often require attention are discussed below.

Transportation   Perhaps no single operational problem has caused as much frustration for service providers as getting children and families to and from programs. Whether plans call for the program providing transportation or caregivers ferrying children back and forth, adequate time must be spent on designing a system that will work. Such a system should include procedures for emergencies (e.g., flat tires, ill bus drivers, and hazardous road conditions).

Supplies   This category includes equipment, disposable items, curricular materials, and office supplies. Procedures must be established for storing materials, ordering replacements, receiving items, and paying vendors. In many agencies, the ordering of supplies is a lengthy process, therefore, reorder schedules must be established so that the program is not faced with a lack of critical items.

Personnel   Procedures for hiring, firing, and evaluation of staff must be developed. Often such practices are dictated by the agency with which the program is affiliated. Personnel policies may be involved and, again, necessitate familiarity and planning to be executed appropriately. Policies for vacations, sick leave, and emergencies need to be formulated.

Facilities   Careful attention to the function and safety of the physical environment of the program is necessary. Unless totally home-based, bathroom and food preparation are essential. Also essential is compliance with local fire ordinances and other safety regulations (e.g., nonflammable rugs, fire evacuation drills) for the protection of the children and staff.

Licensing   Most states require programs serving preschool children to be licensed. Such licensing is for the protection of the children. Again, requirements are often extensive and require preparation and implementation time.

Reports   Most programs are faced with significant report preparation throughout the year for a variety of purposes. Keeping enrolled children's records up to date is often a time-consuming task, as is the dissemination of information to other agencies and the preparation of progress reports for administrative personnel or funding agencies. Efficient procedures for coping with report preparation are necessary.

How will program effectiveness be monitored and evaluated?

Intervention programs should monitor or evaluate child progress at two levels: acquisition of individual short-term objectives, and acquisition of more global, long-term objectives. Ultimately, these two levels should combine in an overall program evaluation system (as is described in another chapter of this book).

Monitoring acquisition of short-term training goals requires systematic data collection. That is, if a response is to be accelerated or decelerated, frequency or rate measures should be recorded during baseline and intervention. If the target behavior involves time measures, such as delay in responding to a stimulus, or length of a response, latency and duration measures, respectively, should be taken.

When the problem is one of measuring acquisition of behavior, a procedure for collecting data called the Mandate-Prompt-Cue-Independent system (MPCI), which was developed at the Experimental Education Unit at the University of Washington, may be suitable. This system allows the teacher to keep a record of the degree to which the child must be moved passively through a desired response pattern or the degree to which the child independently executes the response under appropriate stimulus control. First the child is presented with an appropriate stimulus situation. Then time is allowed for him or her to execute the response *independently*. If the child responds appropriately, an independent response is recorded; if not, the child is cued, perhaps verbally or with the teacher modeling the response, and the response is then credited in the *cue* column. If the response is not executed within the allotted time, the child is *prompted* by the teacher with more support and passive movement, allowing the child the opportunity at various points to complete the response. If the child still fails, the teacher ultimately moves the child through the entire range of motion of the desired response, and a *mandate* is scored. The data sheet, scored properly, allows an immediate visual record, across sessions, of decreases in less dependent modes of responding and increases in independent execution.

In addition to setting up a data system that measures progress toward short-term objectives, decision-rules must be established in advance for determining how and when to continue or change a program, based on the data. The principal function of the decision rules is to ensure that warning signals are heeded and that evaluation of intervention strategies occurs on a regular basis. Time lines should be established for rate changes or successful acquisition of new behaviors. If the plotted data deviate from established time-lines, or if criterion levels of behavioral objectives have not been reached, staff should regard this as a signal for possible change. At this point the target behavior and program are reevaluated to determine whether the goal itself is inappropriate or whether the activities implemented to achieve it are inadequate.

To monitor acquisition of long-term targets or more generic responses, a programmatic assessment instrument should be administered three or four times per year. There are a variety of instruments available for assessing infants ranging from brief checklists to extensive developmental sequences, although as discussed elsewhere none of these tests are without limitation (Bricker, 1978; Haring, 1976; McCall, Hogarty, and Hurlburt, 1972; Lewis, 1976).

What are the mechanisms that ensure a smooth transition of infants from the program?

An important goal for most early intervention programs is the subsequent placement of each child in the least restrictive environment. For many programs, that means placement in a public school kindergarten program. Whether the child's subsequent placement is in a public school, a private agency, or in another early intervention program, the process can be significantly enhanced with an established plan. In general, procedures are needed for two distinct transition times: 1) transfer to another program during the year, or 2) transfer to another program at the termination of the year. Planning for transition should begin at the time of the infant's enrollment. That is, parents or caregivers should be reminded of the importance of informing staff members well in advance of an impending family move or desired change for the child. In addition, staff should share information about future placement possibilities for the child in the community. Compiling records and information takes time, and everyone involved should be alerted to the requirement for preparation of the necessary material.

The child's transition from one program to another should be a major concern for the staff. After spending months or years on the education of an infant, leaving his or her subsequent placement, and thus progress, to chance is unconscionable. In order to minimize problems, a program should develop a set of standard procedures to be followed when a child is shifting to another program. Below is a suggested strategy.

Step one: Establish mechanisms for monitoring records on a quarterly basis to ensure that information is current. Having accurate, up-to-date files will assist immensely in the transition process.

Step two: Have appropriate release forms developed so that parents can give permission for the transmission of information to the child's new program.

Step three: Meet with the parents and discuss the child's progress to date and information to be shared with the child's new program.

Step four: After the new program has received written records on the child, have a meeting, if at all possible, with the teaching staff from the old and new programs, and the parents. At this meeting the staff should offer ongoing assistance until the new staff members become thoroughly acquainted with the child.

Step five: Develop a procedure for assessing the appropriateness of the new program for the child and his or her family. Such information is important for future referrals and placements.

What system has been devised to track previously enrolled children?

All the effort involved in an early intervention program is of little consequence if a child consistently makes poor future adjustments. That is not to say that the child's failure is necessarily the fault of the program, but it is the responsibility of the program to prepare him or her as adequately as possible for subsequent placements. For this reason it is essential that the program make a cost-effective attempt to ascertain regularly how each previously enrolled child is doing. Extensive, longitudinal follow-up is time-consuming and expensive, and beyond the scope of most early intervention programs. However, a few simple methods can be used for collecting some general information.

In many instances both families and teaching personnel who have had subsequent contact with the child may be willing to fill out a short questionnaire. One secret to success is developing a form that is brief and to the point. An end-of-the-year gathering to which previously enrolled children and their families are invited could be an opportunity to collect information on the appropriateness of the child's current placement. Equally as important would be an evaluation by that placement's program staff. Asking specific staff members to complete short questionnaires might, again, be most efficient.

All intervention efforts can be improved. The magnitude of the improvement will depend, in part, on the development of feedback systems that can lead to changes that will enhance the program.

CONCLUSIONS

The question-response format of this chapter was designed to call attention to critical issues for program planning and implementation for infants. Responses were offered as potentially useful approaches for efficient and effective operation of an early intervention program. Underlying these approaches are some basic organizational schemes, which are discussed briefly below:

1. Thorough planning and preparation time are essential for recognizing potential problems and increasing the chances that appropriate solutions are available.
2. It is important to compile necessary information prior to making consequential decisions. Choosing a transportation system without the proper cost data could result in adopting a system that severely taxes the resources of the program over the year. An alternative system might be less ideal, but more affordable, and thus a wiser choice.
3. Consensus by staff members on solutions to problems is a goal worthy of pursuit. Although decisions cannot always please everyone, an effort should be made to consider different opinions and develop compromise positions whenever possible. Such an approach builds effective participation by the staff.
4. Mechanisms should be developed for effective communication between program components. Such mechanisms should encourage communication and feedback between staff members that will enhance the quality of services delivered to the handicapped infant and his or her family.

Efforts expended on program planning will be visible in our end product—children better able to cope with the daily vicissitudes of their environment.

ACKNOWLEDGMENTS

The author would like to thank Laurel Carlson and Mary Beth Bruder for their editorial assistance with this chapter.

REFERENCES

Bricker, D.   Early intervention: The criteria of success. *Allied Health and Behavioral Sciences Journal,* 1978 *1,* 567-582.

Bricker, D., and Carlson, L.   Issues in early language intervention. In R.L. Schiefelbusch and D. Bricker (Eds.), *Early language intervention.* Baltimore: University Park Press, 1981.

Bricker, D., and Casuso, V.   Family involvement: A critical components of early intervention. *Exceptional Children,* 1979, *46,* 108-116.

Bricker, D., and Dow, M.   Early intervention with the young severely handicapped child. *The Journal of the Severely Handicapped,* 1980, *5,* 130-142.

Bricker, D., Seibert, J., and Casuso, V.   Early intervention. In J. Hogg and P. Mittler (Eds.), *Advances in mental handicap research*. London: Wiley, 1980.

Bricker, D., Seibert, J., and Scott, K.   Early intervention: History, current status and the problems of evaluation. In D. Doleys, T. Vaughn, and M. Cantrell (Eds.), *Interdisciplinary assessment and treatment of developmental problems*. New York: Spectrum, in press.

Cohen, M., and Gross, P.   *The developmental resource: Behavioral sequences for assessment and program planning*. New York: Grune & Stratton, 1979.

Finnie, N.   *Handling the young cerebral palsied child at home*. New York: Dutton-Sunrise, 1975.

Flavell, J.   *Cognitive development*. Englewood Cliffs, N.J.: Prentice-Hall, 1977.

Ford, F.   Normal motor development in infancy. In E. Bleck and D. Nagel (Eds.), *Physically handicapped children: A medical atlas for teachers*. New York: Grune & Stratton, 1975.

Haring, N.   Infant identification. In A. Thomas (Ed.), *Hey, don't forget about me: Education's investment in the severely, profoundly, and multiply handicapped*. Reston, Va.: Council for Exceptional Children, 1976.

Hayden, A., and Dmitriev, V.   The Multidisciplinary Preschool for Down's Syndrome Children at the University of Washington Model Preschool Center. In B. Friedlander, G. Sterritt, and G. Kirk (Eds.), *Exceptional infant* (Vol. 3). New York: Brunner/Mazel, 1975.

Karnes, M., and Teska, J.   Children's response to intervention programs. In J. Gallagher (Ed.), *The application of child development research to exceptional children*. Reston, Va.: The Council for Exceptional Children, 1975.

Lewis, M.   What do we mean when we say "infant intelligence scores?" A sociopolitical question. In M. Lewis (Ed.), *Origins of intelligence*. New York: Plenum Press, 1976.

McCall, R. B., Hogarty, P.S., and Hurlburt, N.   Transitions in infant sensorimotor development and the prediction of childhood IQ. *American Psychologist*, 1972, *27*, 728-748.

Meier, J., and Malone, P.   *Facilitating children's development—A systematic guide for opening learning*. Baltimore: University Park Press, 1979.

Saarni, C.   Cognitive and communicative features of emotional experience, or Do you show what you think you feel? In M. Lewis and L. Rosenblum (Eds.), *The development of affect*. New York: Plenum, 1978.

Shearer, D., and Shearer, M.   The Portage Project: A model for early childhood intervention. In T. Tjossem (Ed.), *Intervention strategies for high risk infants and young children*. Baltimore: University Park Press, 1976.

Sroufe, A.   Socioemotional development. In J. Osofsky (Ed.), *Handbook of infant development*. New York: Wiley, 1979.

Turnbull, A., and Turnbull, R. (Eds.), *Parents speak out*. Columbus, Ohio: Charles Merrill, 1978.

Uzgiris, I.   Organization of sensorimotor intelligence. In M. Lewis (Ed.), *Origins of intelligence: Infancy and early childhood*. New York: Plenum Press, 1976.

White, O., Edgar, E., and Haring, N.   *Uniform Performance Assessment System*. Seattle: College of Education, Experimental Education Unit, Child Development and Mental Retardation Center, University of Washington, 1978.

Williams, W., and York, R.   Developing instructional programs for severely handicapped students. In N. Haring and D. Bricker (Eds.), *Teaching the severely handicapped* (Vol. 3). Columbus, Ohio: Special Press, 1978.

8

A Family Focus
for Intervention

Marie M. Bristol and James J. Gallagher

Parents differ in their responses to their handicapped infant and in their
willingness or ability to participate in intervention programs. Yet, it is
widely recognized today that parents play the central role as educators as
well as nurturers of their own children. This chapter explores the evolution of this conception of the role of parents, the nature of parent/infant
interactions, and implications for intervention strategies.

THE CHANGING PARENT ROLE

In the early fifties the parents of handicapped children were generally expected to seek competent professional advice for their handicapped child

MARIE M. BRISTOL is assistant director for Family Sudies in the Carolina Institute for
Research on Early Education of the Handicapped (CIREEH) at the Frank Porter Graham
Child Development Center, and Research Assistant Professor in the Department of
Psychiatry, the University of North Carolina at Chapel Hill.

JAMES J. GALLAGHER is director of the Frank Porter Graham Child Development
Center and Kenan Professor of Education, the University of North Carolina at Chapel Hill.

The preparation of this chapter was supported in part by the Special Education Program, U.S. Department of Education, DHEW, Contract Number 300-77-0309. However,
the opinions expressed do not necessarily reflect the position or policy of the U.S. Special
Education Program, and no official endorsement should be inferred.

and to do what the professionals prescribed. Often, particularly in the case of mentally retarded or autistic children, the advice was to place the child in a state or private institution.

In too many instances the professional service deliverers added to the burden of the parents by suggesting that they were not accepting of their handicapped child. Gallagher (1956) took professionals to task for not providing sympathy and support for the parents. Instead, they implied that these parents reject their handicapped child. He observed

"Needless to say, every parent can be indicted at one time or another if expression of negative values is the only criterion for parental rejection, especially if the observer happens to catch the parent under conditions of stress. When we think of the problems that parents of normal children face and then consider the extra stress that is placed on the parents of handicapped children, it is little wonder that the term [rejected] used loosely could apply to almost any mother or father. What parent could be completely happy or positively oriented to a child who is quadriplegic, blind, or severely mentally retarded, or, for that matter, completely normal in every respect?" (p. 273).

Since that time there has been a significant movement toward a parent/professional partnership based on mutual respect and decision-making. Turnbull and Turnbull (1978) list several reasons why the change has occurred:

1. The experimental evidence that parents can influence positively the development of their children through teaching them at home.
2. The encouraging results of early intervention in ameliorating some of the developmental deficits associated with moderate and severe handicaps.
3. The success of parents in bringing litigation to establish the educational rights of their children.
4. Federal legislation, notably PL 94-142, that sets forth clear standards for parental involvement in the educational process.

The influence of organized parent advocacy on the changing roles of parents, and professionals, cannot be overstated. Increased parent assertiveness has led to action by state legislatures, the U.S. Congress, and the judicial system. Gorham et al. (1975), in their advice to parents, portray well the new parent role and its relationship to advocacy:

"You are the primary helper, monitor, coordinator, observer, record keeper, and decision maker for your child. Insist that you be treated as such. It is your right to understand your child's diagnosis and the reasons for treatment, recommendations, and for educational placement. No changes in his treatment or educational placement should take place without previous consultation with you" (p. 184-185).

The role changes described above, although welcome, do not come without substantial psychological costs, however.

FAMILY DYNAMICS AND PROGRAM PLANNING

The increasing trend to educate and raise handicapped children in their own homes and communities, instead of sending them to a distant institution, raises a whole new set of problems. The parents now must adjust to their handicapped child on a continuous basis, and the relevant professional(s) must interact with the parents on a continuous basis. A more sophisticated understanding of family dynamics is now necessary to plan programs appropriate for the handicapped child and family. A variety of factors are discussed.

Program Focus

Before deciding how parents should be involved in infant programs, we must first determine the focus of the program. If the focus is exclusively on the child, the program goal becomes one of recruiting parents to assist the program in facilitating child progress. If the focus is on the family, however, the goal becomes one of determining how the program can assist in facilitating optimal family adaptation to the handicapped child. Since the compensatory education programs of the sixties we have been exploring ways to do the former. We have just begun to grapple in a systematic way with an understanding of the dynamics and implications of the latter. If we focus exclusively on the child instead of on the family we may find that we have facilitated the development of one at the expense of the other.

Just as we would not consider designing an intervention program for an infant without assessing his present functioning, we should not proceed to plan programs for parents without some understanding and assessment of the larger context in which parents live and their current adaptations to their young handicapped child.

The Dual Crisis of the Handicapped Child's Family

Adaptation to a handicapped infant involves both an acute and a chronic phase. At the time of birth or recognition of the child's handicap, the parents feel the acute sense of loss of the "ideal" child that might have been and experience a grieving process similar to that of bereavement (Solnit and Stark, 1961). The parents may first deny either the existence or the severity of the child's handicap. Intellectual acceptance of the truth of the handicap comes gradually, but the parents may first pass through stages of anger, guilt, depression, and grief. Finally a realistic acceptance of the child and his or her handicap is reached, not only intellectually, but emotionally. This is a gradual process and one which father and mother may move through at different rates. Parental expectations for the child and their willingness to participate in the child's program may reflect the stage of acceptance the parent has achieved. This process of adaptation to handicapped infants is described more fully in Chapter 3.

The more difficult adaptation to the child, however, is not the shock of discovery and the acceptance of the diagnostic label by parents. It is the "chronic sorrow" (Olshansky, 1962) experienced in their day-to-day struggle to meet the needs of the handicapped child while maintaining their self-esteem as persons, their integrity as a family, and their place in the community of which they are a part (Turnbull and Turnbull, 1978).

One aspect of the crisis suffered by parents of severely handicapped children is the extreme modification that must take place in parental roles. Normal roles are based on the expectation that the child will go through a gradual and predictable evolution in terms of increasing levels of self-care, social adaptation, and intellectual and academic competence. This includes performing competently in school, the major occupation in a child's life.

The introduction of a handicapped child into this family causes the "symbolic death" reported by many observers. It is the symbolic death of the "child-who-will-never-be" and thus the death of all the role expectations that the parents had projected for themselves. A program designed to aid parents in making adaptations must understand and take into account the various stresses, supports, and role disjunctions that the situation creates.

The Reciprocal Nature of Parent/Child Interaction

One of the fundamental keys to the understanding of family dynamics is to grasp the essence of the continuing and sequential effects of parent/child interactions. Infants, including severely handicapped infants, profoundly affect their parents and some knowledge of the nature and extent of this impact is necessary to design parent programs that meet the needs, not only of the child, but of the parent. Consideration of the impact of the child on the parent is a relatively recent phenomenon. An exclusive focus on the effect of the parent on the child has been the cornerstone upon which most theories of socialization have been built and is the philosophy behind many parent programs.

Although some authors (Gallagher, 1956; Sears, Maccoby, and Levin, 1957) had openly questioned the adequacy of the unidirectional parent-to-child causal model more than 10 years earlier, it was not until the publication of Bell's work (1968; 1971) on the reinterpretation of the direction of effect in studies of socialization that serious attention was paid to the contribution of the child's behavior to the relationship between parents and child. In place of a parent/cause model, Bell proposed an interactional model that included not only the effect of the parents' behavior on the child, but also the effect of the child's behavior on the parents.

Bell's model organizes parental social response and control behaviors in hierarchical caretaking repertoires. Congenital child characteristics, including impaired sensory-motor capacities, responsiveness to parents, and activity levels, elicit different levels and intensities of parent caretaking responses, and differentially reinforce parent behaviors.

Since the publication of Bell's original studies, a number of other researchers have reported on behaviors of normal and handicapped infants that affect maternal caretaking behaviors and attitudes. These include eye contact (Stern, 1974; Fraiberg, 1974), ability to discriminate mothers from strangers (Lewis and Rosenblum, 1974), imitation and reciprocal play ability (Stern, 1974), state of being (Lewis, 1972), effective prelinguistic communication, including differential crying and hand gestures (Zeskind and Lester, 1978; Bernal, 1972), and vocalization (Anderson, Vietze, and Dokecki, 1977).

Bell (1974) describes how the "signal" aspects of the infant's repertoire (smiling, crying, vocalizing) and the "executive aspects" (clinging, approaching, and following) initiate and maintain close contact with the parent. Through these behaviors the child signals needs to the parent, communicates that the parent has special meaning to the child, and reinforces the parent for initiating some exchange or responding to the infant's overtures.

The Effect of Infant Handicaps on Maternal Attachment

A mother's self-esteem is often seriously affected by her handicapped infant's failure or delay in communicating to her that she is loved and cared for in a unique way. This can hamper development of the special affectional bond called attachment that normally forms between mother and child.

The development of attachment behavior such as the preference for the mother in times of stress (Tracy, Lamb, and Ainsworth, 1976) by the infant clearly signals to the mother that she has a central and essential role in the child's life. This in turn is postulated to result in more frequent and positive interaction between mother and child, leading to greater competence in both and subsequent strengthening of this affectional tie. It follows, then, that strengthening this attachment bond between mother and infant should be one of the primary goals of intervention programs.

It has been suggested, but not demonstrated, in some reviews of the efficacy of early intervention programs (Bronfenbrenner, 1975; Karnes and Teska, 1975), that one program outcome is the strengthening of mother/child attachment and an increase in the quality and quantity of the pair's interaction. These changes are, in turn, thought to lead to improved child outcome. Reports of "vertical diffusion" of effects of intervention from the child under direct study to younger siblings who were never directly involved in the intervention program seem to substantiate this conclusion (Gray and Klaus, 1965; Gilmer, Miller, and Gray, 1970). In a recent study of maternal attachment, Ramey, Sparling, Wasik, and Bryant (1979) demonstrated that the level of what they called "Functional Maternal Concern," a measure of mutual mother/child involvement, was modified by a parent education program. Mothers in a home education group interacted more frequently with their infants, engaged in mutual play more frequently, engaged in mutual play for longer periods of time, and joined the child's activity more often than did comparable mothers not enrolled in the parent education program.

In an earlier longitudinal study, this index of Functional Maternal Concern, or dyadic mutual involvement, was significantly related to positive temperament characteristics of the child. The index, measured when the child was 6 months of age, was not related to the child's 6-month Bayley mental development index (MDI), but was significantly related to the child's developmental and intellectual status as measured by the Bayley at 18 months and the Stanford-Binet at 48 months. This ability of the Functional Maternal Concern Index at 6 months to predict later intellectual status is more striking in light of the fact that the Bayley score at 6 months did not predict intellectual status at 48 months. The study provides some empirical support for the relationship of attachment to program intervention and outcome for non-institutionalized infants (Ramey and Farran, 1981).

Handicapped infants are often deficient in the behaviors that facilitate interaction and attachment. In a literature review of the effect of the handicapped infant on the parent (Ramey, Bell, and Gowen, 1980), the authors found that handicapped infants may differ from normal peers in rate of development; temperament, including quality and duration of crying, irritability, consolability, and adaptability; social responsiveness, including smiling, eye contact, responsiveness to holding, and nonverbal communication; repetitive behavior patterns; and caregiving demands. The data suggest that these deficits affect both the quality and the quantity of interactions between parents and their handicapped children.

Eye contact, for example, has been shown to be a powerful initiator and sustainer of maternal interaction (Robson, 1967; Stern, 1974; Wolff, 1963) as early as the second week of life. In fact, it has been termed the "cornerstone of a mother's attachment to her infant," and it is the infant, not the mother, who makes and breaks the majority of mutual gazes (Stern, 1974). Lack of such eye contact in blind or autistic babies, or distortions of that contact found in cerebral palsied infants, may have profound effects on the quantity and quality of maternal/child interactions.

As important as the child's ability to initiate interactions with the mother is the child's ability to sustain or reinforce the mother's attempts to care for and interact with the child. In a study of attachment behaviors in 15 pairs of mothers and their handicapped infants, Stone and Chesney (1978) noted that each of these children showed disturbances in one or more behaviors that would be expected to initiate and reinforce mother/child interactions and subsequent attachment. The majority of the infants did not cease crying with maternal handling; they seldom, if ever, smiled in response to maternal caretaking behavior, and they provided few vocalizations in response to maternal vocalizations or interventions. This failure of the handicapped infant to reward the mother may lead to fewer and less positive interactions, consequent reduction in stimulation, and further delay in development.

For the attachment bond to grow between mother and child, the mother must be sensitive in responding to the signals her infant is capable of, and must interact frequently and positively with the child (Bowlby, 1969; Schaffer and Emerson, 1964). It is relatively easy to see the responsibility of the mother in this situation. On the other hand, it is rather easy, while working with handicapped and seemingly helpless infants, to overlook the contribution the infant makes to difficulties in these parent/child interactions.

Stress in Mother/Child Interaction

Another key to the understanding of family dynamics which is helpful for designing programs relates to mother/child stress.

Evidence that specific child characteristics not only elicit specific maternal behaviors in observed interactions, but have a more global effect on the mother has been found in studies of stress at the Frank Porter Graham Child Development Center. In a study of the stresses and supports reported by 40 mothers of autistic children, Bristol (1979) found that the majority of the variance in predicting family and parent stress could be accounted for by specific characteristics of the child and his or her environment. These included difficult personality characteristics, degree of severity of the child's physical incapacitation, degree of severity of the child's overall dependency, lack of appropriate activities for the child, lack of services, and limited prospects for independent living.

Bell (1980) examined the effect of child characteristics on mothers of infants with a variety of handicapping conditions. She found that the child's caretaking demands, social responsiveness, and repetitive behavior patterns were predictive of parental stress, with the level of caretaking demands accounting for the majority of the variance. These demands might be expected to be related to degree of dependency found in the Bristol study. The similarity of the findings by both investigators working with different ages and types of populations adds support to the notion that specific child characteristics potentially amenable to intervention are predictive of parental stress and worthy of note in planning parent programs.

Identifying child behaviors that are a particular source of stress to parents may ultimately have implications for intervention programs, particularly because all of the stressors identified above are amenable to intervention. In some cases, this may mean implementing a behavioral intervention program to improve management problems the parent is experiencing with the child's difficult behavior, or, in keeping with Thomas and Chess's (1977) caveats regarding goodness of fit between child and parent temperament, it may imply working with parents to help them understand and adapt to the particular personality and needs of the child.

Parental and Staff Perceptions

Not only do infant behaviors directly affect overt parental responses, but there is another, perhaps more important level on which child behaviors impact on parents and professionals. Fraiberg (1974) describes the impact that a lack of eye contact can have, not only on mothers, but on therapists working with handicapped infants:

> "I have described some of the reactions of professional observers in social exchanges with blind babies. The blind eyes that do not engage our eyes, that do not regard our faces, have an effect upon the observer which is never completely overcome. When the eyes do not meet ours in acknowledgement of our presence, it feels curiously like a rebuff" (p. 220).

Parents and therapists are not simply black box reactors to infant stimuli. They are cognitive human beings who not only objectively observe infant behaviors, but also attach subjective meanings to them (Parke, 1978). Without assistance, parents and therapists may not interpret their child's lack of response as a lack of development in the child, but as a conscious rejection of them as persons or as evidence of their incompetence as parents, setting up a vicious cycle that reduces positive interaction with the infant. In addition to objective knowledge about parent and child behavior, it is essential to be aware of the subjective world of the parent through knowledge of parental perceptions, values, and attitudes. As Parke (1978) points out, parental reports about the ways in which parents perceive and understand both their infants and their roles are legitimate and important sources of data not easily derived from observation alone.

For example, Kilbride, Johnson, and Streissguth (1971) found that lower-class mothers who provided less visual stimulation than middle-class mothers for their 2-week-old infants were less aware that their infants could see at birth. The parents were acting in accord, not with reality, but with their perception or misperception of that reality. Part of the "goodness of fit" between child and parent cited in the Thomas and Chess studies (Thomas et al., 1963; Thomas and Chess, 1977) is the differential perception and response of parents to children with similar individual characteristics. Some understanding of these subjective perceptions is essential for correcting misperceptions or for responding to parents' needs within the social or cultural framework that shapes those perceptions.

We need to learn much more about the ways in which parental perceptions about a handicapped infant's capacities affect interaction, and ultimately, outcome.

The Father Is Also Affected by the Infant's Handicap

Another factor of family dynamics that must be considered when planning programs is that of the father. Traditionally, the role of the father in infancy has been de-emphasized. Particularly in discussing the concept of attachment, virtually all theorists have focused on the importance of the mother/child relationship to the exclusion of the father (Bowlby, 1951, 1958, 1959; Bijou and Baer, 1961; Freud, 1940; Maccoby and Masters, 1970).

Recent research reviewed by Lamb (1976), however, suggests that many fathers are accessible and responsive to their infants and are important figures in their infants' lives. He presents a review of evidence of an attachment bond between fathers and infants and concludes that there is no demonstrable preference by infants for either parent in the home or the laboratory, except in stress situations when they show some preference for their mothers.

Because there is empirical evidence that the amount of time spent together is a poor predictor of the quality of the infant's relationships with either father or mother, Lamb concludes that the time spent between father and child, though limited, has important implications for child development. Among his many roles, the father serves as the medium through which the values and role demands of the social system are interpreted to the child. On the basis of data showing that father absence is more acute for young children and that sex-role assignment may be made before 18 months of age, Lamb concludes that although the influence of the father is felt throughout the lifespan of the child, it is particularly critical in infancy.

Research on families clearly shows that the father is affected by the birth of a handicapped child. In a review by Price-Bonham and Addison (1978), the authors report major sources of stress for fathers of retarded children including financial strain, emotional tension, and limitations in social activities. The desertion rate for fathers of retarded children is high (Reed and Reed, 1965), and the divorce rate among parents of mentally retarded children is triple that among parents of nonhandicapped children (Love, 1973). The suicide rate among parents of retarded children is double the national average (Love, 1973).

Price-Bonham and Addison also review studies that demonstrate that the impact on fathers is different from that on mothers. Fathers appear to accept the diagnosis of a handicap with less emotion, to exhibit more knowledge, to be more objective, to be less emotionally involved, and to be more future-oriented than mothers. There is also evidence that fathers determine the pattern for rejection or acceptance of the child in the family.

Fathers appear to be more affected by attributes that stigmatize the family's social and community image and are particularly affected by the birth of a handicapped son, often reacting in extremes of total involvement or total withdrawal. Tallman (1965) points out that the father's role is often conceived of as an instrumental or task-oriented one and is geared toward achievement in the outside world. Because of his traditional orientation to the world outside the family, the father may experience more acute stress at those times when the child comes into contact with the outside world and fails to conform to its norms (e.g., at school entry).

Ordinarily, a father would be involved in preparing his children, particularly his sons, for activities related to competing for status and prestige outside the home, such as sports or employment. Handicapped children are able to develop domestic skills often associated with the feminine role, but may not develop as readily the competitive skills often associated with the father's role. The father's unique training skills, then, may be seen by him as superfluous in interacting with his handicapped child. Fathers, then, have fewer opportunities to feel that they have contributed to the child's well-being.

Cummings et al. (1976) studied 240 fathers of mentally retarded, chronically ill, neurotic, and healthy children and found that fathers reported more stress than mothers of similar children. They found that fathers of mentally retarded children undergo long-term personality changes of a neurotic type and have few constructive outlets for such stress. They report awareness of the negative aspects of the child's care, but are involved in few of the rehabilitative aspects.

Effects of an Infant's Handicap on Siblings

Another largely neglected topic concerning family dynamics has been the effect of the handicapped child upon normal siblings within the family. Studies of siblings of handicapped children indicate that the normal sibling is at risk for emotional and behavioral disorders (Farber, 1959; Cohen, 1962; Schwirian, 1976). Gath (1972) found evidence of poor peer relationships, behavior problems, and depression, particularly in siblings in large families of Down's syndrome children. The age and sex of both the siblings and the handicapped child have been related to sibling maladjustment (Farber, 1959, 1976; Schild, 1971; Schwirian, 1976). Whether or not the handicapped child remained at home or was institutionalized was also related to sibling adjustment (Farber et al., 1960; Fowle, 1968). The pervasive nature of this impact is highlighted by studies indicating that these negative effects on siblings continue into adult life (Grossman, 1972; Cleveland and Miller, 1977) and are not merely a temporary reaction to the increased child-rearing demands posed by the handicapped child. The case for stress in families of handicapped children, then, is rather well documented.

General Family Adaptation

In addition to the effect felt by the individual members of the family, there is clear evidence that the presence of the handicapped child affects the social entity of the family (Farber, 1959; Farber and Ryckman, 1965; Fotheringham, Skelton, and Hoddinott, 1972; Martin, 1975; Price-Bonham and Addison, 1978; Fotheringham and Creal, 1974; Marcus, 1977).

Tavormina and his associates (1977) have noted four major parent styles of adapting to the reality of having a handicapped child. In the first case, the father "emotionally divorces" himself from the child, leaving the care of the child entirely up to the mother and involving himself fully in outside activities, such as his job and organizations unrelated to the child. A second style of adaptation occurs when the parents join together in rejecting the child. The child in this type of family is most apt to be institutionalized, regardless of the severity of his handicap.

In the third style, the parents make the child the center of their universe, subordinating all of their own desires and pleasures to the service of the handicapped child. The child is usually quick to sense such an arrangement and to take advantage of it by making the parents feel guilty for wanting a life of their own. A final style is one in which the parents join in mutual support of the child and each other, but maintain a sense of their own identities and a semblance of a normal life.

Although the last style seems by far the most adaptive, Tavormina is quick to point out that there is no single best style for all families, or, at least, that it is unrealistic to expect that all parents will use only this most adaptive style. In fact, it is likely that mixtures of these adaptive styles exist in any one family at different times.

The results of studies on the effects of marital integration on having a handicapped child have yielded mixed results. At least in the United States, they show that handicapped children tend either to severely disrupt the marital relationship or, alternatively, to strengthen it.

The stresses to be dealt with by families of handicapped children are so manifest that it is easy to forget that many families are coping successfully with their handicapped children. There are studies which indicate that at least some families are even enriched by the presence of a handicapped child (Caldwell and Guze, 1960; Gralicker, Fischler and Koch, 1962; Grossman, 1972).

Characteristics of Successful Families

Bristol (1979) studied 40 mothers of autistic children and identified successful mothers as those reporting the lowest levels of parent and family stress related to the child (lowest quartile). These "successful" mothers were comparable to the high-stress (top quartile) mothers on a number of factors. These included the mothers' ages and number of hours of paid employment, as well as the number of children in the family, the degree of child dependency, and the children's birth order.

Successful mothers did differ significantly from the highest stress mothers in terms of the severity of their children's physical and social handicaps and in the mothers' informal support networks. The study indicated that the composite "successful" mother (coping well with her autistic child) had a husband who was extremely helpful, and had relatives who were available and helpful. (Eight of ten high-stress mothers had relatives who were available but not helpful.) The mother was also apt to have an autistic girl rather than an autistic boy, a child who was less severely handicapped socially and physically, a younger child and a family experiencing less general stress. The successful mother was less isolated from friends and other parents of handicapped children and had access to services for her autistic child.

Gallagher (1979) studied a sample of 50 families, comparing successful versus average parents (so determined by staff ratings), whose handicapped children were enrolled in five programs across the country. Although the similarities were greater than the differences between the two types of parents in terms of stress, family role, and support, the successful parents, particularly mothers, seemed to have stronger ego controls and personal value systems that sustained them through the crisis and gave them a positive and up-beat outlook on life.

Summary

The handicapped child impacts on each family member as well as on the family as a social entity. How those involved respond depends on a variety of factors that impinge on the key reciprocal interactions of the child and mother.

The ability of a significant number of families to cope effectively lends promise to professional attempts to intervene positively to increase the capabilities of families to find adequate coping mechanisms.

IMPLICATIONS FOR INTERVENTION

The central roles parents play in their infants' lives make a partnership between parents and professionals of critical importance. The type and level of that involvement, however, should vary depending upon the individual needs of the family. Yet, it is not unusual to visit programs for high-risk or handicapped infants that have highly individualized programs for each infant, but only a single "package" for involving parents. Several recommendations are offered.

Create Individualized Family Plans

In place of developing individualized education programs (IEP) or individualized habilitation plans (IHP) for each child, we need to develop individualized family plans (IFP) that consider assessment, programming, and evaluation in the broader context of family development. Some efforts have been made in this regard (Karnes, Zehrbach, and Teska, 1972). Bricker and Casuso (1979) describe an individualized parent program calling for assessment of family needs, determination of objectives, and development of an individual parent plan (IPP) that includes activities and evaluation criteria for meeting each objective. The authors suggest an ongoing recycling process that continues until all objectives have been reached.

The National Collaborative Infant Project has developed a set of objectives and evaluation criteria for programs working with parents (Meisel, 1977). Objectives include helping families to integrate the handicapped child into the family with an equitable distribution of resources among all family members and a minimal negative impact on the financial, physical, and emotional status of the family; assisting parents in coping with their feelings about the child and with the feelings and responses of the siblings; and assisting parents in feeling competent as parents. Evaluation criteria are suggested for each goal.

The activities developed to help meet these goals must be based on an assessment of parent needs. WESTAR (1979) has published a 19-point family needs assessent checklist developed by Project KIDS Outreach of Dallas, Texas, which assesses parent concerns about community resources, educational programming, support services, normal development, and tests and measurements, and asks parents about priorities for involvement and intervention. Similarly, Wiegerink, Hocutt, Bristol, and Bell (1980) have developed a Parents Need and Expectations Questionnaire that assesses parents' expectations and priorities for involvement in 36 different activities and support services.

A corollary of this individualization is the necessity of providing, within existing financial constraints, a continuum of services to parents in response to differences in level of service needed, severity of the child's handicap, geographic distance from services, and social and cultural diversity. Such a continuum of services was developed for a rural area by the Southeast Mental Health and Retardation Center (Bristol, 1977) when it was found that the center-based services traditionally offered attracted, or at least retained, primarily middle-class, relatively articulate parents. The continuum of services ranges from community-based screening programs and parent-to-parent support "clubs" held in parents' homes, through home teaching for individual families, and intensive parent and professional training in a center-based Therapeutic Evaluation and Treatment Center.

Fit Programs to the Clients

Individualization of the program must relate not only to program content but to flexibility of other administrative arrangements as well. If we are serious about involving fathers in programs and hope to reach fathers other than middle- and upper-class professionals, we must provide flexibility of scheduling. The majority of programs for infants are conducted from 9 to 3, making them inaccessible not only for most fathers, but also for working mothers. The reality with which we must deal in designing parent programs is that 43 percent of all mothers with children under 6 are now working outside the home.

Consideration of other stresses and forces acting upon the family is critical. In the course of studying the effects of the autistic child on the family, Bristol (1979) discovered examples of middle-class families struggling simultaneously not only with their handicapped child but with a collection of crises, such as financial problems, a spouse suffering from Parkinson's disease, a sibling dying of leukemia, a mother herself ill with cancer, and parents responsible for the care of ailing and aged grandparents. These demands on parents' time are substantial and must be respected.

Providing supplementary services for these parents may make their involvement possible. Social services, such as help in obtaining food stamps, respite care, or transportation for parents unable to reach the program on their own are examples of individualization that may make the difference between apparent parent apathy and active involvement.

In the Bristol (1980) study of families of autistic children, more than two-thirds of the parents cited the critical need for trained babysitters or respite care for their child and themselves. Almost a fourth of the mothers also reported that they knew of services available for their children that could not be obtained, or obtained regularly, because of transportation problems. One mother drove 250 miles a day to obtain school services.

Build Meaningful Parental Roles into Programs

An appreciation of the multiple roles played by parents should also encourage professionals to evidence respect for parents' time by involving them in programs in meaningful roles, not just as program assistants. They should be respected members of the intervention team involved in program planning and evaluation. A review of parent involvement in the different roles of learner, teacher, and decision maker by Wiegerink, Hocutt, Posante-Loro, and Bristol (1980) concluded that the role the parent plays in the program affects the outcome for the child, the parent, and the community.

Programs operating within the aegis of PL 94-142, Education for All Handicapped Children Act, have a legal and moral obligation to involve parents as decision-makers in all phases of diagnosis and assessment, placement, programming, and evaluation of progress. These legal requirements have been discussed in detail by various authors (Turnbull, 1978; Pelosi and Hocutt, 1977) and should be familiar to all professionals conducting programs for the families of young children.

A recent policy study (Hocutt, 1979) used a Delphi procedure to generate norms for parent involvement by a panel of 20 experts (high-level staff from congressional committees dealing with handicapped children, government bureaucrats, directors of validated Handicapped Children's Early Education Program Projects of the U.S. Special Education Programs, parents, and early childhood experts). The panel proposed 36 different parent activities ranging from parent training and involvement in educational and therapeutic services, to participation in program planning, operation, and evaluation.

Weigerink and Hocutt (1979) reported that, in spite of legislative mandates for more policy-oriented involvement and the opinions of this panel of experts, the majority of parents are involved in recipient activities such as parent training rather than in roles that make programs more accountable to their consumers.

Plan for Father Involvement

Traditionally, program roles for parents have been defined in terms of the mother's role. The separate role of the father should also be considered in planning program activities. In a study by Gallagher (1979), both fathers and mothers were asked to rank ideal role behavior as well as current role allocations in the family. The fathers strongly indicated that they believed they should be playing a more active role in the lives of their handicapped children. The mothers, rather naturally, agreed. Fathers, however, have been consciously or unconsciously excluded from receiving assistance from intervention programs, if only by virtue of the fact that most infant intervention programs are held while the father is at work.

Research on fathers of handicapped children suggests that fathers have few constructive ways in which they contribute to the welfare of the child, few opportunities to share their stress with other fathers of handicapped children, and few opportunities to work through the mourning process, the sense of loss, frustration, and anger related to having a handicapped child. Their contact with the child and his or her handicap is often indirect, through bill paying, or arbitrating and serving as a sounding board for the complaints of the mother and the siblings about the handicapped child.

How should fathers be involved? The temptation in reacting to the exclusion of fathers is now to overreact and imply that fathers play the same role as mothers, with interventions designed to make fathers mini-mothers or mother substitutes. Some caretaking balance is clearly called for, but maximizing the possibility of a unique role for the fathers while avoiding sex stereotyping should be the goal. At one time it was thought that "fatherese" (paternal language) was inadequate when compared with "motherese" in meeting the needs of young children. Recent evidence suggests that the fathers' greater demands for linguistic clarity may provide the critical transition between the mother's nonevaluative acceptance and the critical judgment of the real world.

Lamb (1976) suggests that different parental roles exist in early infancy. Infants tend to be involved more in play with fathers and in caretaking with mothers. Fathers engage in more rigorous and rough and tumble play, and infants tend to prefer play with fathers to play with mothers. Pedersen (1976) points out that because of the time spent away from the child, the father has a novelty value for the child that the ever-present nonworking mother does not have. Conversely, the infant may also be more interesting to the father, enabling him to interact with the child more intensely than he might if he were with the child all day. The additional mutual interest can enable the father to play an important role in programming for the handicapped child.

Keep in Mind Sibling Needs

Parents of handicapped children often express concern about the effect of the handicapped child on siblings. Although this is less of a concern while the child is still an infant, parents should at least have the opportunity to be aware of and discuss the issues. Program staff can counsel parents to arrange their lives so that siblings receive adequate attention. They can caution them against expecting older siblings to assume caretaking responsibilities for the handicapped brother or sister that exceed their level of maturity and their own needs as children.

Siblings may also have fears that they, too, will become handicapped. If older, they may fear that they will have handicapped children when they marry. Program staff can help siblings deal with these expressed and unexpressed fears. Cansler, Martin, and Valand (1975) have developed a model for a week-long workshop that includes an agenda, a sample letter to parents, and an evaluation instrument.

One of the best contributions a program can make to sibling welfare is to assist parents in obtaining adequate support services. Mothers and fathers with access to reliable babysitting and respite care are more likely to have sufficient time and energy for their other children. If neither assistance from the father nor outside help is available, a mother may be too drained to respond to the needs of the infant's brothers and sisters.

Create a Responsive Environment that Fosters Parental Involvement

One continuing issue is maintaining active parent participation and involvement. Some program factors appear to be related to levels of parental involvement. The smallest programs have a higher percentage of parents involved (Wiegerink and Hocutt, 1979; Bauch, Vietze, and Morris, 1973). Behaviorally oriented programs have higher levels of involvement than other types (Reisenger, Ora, and Frangia, 1970); and programs with transportation available have greater participation (Schaefer et al., 1976) than those that do not. School-based programs may have lower levels of parent involvement because a bureaucratic or hierarchical system may have no meaningful role for parents (Ora, 1973).

Another critical element in successfully including families is the extent of the program commitment to support such activities. Karnes and Zehrbach (1975) cited the need for funding trained staff with time specifically allocated to parent programming. Wiegerink and Hocutt (1979) concluded that programs with at least one three-quarter-time staff member specifically designated to work with parents had higher levels of parent involvement than those that did not. This reinforces the need for a family focus where parent activities are not afterthoughts to child programming but are themselves program goals worthy of scarce resources.

Identify Parental Expectation

To ensure continued parental involvement, intervention programs must focus on goals that are important to the family. Research studies indicate that parents who are committed to program goals are more likely to carry out suggested activities, will become more skilled as teachers, and are more likely to have children who show measurable progress (Rosenberg, 1977). Conversely, parents whose children show measurable progress and who receive feedback that they are effective teachers are more likely to be committed to program goals and to carry out suggested activities.

Kogan, Tyler, and Turner (1974) observed children with cerebral palsy and their mothers in both play and therapy sessions over a 2-year period. A report of initial observations indicated that both children and mothers exhibited more negative feelings during therapy sessions than they did when playing together. This suggests that the therapy sessions with the child were at least a potential source of stress. The "parent as therapist" role apparently was a new one for the mother and one in which she may not have been comfortable at first. However, these behaviors persisted over a 2-year period and, in addition, there was a significant decrease in warm and positive behaviors between both mother and child and, significantly, between therapist and child over the same period.

The "affect turn-off" or burnout that parents displayed was significantly related to the absolute deficit in motor skills of the child and inversely related to the size of the child's gain in motor areas, though not to gains in language or personality areas. The less progress the child made, the greater the reduction in warmth. Particularly, there was a clear relationship between warmth of interaction and whether the child was walking at the end of the 2-year period of the study.

The authors suggested that parents (and perhaps therapists) expected that initial spurts on program entry would continue over time and were disappointed when that expectation did not materialize. An alternative explanation offered was that because treatment generally is often directed toward deficits, parents may focus on these deficits to the exclusion of gains in other areas. Shere and Kastenbaum (1966) noted that medical professionals often tended to limit parents' attention to physical handicaps to the point that parents were not aware of intellectual or social gains made by their physically handicapped patients.

Ideally, the reinforcement for parental involvement in programs for handicapped infants is progress observed in the child or the family. The extent to which parental burnout may be a function of the amount of investment of time and energy they have made and the positive feedback they receive that their efforts are worthwhile. A mother who works for 2 years in the belief (however mistaken) that her efforts will enable her child to walk, will understandably become discouraged when she fails to see the goal attained. Just as we talk of providing the child with a contingent environment over which he has some control (Vietze et al., 1978), we must provide parents with a responsive environment that gives them feedback that they are effective persons and that their efforts are making a difference.

This includes checking parental expectations for reality before beginning the program. It also means helping parents to be aware of areas in which the child is making gains, and finally, it means monitoring and altering the intervention when no progress is being made.

In a follow-up study by Tyler and Kogan (1977), the authors demonstrated that an 8-week intervention involving immediate videotape feedback to the mother and individualized program modification could reduce stressful, negative interactions between mother and child, with the improvements maintained 9 months later. Equally important, there was no reduction in warmth (no affect turn-off) over the course of the 9 months.

Parents Can Be Helped To "See Progress"

We must also help parents find alternate ways of understanding and eliciting responses from their handicapped infants. Fraiberg and her associates (Fraiberg, 1974; Fraiberg, Smith, and Adelson, 1969) demonstrated that parents of blind children can be taught to "read" their children's hands in the absence of eye contact signals, as well as taught to stimulate a nonvisual motoric dialogue between parents and infants that enables the infants to develop social responses such as smiling at approximately the same age as nonhandicapped children. This, in turn, enables the infants to respond to and reinforce their parents' efforts and effectively keeps the parent interacting positively with the now responsive infant.

Progress in many areas, especially with severely handicapped infants, is extremely slow. We must find ways to help parents appreciate the value of small increments in skill progress. In addition, the system must provide feedback to the parents and direct input into program modification to avoid the feeling of helplessness that many parents face in interacting with their young handicapped children. It is possible that this lack of a responsive environment experienced by the parent leads to a form of "learned helplessness" (Seligman, 1975) and is partially responsible for the high incidence of depression among parents of handicapped children.

Help Build a Support Network

The intervention program would be well-advised to stimulate the parents' own support network of friends and relatives or to assist the parent in building an expanded network, perhaps through formal or informal contacts with other parents of handicapped children. For this reason, parents should also be encouraged to join parent organizations, such as the National Association for Retarded Citizens or the National Society for Autistic Children. In effectively working through these organizations to obtain services for their children, parents not only serve children, but they also regain a sense of their own competence as persons and a clearer sense of having some mastery over their own destiny.

SUMMARY

Parent intervention programs have not reflected the information now available about families of handicapped children. The highly individualized nature of a particular family's problems call for a more individualized approach to parents, as we have already attempted through the IEP for their children. We need to realize that the presence of a handicapped infant is one of many important events in the life of a family and should not be assumed by professionals to be the one overriding factor. The role of the father has been largely ignored and obviously needs more study and attention.

Another area of needed attention is how we can support the family with professional help to ease the strain or feelings of burnout that are observable. Although we have accepted the use of contingent reinforcement as one of the clearest advances in programs for children, we have not yet transferred that knowledge to programs for parents. The best means of providing community support still needs much discussion and study. It seems that we are on the threshold of a new era of understanding and cooperative relationships with parents if only we can effectively use the knowledge we already have about these families and their strengths and weaknesses.

REFERENCES

Anderson, B. J., Vietze, P., and Dokecki, P. R.   Reciprocity in vocal interactions of mothers and infant. *Child Development,* 1977, *48,* 1976-1981.

Bauch, J. P., Vietze, R. M., and Morris, V. D.   What makes the difference in parental participation? *Childhood Education,* 1973, *49,* 47-51.

Bell, P. B.   *Characteristics of handicapped infants: A study of the relationship between child characteristics and stress as reported by mothers.* Unpublished doctoral dissertation. Chapel Hill, N.C.: University of North Carolina, 1980.

Bell, R. Q.   A reinterpretation of the direction of effects in studies of socialization. *Psychological Review,* 1968, *75,* 2, 81-95.

Bell, R. Q.   Stimulus control of parent or caretaker behavior by offspring. *Developmental Psychology,* 1971, *4,* 63-72.

Bell, R. Q.   Contributions of human infants to caregiving and social interaction. In M. Lewis and L. A. Rosenblum (Eds.), *The effect of the infant on its caregiver.* New York: Wiley, 1974.

Bernal, J.   Crying during the first ten days of life and the maternal responses. *Developmental Medicine and Child Neurology,* 1972, *14,* 362-372.

Bijou, S. W., and Baer, D. M.   *Child development: I   A systematic and empirical theory.* New York: Appleton-Century-Crofts, 1961.

Bowlby, J.   *Maternal care and mental health.* Geneva: World Health Organization, 1951.

Bowlby, J.   The nature of the child's tie to his mother. *International Journal of Psychoanalysis,* 1958, *39,* 350-373.

Bowlby, J.   *Attachment and loss* (Vol. 1). New York: Basic Books, 1959.

Bricker, D., and Casuso, V.   Family involvement: A critical component of early intervention. *Exceptional Children,* 1979, *46,* 108-117.

Bristol, M. M.   Continuum of service delivery to preschool handicapped children and their families. In P. Mittler (Ed.), *Research to practice in mental retardation* (Vol. 1). Baltimore: University Park Press, 1977.

Bristol, M. M.   *Maternal coping with autistic children: The effect of child-characteristics and interpersonal support.* Unpublished doctoral dissertation. Chapel Hill, N.C.: University of North Carolina, 1979.

Bristol, M. M.   Impact of handicapped children on mothers: Some research results. In S. Freedman (Ed.), Proceedings of the 1980 OSE Handicapped Children's Early Education Program Conference, Washington, D.C. 1980.

Bronfenbrenner, U.   Is early intervention effective? In M. Guttentag and E. Struening (Eds.), *Handbook of evaluation and research. Beverly Hills: Sage Publications, 1975.*

Caldwell, B. M., and Guze, S. B.   A study of the adjustment of parents and siblings of institutionalized and noninstitutionalized retarded children. *American Journal of Mental Deficiency,* 1960, *64,* 845-861.

Cansler, D. P., Martin, G. H., and Valand, M. C.   *Working with families.* Winston-Salem, N.C.: Kaplan Press, 1975.

Cleveland, D. W., and Miller, N. B.   Attitudes and life commitments of older siblings of mentally retarded adults: An exploratory study. *Mental Retardation,* 1977, *15,* 38-41.

Cohen, P. C.   The impact of the handicapped child on the family. *Social Casework,* 1962, *43,* 137-142.

Cummings, S. T.   The impact of the child's deficiency on the father: A study of fathers of mentally retarded and chronically ill children. *American Journal of Orthopsychiatry,* 1976, *46,* 246-255.

Farber, B.   Effects of severely mentally retarded child on family integration. *Monographs of the Society for Research in Child Development* 1959, *24,* No. 2, Serial 71.

Farber, B.   Family adaptations to severely mentally retarded children. In M. Begab and S. Richardson (Eds.), *Mentally retarded in society.* Baltimore: University Park Press, 1976.

Farber, B., and Ryckman, D. B.   Effects of severely mentally retarded children and family relationships. *Mental Retardation Abstracts,* 1965, *2,* 1, 1-17.

Fotheringham, J., and Creal, D.   Handicapped children and handicapped families. *International Review of Education,* 1974, *20,* 355-373.

Fotheringham, J. B., Skelton, M., and Hoddinott, B. A.   The effects on the family of the presence of a mentally retarded child. *Canadian Psychiatric Association Journal,* 1972, *17,* 283-290.

Fowle, C. M. The effect of the severely mentally retarded child on his family. *American Journal of Mental Deficiency,* 1968, *73,* 468-473.

Fraiberg, S. Blind infants and their mothers: An examination of the sign system. In M. Lewis and L. A. Rosenblum (Eds.), *The effects of the infant on its caregiver.* New York: Wiley, 1974.

Fraiberg, S., Smith, M., and Adelson, E. An education program for blind infants. *Journal of Special Education,* 1969, *3,* 121-139.

Freud, S. *An outline of psychoanalysis.* New York: Norton, 1940.

Gallagher, J. J. Rejecting parents? *Exceptional Children,* 1956, *22,* 273-276.

Gallagher, J. J. *Characteristics of successful parents of moderately/severely handicapped children.* Paper presented at Handicapped Children's Early Education Conference, Washington, D.C., December 6, 1979.

Gallagher, J. J., Cross, A., and Scharfman, W. Parental adaptation to a young handicapped child: The father's role. *Journal of the Division for Early Childhood,* 1981, *3,* 3-14.

Gath, A. The effects of mental subnormality on the family. *British Journal of Hospital Medicine,* 1972, *8,* 147-150.

Gilmer, B., Miller, J. O., and Gray, S. W. *Intervention with mothers and young children: A study of intrafamily effects.* Demonstration and Research Center for Early Education (DARCEE), papers and reports Vol. 4, No. 11, Nashville, Tenn.: George Peabody College for Teachers, 1970.

Gorham, K., Des Jardins, R., Page, E., and Scheiber, B. The effect on parents of the labeling of their children. In N. Hobbs (Ed.), *Issues in the classification of children: A handbook on categories, labels and their consequences.* San Francisco, Ca.: Jossey-Bass, 1975.

Gralicker, B. V., Fishler, K., and Koch, R. Teenage reaction to a mentally retarded sibling. *American Journal of Mental Deficiency,* 1962, *66,* 838-843.

Gray, S. W., and Klaus, R.A. Experimental preschool program for culturally deprived children. *Child Development,* 1965, *36,* 887-898.

Grossman, F. K. *Brothers and sisters of retarded children: An exploratory study.* Syracuse, N.Y.: Syracuse University Press, 1972.

Hare, E. H., Laurence, K. M., Paynes, H., and Rawnsly, R. Spina bifida cystica and family stress. *British Medical Journal,* 1966, *2,* 757-760.

Haring, N. *Individualized parent involvement.* Seattle, Wash.: Western States Technical Assistance Resource (WESTAR), 1979.

Hocutt, A. M. *Parent involvement policy and practice: A study of parental participation in early education projects for handicapped children.* Unpublished doctoral dissertation, University of North Carolina, Chapel Hill, N.C., 1979.

Karnes, M. B., and Teska, J. A. Children's response to intervention programs. In J. J. Gallagher (Ed.), *The application of child development research to exceptional children.* Reston, Va.: Council for Exceptional Children, 1975.

Karnes, M. B., and Zehrbach, R. Parental attitudes and education in the culture of poverty. *Journal of Research and Development in Education,* 1975, *8,* 45-53.

Karnes, M. B., Zehrbach, R., and Teska, J. A. A family involvement model, implementation with families of multihandicapped children. *Theory into Practice,* 1972, *11,* 150-156.

Kilbride, H., Johnson, D., and Streissguth, A. P. Early home experience of newborns as a function of social class, infant sex and birth order. Unpublished manuscript, University of Washington, Seattle, 1971.

Kogan, K. L., Tyler, N., and Turner, P. The process of interpersonal adaptation between mothers and their cerebral palsied children. *Developmental Medicine and Child Neurology,* 1974, *16,* 518-527.

Lamb, M. E. (Ed.). *The role of the father in child development.* New York: Wiley, 1976.

Lewis, M.   State as an infant—Environment interaction: An analysis of mother-infant interaction as a function of sex. *Merrill-Palmer Quarterly,* 1972, *18,* 95-121.

Lewis, M., and Rosenblum, L. A. *The effect of the infant on its caregiver.* New York: Wiley, 1974.

Love, H. *The mentally retarded child and his family.* Springfield, Ill.: Charles C Thomas, 1973.

Maccoby, E. E., and Masters, J. C.   Attachment and dependency. In P. H. Mussen (Ed.), *Carmichael's manual of child psychology* (Vol. 2.) (3rd ed.), New York: Wiley, 1970.

Marcus, L.   Patterns of coping in families of psychotic children. *American Journal of Orthopsychiatry,* 1977, *47,* 3, 383-399.

Martin, B.   Marital breakdown in families of children with spina bifida ceptica. *Developmental Medicine and Child Neurology,* 1975, *17,* 757-764.

Meisel, J.   *Programming for atypical infants and their families: Guidelines for program evaluation.* Monograph No. 5 of the Nationally Organized Collaborative Project to Provide Comprehensive Services for Atypical Infants and Their Families. New York: United Cerebral Palsy, June 1977.

Olshansky, S.   Chronic sorrow: A response to having mentally defective children. *Social Casework,* 1962, *43,* 190-192.

Ora, J.   Involvement and training of parents and citizen workers in early education for the handicapped. In M. B. Karnes (Ed.), *Not all little wagons are red.* Reston, Va.: Council for Exceptional Children, 1973.

Parke, R. D.   Parent/infant interaction: Progress, paradigms and problems. In G. P. Sackett (Ed.), *Observing behavior. Vol. I: Theory and applications in mental retardation.* Baltimore: University Park Press, 1978.

Pedersen, F.A.   Does research on children reared in father-absent families yield information on father influences? *Family Coordinator,* 1976, *25,* 4, 459-464.

Pelosi, J., and Hocutt, A. *The Education for All Handicapped Children Act: Issues and implications.* Chapel Hill, N.C.: Developmental Disabilities Technical Assistance System, 1977.

Price-Bonham, S., and Addison, S.   Families and mentally retarded children: Emphasis on the father. *Family Coordinator,* 1978, *27,* 3, 221-230.

Ramey, C. T., and Farran, D.   The functional concern of mothers for their infants. *Infant Mental Health Journal,* 1981, *2,* 48-55.

Ramey, C. T., Bell, P. B., and Gowen, J. W.   Parents as educators during infancy: Implications from research for handicapped infants. In J. J. Gallagher (Ed.), *New directions in exceptional children,* pp. 59-84. San Francisco, Ca.: Jossey-Bass, 1980.

Ramey, C. T., Sparling, J. J., Wasik, B. H., and Bryant, D. *A model for educating parents of high-risk infants.* Paper presented at the Ira J. Gordon Memorial Conference on Parent Education and Involvement. Chapel Hill, N.C., June, 1979.

Reed, E. W., and Reed, S. C. *Mental retardation: A family study.* Philadelphia: W. B. Saunders Publishing Co., 1965.

Reisinger, J. J., Ora, J. P., and Frangia, G. M.   Parents as change agents for their children: A review. *Journal of Consulting Psychology, 1970, 4,* 108-123.

Robson, K. S.   The role of eye-to-eye contact in maternal-infant attachment. *Journal of Child Psychology and Psychiatry*, 1967, *8*, 13-25.

Rosenberg, S.   *Family and parent variables affected outcomes of a parent-mediated intervention.* Unpublished doctoral dissertation, George Peabody College, Nashville, Tenn., 1977.

Schaefer, E. S.   *Parent-professional-child interaction and involvement.* Progress report. Submitted to the U.S. Office of Child Development, 1976.

Schaffer, H. R., and Emerson, P. E.   The development of social attachments in infancy. *Monographs of the Society for Research in Child Develoment,* 1964, *29*, 3, 1-77.

Schild, S.   The family of the retarded child. In R. Koch and J. C. Dobson (Eds.), *The mentally retarded child and his family.* New York: Brunner/Mazel, 1971.

Schwirian, P. M.   Effects of the presence of a hearing-impaired preschool child in the family on behavior of older "normal" siblings. *American Annals of the Deaf,* 1976, *121*, 373-380.

Sears, R. R., Maccoby, E. E., and Levin, H.   *Patterns of child rearing.* New York: Harper & Row, 1957.

Seligman, M. E. P.   *Helplessness: On depression and death.* San Francisco: Freeman Publishers, 1975.

Shere, E., and Kastenbaum, R.   Mother-child interaction in cerebral palsy: Environmental and psychosocial obstacles to cognitive development. *Genetic Psychology Monographs,* 1966, *73*, 255-335.

Solnit, J., and Stark, M. H.   Mourning the birth of a defective child. *Psycho-analytic Study of the Child, 16,* 1961, 523-537.

Stern, D. N.   Mother and infant at play: The dyadic interaction involving facial, vocal, and gaze behaviors. In M. Lewis and L. A. Rosenblum (Eds.), *The effect of the infant on its caregiver.* New York: Wiley, 1974.

Stone, N. W., and Chesney, B. H.   Attachment behaviors in handicapped infants. *Mental Retardation,* 1978, *16*, 8-12.

Tallman, I.   Spousal role differentiation and the socialization of severely retarded children. *Journal of Marriage and the Family,* 1965,*27*, 37-42.

Tavormina, J. B., Ball, N. J., Dunn, R. C., Luscomb, B., and Taylor, J. R. *Psychosocial effects of raising a physically handicapped child on parents.* Unpublished manuscript, University of Virginia, Charlottesville, 1977.

Thomas, A. and Chess, S.   *Temperament and development.* New York: Brunner/Mazel, 1977.

Thomas, A., Chess, S., Birch, H. G., Hertyig, M., and Korn, S.   *Behavioral individuality in early childhood.* New York: New York University Press, 1963.

Tracy, R. L., Lamb, M. E., and Ainsworth, M.D.S.   Infant approach behavior as related to attachment. *Child Development,* 1976, *47*, 571-578.

Turnbull, A. P.   Parent-professional relationships. In M. Snell (Ed.), *Curriculum for the moderately and severely handicapped.* Columbus, Ohio: Charles E. Merrill, 1978.

Turnbull, S. P., and Turnbull, H. R.   *Parents speak out: Views from the other side of the two-way mirror.* Columbus, Ohio: Charles E. Merrill, 1978.

Tyler, N. B., and Kogan, K. L.   Reduction of stress between mothers and their handicapped children. *American Journal of Occupational Therapy,* 1977, *31*, 151-155.

Vietze, P. M., Abernathy, S. R., Ashe, M. L., and Farelstich, G.   Contingency interaction between mothers and their developmentally delayed infants. In G. P. Sachett (Ed.), *Observing behavior: Theory and application in mental retardation* (Vol. 1). Baltimore: University Park Press, 1978.

Wiegerink, R., and Hocutt, A.   *The policy perspective: Congruence between the policy of parent involvement and its implementation.* Paper presented at the annual meeting of the American Educational Research Association, April 1979.

Wiegerink, R., Hocutt, A., Bristol, M. M., and Bell, P. B.   Parent needs and expectations questionnaire: Experimental edition. Chapel Hill, N.C.: University of North Carolina, 1980.

Wiegerink, R., Hocutt, A., Posante-Loro, R., and Bristol, M. M.   Parent involvement in Early Education Programs for Handicapped Children. In J. J. Gallagher (Ed.), *New directions for exceptional children,* 1980, *1,* 67-85.

Wolff, P. H.   Observations on the early development of smiling. In B. M. Foss (Ed.), *Determinants in infant behavior.* New York: Wiley, 1963.

Zeskind, P. S., and Lester, B. M.   Acoustic features and auditory perceptions of the cries of newborns with prenatal and perinatal complications. *Child Development,* 1978, *49,* 580-589.

A Report on Selected
Demonstration Programs
for Infant Intervention

*Pascal L. Trohanis, James O. Cox, and
Ruth A. Meyer*

Infant intervention programs provide early, comprehensive, and effective treatment to handicapped infants or those at risk for developmental disorders. Whether the intervention is preventive, ameliorative, or remedial in nature, the goal is the same for infants to have a better opportunity for a full and productive life.

This chapter provides timely information for developing new intervention programs or maintaining and improving existing practices.

PASCAL L.TROHANIS is director of the Technical Assistance Development System (TADS) of the Frank Porter Graham Child Development Center, and associate professor of education at the University of North Carolina at Chapel Hill.

JAMES O. COX is technical assistance coordinator for demonstration projects at the Technical Assistance Development System (TADS), Frank Porter Graham Child Development Center, University of North Carolina at Chapel Hill.

RUTH A. MEYER is a writer and editor based in Atlanta, Georgia, and a former publications coordinator for the Technical Assistance Development System (TADS), Frank Porter Graham Child Development Center, University of North Carolina at Chapel Hill.

First, it reports the results of a survey of programs that offer educational/ developmental intervention services to very young children and their families. Second, it provides detailed descriptions of nine diverse demonstration programs. And finally, the chapter concludes with the identification of key issues that infant service planners and providers must contemplate as they seek to initiate, maintain, or improve services in their community.

As was noted by Merle Karnes in the foreword of this book, there is only limited research data that supports the efficacy of early identification and programming for the high-risk or handicapped infant. In fact, intervention with infants and their families is a relatively new endeavor that has only been gradually initiated during the last 10 years in the United States. Although there have been a few efficacy research studies conducted and some currently being conducted (refer to Chapter 1 for some information on this topic), it is not the purpose of this chapter to report the results of these studies. Rather, the authors attempted to identify and describe selected exemplary demonstration practices that have been developed and are being used by programs across the nation. The infant intervention projects that provided the information for this chapter are, for the most part, funded as service or demonstration programs, not efficacy research projects. Although most are encouraged by their funding sources to document the effectiveness of their efforts, the documentation approaches usually do not include the experimental approach or methodological rigor that characterizes research projects. The reader should keep this limitation in mind when reviewing the information in this chapter.

THE SURVEY

The nine exemplary intervention practices described in this chapter provide an opportunity for learning from other programs' experiences. They were chosen from respondents to a survey that was conducted in the fall of 1979 in order to locate programs serving high-risk and handicapped infants, birth to 3 years old, and their families.

Packets containing two questionnaires, one about screening infants and one about intervening with infants, were sent out in October to 142 programs considered likely to have been providing either type of services for 3 or more years. A total of 56 programs (about 40 percent) responded. Among the responses were 45 completed intervention questionnaires and 16 completed screening questionnaires, including forms from 12 programs reporting both types of service delivery. Nine of the intervention programs were chosen for description in this chapter, and six screening programs are described in Chapter 5, "A Report on Selected

Screening Programs for High-Risk and Handicapped Infants.'' Also, addresses and brief annotations of all projects that responded to the survey are provided in Appendices A and B.

There is no easy way to identify the programs throughout the nation that are providing services to infants, because the sources of their funding and the agencies with which they are affiliated are diverse. The projects contacted for this survey include: Mental Retardation Research Centers; American Association of University-Affiliated Programs for the developmentally disabled; current and former demonstration projects and outreach projects of the Handicapped Children's Early Education Program (HCEEP); and many others located through a search of the current literature and recommendations by educational, medical, and other professionals.

The criteria for exemplary status that were developed for the survey are reflected in the individual questions of the intervention survey form (see Appendix D). They include such factors as: clearly defined model and implementation methods, service history of 3 or more years, high level of participation (service to at least 100 children), documentation of effectiveness, availability of dissemination materials, and replication assistance. Most of the respondents to the survey met the criteria for exemplary status. Those described in this chapter, however, were chosen because they are representative also of the many variations in the settings in which infant programs operate and the populations they serve.

General Impressions of the Survey Results

A large majority of the 45 programs (80 percent) that returned the intervention questionnaire were funded during their early development as model demonstration projects by the federal government's Handicapped Children's Early Education Program (HCEEP). These projects are encouraged not only to provide quality services for children and parents, but also to rigorously evaluate their efforts, develop and disseminate materials, stimulate new programs, and secure long-term funding. The reader should keep in mind that these are some of the very criteria that were set forth to define exemplary infant intervention programs for the survey. Also, TADS, the organization that conducted the survey, is a support system for these programs while they receive HCEEP funding; therefore, previously funded HCEEP programs may have more readily responded to a survey from TADS and it is uncertain to what degree the survey results can be generalized.

Chapter 7 offers a list of essential questions for program planners. The survey results, by providing a summary of project experiences, suggest answers to some of these questions. For those already operating infant programs, the survey results provide an opportunity to compare program strategies.

Eighty-two percent of the programs that responded to the survey reported that their direct services programs for infants and their families have been funded for 5 or more years. In addition, 40 percent reported that their current funding sources are stable and that they expect to receive continuing funding for the foreseeable future. An equal percentage reported that they expect to be funded by their current sources for the next 2 to 6 years. Figure 1 indicates the nature of current funding for the programs.

All of the programs surveyed begin services for infants at or very near birth with varying upper age limits, some as high as age 5 or 6. About half the programs serve an average of 32 infants and families annually; another third serve an average of 112 infants and families; the remainder serve a relatively large number of infants, between 200 and 800 annually. Over three-quarters of the programs (76 percent) reported serving infants who exhibit any of the ten PL 94-142 categories of handicapping conditions, although a number did not indicate serving learning-disabled or seriously emotionally disturbed infants because diagnosing these types of handicaps is difficult during the first 2 years of life. (PL 94-142 categories for children with handicapping conditions are: mentally retarded, hard-of-hearing, deaf, speech-impaired, visually handicapped, deaf/blind, seriously emotionally disturbed, learning-disabled, orthopedically impaired, and other health-impaired.) Thirteen percent of the programs reported serving only one type of handicapped infant (e.g., deaf or visually handicapped). The remaining programs (11 percent) reported selectively serving infants who may exhibit any of four to five conditions (the most commonly listed categories were mentally retarded, orthopedically impaired, or other health impairments, visually handicapped, and hard-of-hearing). Figure 2 shows the distribution.

All of the programs responding to the survey indicated delivering some type of services to families and/or involving parents in project activities such as teaching their own children or participating in educational and therapeutic components of the project. Parents also are involved in information dissemination and programming planning. Average reported parent participation was 87 percent with a range from 100 percent to a low of about 34 percent. One-quarter of the programs reported primarily targeting and getting participation from only one member of the family (usually the mother), while half indicated targeting activities and involvement by two or more family members.

The majority of programs (58 percent) indicate that they are primarily engaged in developmental/educational intervention. Another 11 percent indicated that they are primarily engaged in therapeutic intervention (physical therapy, occupational therapy, and other specialized in therapies). Nine percent indicated delivering both educational/develop-

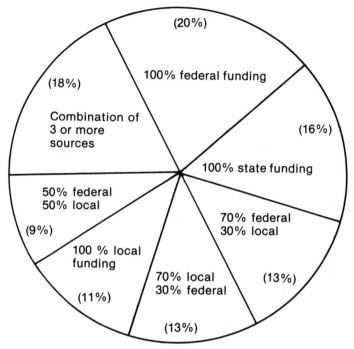

Figure 1.   Distribution of funding sources.

mental and therapeutic intervention. The remaining 15 percent combine medical intervention with other interventions.

When programs were asked to provide the best description of the theoretical construct upon which their intervention services are based, approximately one-fourth indicated a developmental base with another fourth indicating a developmental/behavioral base. A neurodevelopmental approach was indicated by 11 percent with an equal percentage indicating Piagetian theory as the base for their intervention (often Piagetian theory was combined with other approaches, such as developmental or neurodevelopmental). Seven percent of the programs reported basing their intervention on the medical model. The remaining programs indicated origins in a variety of other theoretical constructs, such as information processing, eclectic, or transdisciplinary.

Figure 3 indicates the settings in which the responding programs deliver their services. The most common setting is a combination of home and center programs.

Usually programs serve either an urban (47 percent), rural (35 percent), or suburban (9 percent) community. But 9 percent indicated they serve a combination of all three types. Almost half (47 percent) work with families in a multicounty region, while 26 percent serve a single

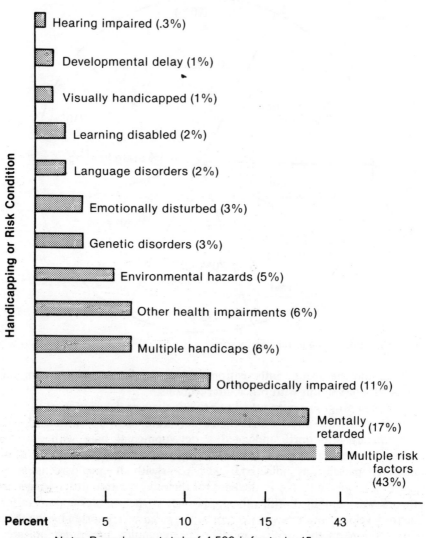

Figure 2.   Handicapping conditions of children served.

community, 18 percent a single county, 7 percent an entire state, and 2 percent the entire nation.

The most common fiscal agencies for programs were institutions of higher education (37 percent), followed by hospitals (18 percent), private nonprofit organizations (18 percent), public educational agencies (15 percent), and other public agencies (7 percent).

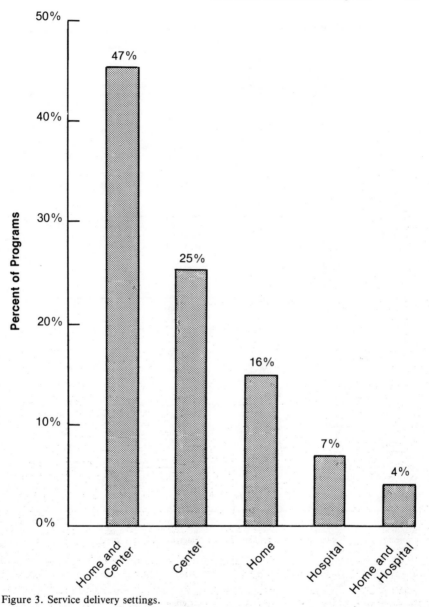

Figure 3. Service delivery settings.

When asked to describe their staffing patterns, 45 percent reported being operated by all full-time staff, 22 percent reported all part-time staff, and 29 percent indicated an approximately equal mix of full-time and part-time staff. In addition to teachers, programs employ therapists, social workers, administrators, nurses, and physicians.

Table 1. Selected comparative information about nine demonstration programs

		Areas of comparison			
Project name and location	Type of handicapping condition served (10 PL 94-142 categories)	Age range and approximate number of clients served annually	Type of approach	Service delivery mode	Geographic service area
Peoria 0-3 Replication Project Peoria, IL	All except learning disabled	0 to 3 years 66 clients	Medical/educational based on developmental task analysis	Home- and center-based	Urban multi-county area
PEERS Project Philadelphia, PA	All	0 to 4 years 33 clients	Developmental	Home- and center-based	Urban area
KIDS Project Dallas, TX	MR, seriously, emotionally disturbed, LD, orthopedically impaired, other health impaired	0 to 3 years 61 clients	Developmental/prescriptive	Home- and center-based	Urban area
Project SKI*HI Logan, UT	Deaf, hard-of-hearing, deaf/blind	0 to 6 years 32 clients	Developmental	Home-based	Statewide area
Kent First Chance Project Kent, OH	All except learning disabled and seriously emotionally disturbed	3 to 13 months 200 clients	Developmental/behavioral	Hospital-based	State and nationwide area
Teaching Research Infant and Child Center Monmouth, OR	All except learning disabled	0 to 3 years 96 clients	Developmental/behavioral	Home- and center-based	Rural single county area
EMI Project Charlottesville, VA	All except seriously emotionally disturbed	0 to 2 years 30 clients	Piagetian/neuro-developmental	Home- and hospital-based	Rural multi-county area
Macomb 0-3 Regional Project Macomb, IL	All except learning disabled	0 to 3 years 50 clients	Developmental/Piagetian	Home-based	Rural multi-county area
The Model Preschool Center for Handicapped Children Seattle, WA	MR, visually handicapped, orthopedically impaired, other health impaired	0 to 3 years 94 clients	Developmental/diagnostic prescriptive/behavioral	Center-based	Statewide area

	Areas of comparison				
Type of fiscal agency	Number of Years in operation as of 12/79	Funding sources	Number of replication sites	U.S. Dept. of Education JDRP approval	Print materials available
Private nonprofit agency	4½	90% state 10% county	99	Yes	Yes
Private nonprofit agency	7	90% local 10% state	1	No	Yes
Local educational agency	4	100% local	4	No	Yes
State school for deaf	7	100% state	17	Yes	Yes
Cooperative: higher education institution and private hospital	6	100% federal	3	No	Yes
Higher education institution	7	85% local 15% state	100	Yes	Yes
Hospital/ medical school	7	90% state 10% fees	4	No	Yes
Cooperative: higher education institution and rehabilita- tion facility	5	90% state 10% local	2	Yes	Yes
Higher education institution (UAF)	10	17% federal 58% state 24% local 1% contri- butions	8	Yes	Yes

DESCRIPTION OF EXEMPLARY DEMONSTRATION PROGRAMS

Following are detailed descriptions of nine of the 45 programs that responded to the survey. They were selected from those programs that met all of the exemplary status criteria because they represent the wide range of theoretical models, intervention practices, types of infants served, geographic areas, funding sources, fiscal agencies, and program evaluation strategies of the respondents. Currently, all nine can respond to requests for information about their approach to serving infants and families. Also, each one can offer assistance to organizations interested in replicating its program model—through on-site visits to the demonstration project, training and technical assistance, or distribution of printed materials. For further information about any program, check with the contact person listed at the end of each program description.

The purpose of this section is to provide enough descriptive information about representative infant intervention programs to assist the reader in selecting a program approach that warrants further investigation. Table 1 provides some comparative information about each of the nine programs, and should assist the reader in making a decision about which program or programs offer the best opportunity to meet their information needs.

PEORIA 0-3 REPLICATION PROJECT/
PEORIA, ILLINOIS—A Home- and Center-Based Program

Background and Overview

The original Peoria 0-3 Project was funded in the summer of 1971 as a 3-year demonstration project by the federal government's Handicapped Children's Early Education Program. Current funding for the direct services program for children and families comes primarily from the state of Illinois with supplemental funds provided by the United Way and the Peoria County Board. The project is jointly sponsored by United Cerebral Palsy of Northwestern Illinois and the Peoria Association for Retarded Citizens, both private nonprofit organizations. Since 1974, the program has also been an HCEEP outreach project, funded to provide training and technical assistance to other agencies interested in improving or expanding their comprehensive services for infants.

During the program's early years, the direct services program provided center-based transdisciplinary diagnostic and evaluation services followed by home-based programming, which was often supplemented with outpatient occupational, physical, and speech/language therapy. After several years of experience, however, need for continued programming was realized, and center-based preschool and developmental training programs were added. The children served are birth to 3 years old and impaired or high risk because of mental retardation, neuromotor handicaps, orthopedic handicaps, visual and hearing impairments, congenital anomalies, social/emotional disorders, psychomotor retardation, and developmental delay. The project model is a medical/educational one based upon a developmental/task analysis approach to individualized prescriptive teaching. A transdisciplinary evaluation and intervention team works to help parents become primary programmers for their children.

The Peoria 0-3 assessment and intervention process begins with a comprehensive diagnostic and evaluation procedure including medical, psychological, social, motor, speech/language, and hearing evaluations. When necessary, these are supplemented with evaluations through outside referrals. If intervention is warranted, the child may participate in the home-based and/or center-based program, depending upon his or her individual needs. In both programs, individual educational plans are written with emphasis on utilization of the child's strengths in the areas of cognition, speech/language, social/emotional, gross motor, fine motor, eating, toileting, and dressing. In the home program, individual lessons are developed by a transdisciplinary team and taken into the home weekly by the child development worker, who observes and directs the parent in implementing the activity and explains procedures for recording the child's responses. As these data and other progress data are collected, program adjustments are made. The center-based 0-3 services include a comprehensive diagnostic and evaluation program; a preschool program that meets twice a week; a developmental training program that meets daily for children 2 to 3 years of age; and outpatient speech and language, occupational, and physical therapy. Parent/family education and support are heavily emphasized.

Evidence of Effectiveness

Using data from the third year of demonstration services, a random sample of 99 children, mildly to profoundly handicapped, was selected. To determine program outcomes, estimates were made of maturational effects and then compared to the actual development of children. Statistically significant gains were found in the personal/social, cognitive/ linguistical/verbal, eating, dressing, and toileting areas. A project-developed scale tested for reliability and validity, the Functional Profile, was used to collect the data. Results were presented to the U.S. Department of Education's Joint Dissemination and Review Panel, which approved Peoria's 0-3 program and validated it in February 1979. In addition to child progress, anecdotal data gathered shows parent gains, including acceptance of the child's handicap, attendance and participation in parent meetings and workshops, parents working with the child on their own initiative, and parents constructing equipment to help their own children and other agency clients. Additional evidence of effectiveness includes the stimulation of 110 full or partial replication sites in 15 states and the distribution of over 500 program manuals, 500 information packets, 1,400 quarterly newsletters, and 4,000 handouts in 41 states and trust territories and seven foreign countries.

Implementation Requirements

Start-up costs for the program range from $1,500 to $2,000 per child during the first year. Once initiated, recurring costs include: 1) $600 per child for initial evaluation, 2) $2,150 per child annually for weekly home services, and 3) $1,050 per child annually for weekly outpatient services. These costs are based on service to approximately 80 infants annually. The current staff requirements are: 5 full-time child development workers, 1 full-time speech therapist, 1 three-quarters-time occupational therapist, 1 three-quarters-time social worker, 1 one-third-time program director, as well as a part-time vision specialist, behavioral consultant, and psychologist (approximately 5 percent time each).

Materials Available

1. The Functional Profile (an ongoing assessment and curriculum planning instrument)
2. "A Replication of a 0-3 Project" (a program manual)
3. A variety of information packets (please contact the project for a complete listing).

For Information, Contact

Karen Hurst, Director
Peoria 0-3 Replication Project
320 East Armstrong Avenue
Peoria, Illinois, 61603
(309) 672-6358

PEERS PROJECT/
(PARENTS ARE EFFECTIVE EARLY EDUCATION RESOURCES)
PHILADELPHIA, PENNSYLVANIA—A Home- and Center-Based Program

Background and Program Overview

The PEERS Project was initiated in 1973 as a volunteer effort by Special People in Northeast (SPIN), a private nonprofit organization. Two years later, it was funded as a 3-year model demonstration project of the federal government's Handicapped Children's Early Education Program. At this time, the project became a joint effort of SPIN and the Philadelphia Association for Retarded Citizens. Since 1978, the program's direct services have been funded primarily by the county, with a small amount—approximately 10 percent—from federal funds (PL 89-313).

The project serves infant and toddlers ages birth to 48 months who have developmental delays which may be caused by any type of handicapping condition (such as mental retardation, deafness, or orthopedic impairment) or no etiologically identifiable problem. The service area is northeast Philadelphia, a large urban area, with services provided both in the home and at a city center.

The PEERS center-based program meets once a week, on Saturday mornings, for approximately 3 hours. During this time the parents work with parent education counselors who cover a defined course content that includes needs identified by the parents, basic concepts in child development, methods and meaning of child assessment, a discussion of community resources, and other related topics. While the parents attend these sessions, a community volunteer who is trained and supervised by the PEERS staff works with the infant. The parents carry out the home program daily using a "prescription" of activities for accomplishment each Saturday. It is suggested that they spend an average of 30 minutes a day working with the infant. Once a month a home visit is made by a project staff member. The program is based on a cognitive/developmental model and the assumption that the parents are the best teachers of their own child during early life.

Evidence of Effectiveness

An independent university-affiliated evaluation of PEERS indicated significant changes in all developmental areas. During the first year of the child's participation, significant differences were found even when a more rigorous analysis was made that controlled for the effects of maturation. The infant measures used by the project are the Bayley Scales of Infant Development; Bzoch-League Receptive-Expressive Language Scales; Vineland Social Maturity Scale; and a project-developed scale, the PEERS Assessment Instrument. A separate investigation was conducted to establish both validity and reliability of the project-developed scale. In addition to assessing child progress, PEERS assesses changes in parents' knowledge and attitudes using an interview and survey format. An additional indication of parent commitment is the high participation rate in Saturday morning sessions, 80 percent for one parent and about 60 percent for both parents. The program also has made presentations at local, regional, and national professional meetings.

Implementation Requirements

The PEERS program is a relatively low-cost model for infant stimulation and parent training when compared with other options in the same geographic area. The costs of approximately $2,000 per year per child are about one-half that of traditional center-based programs and one-fourth, or less, of that for institutional care. The program makes extensive use of volunteers and donated space. All the project staff are part-time and include: a parent education counselor, two group teachers, two assistant teachers, a language specialist, an educational specialist, a physical therapist, and a nurse.

Materials Available

1. A series of how-to-do-it papers about each element of the PEERS Project
2. A series of parent training modules
3. The PEERS Assessment Instrument
4. The Parent Attitude Survey
5. The Parent Knowledge Test

For Information Contact

Trina Losinno, Director of Education
PEERS Project
Special People in Northeast, Inc.
8040 Roosevelt Boulevard
Philadelphia, Pennsylvania 19152
(215) 333-6262

KINDLING INDIVIDUAL DEVELOPMENT SYSTEM (KIDS PROJECT)/ DALLAS, TEXAS—A Home- and Center-Based Program

Background and Program Overview

The KIDS Project was originally funded as a model demonstration project in the summer of 1975 by the federal government's Handicapped Children's Early Education Program (HCEEP). Current funding for direct services for children and their parents is provided by the Dallas Independent School District, a large urban local education agency. KIDS received a second federal grant in the summer of 1978 (HCEEP Outreach) to support training, dissemination, and replication activities.

The KIDS direct services project is a home-to-school transition program for children birth to 6 years of age with developmental delays, mental retardation, serious emotional disturbance, learning disabilities, orthopedic impairments, and other health impairments. Three types of services are provided: home-based training for infants, center-based stimulation classes for toddlers, and early childhood school-based classrooms for preschool children. The project utilizes a developmental/ prescriptive approach in its continuum of services for the child and the family. Its goal is a smooth, uninterrupted transition from the home and center to the public school setting.

Evidence of Effectiveness

The KIDS project maintains a full-time program evaluator who assists the project staff with regular evaluations for modification and improvement and with annual outcome evaluations designed to determine the overall effectiveness of the program. A review of the last three evaluation methods used include time-series designs with repeated-measures analysis of variance, a prediction design with a theoretical control group, and a one-group pretest-posttest. Additional evidence of effectiveness includes total and partial replication of the project model in 25 classrooms in 20 different schools in Texas, and distribution (at cost) of approximately 250 dissemination packages to agencies and personnel in 24 states. A variety of papers about the KIDS Project have been presented at over 15 national, regional, and local conferences and conventions.

Implementation Requirements

There are four major components in the KIDS project: 1) child appraisal and curriculum development, 2) family involvement, 3) staff development, and 4) program evaluation. Each of the three methods of service delivery—home-based, toddler center-based, and school-based—has the four components. To implement them, the project currently employs 1 full-time special education facilitator, 1 full-time home-based teacher, 2 half-time center-based teachers, 4 full-time teacher aides, 1 full-time parent involvement specialist, and 1 full-time program evaluator. Supplemental services and consultation are provided by a local university-affiliated facility and special education program. This project provides services for approximately 60 children and their families annually. The average cost per child and family per year is $1,400 for infant home-based, $2,500 for toddler center-based classrooms, and $3,000 for school-based preschool classrooms.

Materials Available

1. Staff development package
2. Appraisal package (available in English and Spanish)
3. Curriculum package (includes a curriculum activities cross-reference card file)
4. Evaluation package
5. Family involvement package

For Information, Contact

Ruth M. Turner, Director
KIDS Project
Dallas Independent School District

3801 Herschel Avenue
Dallas, Texas 75228
(214) 526-0999 or 824-1620, ext. 342

PROJECT SKI*HI/PROGRAMMING FOR HEARING IMPAIRED
INFANTS THROUGH AMPLIFICATION AND HOME INTERVENTION,
AGES BIRTH TO SIX/
LOGAN, UTAH—A Home-Based Program

Background and Overview

This project was funded in 1973 as a 3-year demonstration project by the federal government's Handicapped Children's Early Education Program. It was initiated by the Department of Communicative disorders at Utah State University in Logan, in cooperation with the Utah School for the Deaf in Ogden, Utah, and provided the state's first services for very young deaf children. In 1976, the State of Utah began funding the delivery of direct services for children and parents that were not totally provided by the Utah School for the Deaf, and Project SKI*HI was funded as an outreach program by HCEEP. With the new outreach funding, it began stimulating development of high-quality services for young hearing-impaired and deaf children in other states.

SKI*HI early intervention programs throughout the country provide comprehensive home-based services for hard-of-hearing and deaf children ages birth to 6 years. The major goal of the model is to provide the hearing-impaired child and the family with a functional communication system and to make the home a linguistically meaningful environment. An important aspect of this goal is the provision of emotional and psychological support—in addition to educational services—to parents during the identification, diagnosis, and intervention periods.

The project has five major components. The first, *identification of users,* is accomplished primarily through a high-risk checklist administered to new mothers during their hospital stay. The second component is *home intervention,* which is primarily targeted at the parents. Immediately upon entry into the program, the child is fitted with a project-loaner hearing aid. After a trial period, the child is then fitted with a permanent aid. Parent advisors teach the parents how to manage use of the hearing aid and detect any operating problems. The advisors also teach the parents how to encourage their child's auditory skills and develop an effective communication system. For children who do not have the auditory capacity for oral language, a program of total communication is introduced. Once the communication system is operating, the parent advisor helps provide a home language foundation through modeling of dialogue and other techniques. The third component, *Provision of train-*

ing and assistance, involves the training of parent advisors in complete home intervention. This is accomplished with an audio-visual training package and periodic in-service sessions. The fourth component, *program management,* includes supervision of the parent advisors who make weekly, 1-hour home visits in their own regions. The final component, *evaluation,* enables the project to monitor progress and revise individualized treatment plans when necessary. It also determines program effectiveness.

Evidence of Effectiveness

Evaluations have been done using both a pre-post design and a cross-sectional design. The results indicate that project children are more likely than other hearing-impaired children to have early confirmation of their hearing loss. The results also show a significant relationship between early initiation of treatment and both unaided and aided auditory response improvement. Expressive and receptive language development also showed improvement as measured by the Receptive-Expressive Emergent Language Scale (REEL), a standardized test of language development. Converted into monthly gains, the scores indicated a gain of 16 months after 11 months of intervention. Progress for parents has also been documented and includes high program participation (e.g., 97 percent of all weekly appointments are kept). The program presented its evaluation data to the U.S. Department of Education's Joint Dissemination Review Panel (JDRP) and was approved as a validated program in May 1978. Additional evidence of effectiveness is that the program has been totally or partially replicated by 30 programs in 26 states.

Implementation Requirements

The average annual cost per child is $1,475. This is based on full services for 48 weeks. As currently implemented in Utah, the staff includes 1 part-time director (10 percent), 1 full-time supervisor, 19 part-time parent advisors, 2 part-time psychologists (10 percent each), and 1 full-time secretary. The maximum client load is 18 families per parent advisor, with each family requiring 2 hours of service time weekly. Assistance is provided by Project SKI*HI Outreach to programs wishing to implement a similar model.

Materials Available

1. "Programming for hearing impaired infants through amplification and home intervention" (program manual)
2. Total Communication in the Home (color video tapes)
3. Slide-tape programs (e.g., home auditory, home hearing aid, home language, and communication)

4. SKI*HI Receptive Language Test
5. Parent Advisor Training Package (video tapes, manual, and transparencies)
6. Contact the project for a complete materials list.

For Information, Contact

Thomas C. Clark, Director or
Dorothy Jensen, Product Development Specialist
Project SKI*HI Outreach
Department of Communicative Disorders, UMC 10
Utah State University
Logan, Utah 84322
(801) 750-1369

KENT FIRST CHANCE PROJECT/
KENT, OHIO—A Hospital-Affiliated Program

Background and Program Overview

Kent State University's First Chance Project began in 1974 as a joint endeavor between the Kent State University psychology department and the Hattie Larlham Foundation, a private, nonprofit intermediate care residential treatment center for catastrophically damaged infants and young children. The project's first funding was a 3-year demonstration grant from the federal Handicapped Children's Early Education Program to develop a responsive social and physical environment for 25 resident young children and to evaluate the results of living in such an environment on their developmental progress. In 1977, the project went into an Outreach phase and the developmental programming in a responsive environment was continued by the Larlham Foundation and the Ohio Board of Mental Health and Mental Retardation. Components of the original service program are now made available to all young children in residence. The local school district also continues an on-site educational program for eligible children.

The project model is designed to serve a broad range of severely and profoundly handicapped young children ages 3 months to 8 years. The components of the model described below are amenable to use in a wide variety of settings and are being used across the country. The intervention approach is developmental/educational and is built upon a base of behavioral theory and practice. The project continues a strong research orientation and is currently involved in a field-initiated study for the federal government's Special Education Program, to continue developing its model and data base. Staff consult on the design and construction of educational/recreational facilities and on the training of personnel to create responsive environments for developmental programming. A good part of the project personnel's energy also goes into developing and refining measurement techniques that are sensitive to the developmental progress of young multihandicapped children.

Evidence of Effectiveness

During its 3 years as a demonstration project, the Kent program documented the effectiveness of its efforts. Positive changes were measured in the rate of development of target children as tested with the Bayley Scales of Infant Development. The project developed and standardized the Kent Infant Development Scale (KID Scale), an inventory of 252 short sentence stems allowing caregivers to check behaviors of developmental significance for infants in the first year of life or for handicapped children who function developmentally below the 1 year level. The direct measurement was conducted for the social milieu of the children over three years using behavioral sampling techniques (Social Ecology Protocol). The results were reported and can be used as a comparison baseline for other similar settings.

Implementation Requirements

The Kent First Chance Project, which has components for assessment, programming, caregiver training, and facility design, can best be implemented in a residential or home treatment setting for severely handicapped young children. Staffing should consist of behaviorally trained administrators as well as trained, highly motivated caregivers who play the major role in assessment and programming. The physical setting should be normalized and amenable to remodeling to become more responsive and homelike. The Learning Accomplishment Profile (LAP) and the Portage Curriculum can be used along with the Kent Infant Development Scale if desired.

Materials Available

1. The Kent Infant Development Scale (KID Scale)
2. The Bayley Scales of Infant Development scoring adaptation and training videotape
3. Reviews of screening and infant tests
4. "A Protocol for Measuring the Social Milieu of a Group Care Setting for Young Multi-Handicapped Children" (a training manual)
5. Assessment and environmental design consultations

For Information, Contact

Jeanette Reuter, Ph.D.

Kent First Chance Project
252 Lowry Hall
Kent State University
Kent, Ohio 44242
(216) 672-7970

TEACHING RESEARCH INFANT AND CHILD CENTER/ MONMOUTH, OREGON—A Home- and Center-Based Program

Background and Program Overview

The Teaching Research (TR) program initially began in July of 1972 as a demonstration project funded for three years by the federal Handicapped Children's Early Education Program. Current support for direct services to children and families comes primarily from sources with some state monies. The program, based in a higher education institution, serves a primarily rural county area.

Services are delivered both in the home and center to children ages 1 to 6 years who are moderately to profoundly handicapped. Included are cerebral palsied, mentally retarded, autistic, emotionally disturbed, and deaf-blind children. A developmental educational intervention approach is used in a noncategorical manner and is underpinned by a behavioral theoretical base. Classrooms are formulated on the principles of individualization within the context of a comprehensive curriculum emphasizing self-help, motor, language, and cognitive skills. Teaching youngsters to manage their social behavior is also stressed. Classroom activities are extended into the home by teaching parents to teach their children.

Evidence of Effectiveness

The TR program follows rigorous evaluation procedures. Multiple baseline technique applied to child performance has documented that the program has a positive impact on skill acquisition. Their data also suggest that the TR procedures and methodologies are well defined and can be replicated to produce similar effects in different educational sites. In addition to the approximately 100 TR classrooms operating throughout Oregon, TR satellite training centers are operating in several other states (Hawaii, Indiana, Rhode Island, New Hampshire, and Iowa). The centers provide training in the use of the TR model. Additional evidence of effectiveness is the availability of diverse project-development print and audiovisual products, as well as inservice training. Finally, in 1978, the TR program was reviewed by the Joint Dissemination Review Panel of the U.S. Department of Education and approved as a validated program.

Implementation Requirements

Recommended physical facilities for each TR classroom of approximately 12 children include a large work area for group play or instruction as well as five individual instruction areas. The *TR Curriculum for Moderately and Severely Handicapped* is utilized along with a special curriculum for expressive oral language. The average annual cost per pupil, including administrative and overhead costs, ranges from $2,365 at the original TR site to $3,100 in some replication sites.

Materials Available

There are many products available. These include:

1. "Toilet Training the Handicapped Child"
2. "Isn't It Time He Outgrew This? or A Training Manual for Parents of the Retarded"
3. "Data-Based Classroom for the Moderately and Severely Handicapped" (3rd ed.)

For Information, Contact

H. D. Bud Fredericks
Research Professor
Teaching Research Infant and Child Center
Monmouth, Oregon 97361
(503) 838-1220

EDUCATION FOR MULTIHANDICAPPED INFANTS (EMI)/ CHARLOTTESVILLE, VIRGINIA—A Hospital-Affiliated Program

Background and Program Overview

The EMI project is a division of the Department of Pediatrics at the University of Virginia Medical Center. It was developed with a 3-year demonstration grant from the federal government's Handicapped Children's Early Education Program in the fall of 1973. Continuation of the direct services program is primarily funded by Virginia's Department of Education, Division of Special Education, with a small portion of funding—about 10 percent—coming from insurance payments. In addition to its continuation of direct services for children and families, EMI operates another component, EMI-Impact, which provides training and technical assistance to medical, educational, and allied health field personnel interested in initiating or improving services to handicapped infants and their parents. EMI-Impact has developed training materials and demonstration workshops for hospital nursery personnel and shares its skills in neonatal assessment and stimulation, prescriptive teaching, and developing referral procedures.

The EMI project is a combined hospital-, home-, and center-based program for infants, ages birth to 2 years, who exhibit a variety of handicapping conditions from mild to severe, such as myelomeningocele, hemiparesis, cerebral palsy, vision or hearing impairments, and other health impairments. The primary goal of the project is to have each child accepted into a public school program by the age of 2 or 3. (Since 1975 the state of Virginia has served handicapped children ages 2 to 21.) The developmental/educational progam is based on a Piagetian/neurodevelopmental approach. Its hospital/center program consists of weekly hour-long individual lessons for the infant and at least one parent. Since the services of this project reach a multicounty rural area, transportation to the center may be provided for both the infant and his or her parents. A written "prescription" of activities for parents and infants to perform at home is supplemented by monthly home visits by EMI staff. A physical therapist and social worker provide additional services for infants and families.

Evidence of Effectiveness

Infants are assessed monthly on the EMI Assessment Scale. The developmental age equivalents it provides are used to assess the project on child progress and guide individualized curriculum planning. A developmental growth rate index, a ratio of the change in developmental age to the change in chronological age, is computed to compare the rate of change over time. Statistical analysis using Wilcoxon's Test for Paired Replicates indicates significant improvement in fine motor skills, cognitive development, social skills, and general developmental growth rate. Also, a composite profile of growth rates compares favorably to the theoretical norm for nonhandicapped infant development. Additional evidence of effectiveness includes assistance in developing 12 partial replication sites in the state of Virginia and distribution of materials both within and outside the state.

Implementation Requirements

Current costs for the EMI project, which serves approximately 30 infants and families annually, are $1,400 per child. As currently implemented, the staffing requirements are one full-time infant teacher, one half-time physical therapist, two part-time social workers, and one quarter-time pediatrician. The program can be implemented in many types of hospital or clinic settings. A variety of project materials are available to those interested in replicating the project model.

Materials Available

1. EMI Asessment Scale
2. EMI curriculum pool materials
3. EMI infant learning packets
4. "The EMI High-Risk Nursery Intervention Manual"
5. Guidelines for working with parents of handicapped infants
6. A list of additional materials and selected bibliographies may be obtained by writing to the project.

For Information, Contact

Kathy Steward, Director
Education for Multihandicapped Infants
University of Virginia Medical Center
Box 232
Charlotesville, Virginia 22908
(804) 924-5161

THE MACOMB 0-3 REGIONAL PROJECT
MACOMB, ILLINOIS—A Home-Based Program

Background and Program Overview

The project was initiated in 1975 at Western Illinois University as a demonstration project of the federal Handicapped Children's Early Education Program to serve three rural counties. These counties contain a population with varied socio-economic backgrounds, occupations, and education. Since the 3-year HCEEP grant ended, service to children and families has been continued with local resources from a nearby county rehabilitation center and a community workshop. Another HCEEP grant has been funding outreach and training activities since 1978.

The Macomb project is a home-based one that provides each child with an individualized remediation and educational program. The project, which provides weekly home visits by a child development specialist (approximately 1 hour in length), stresses active parent/caretaker involvement. A core curriculum follows developmental/Piagetian principles with adaptations for specific handicapping conditions. A second major component of the project is a Sharing Center. Convened biweekly in churches, community buildings, or homes, it brings together six to seven families to participate in activities with their children and to gain new skills and information. Parents also construct toys in special workshops.

Sharing Centers provide an opportunity for handicapped children to participate in activities with nonhandicapped children, which gives them at least a certain amount of experience in a less restrictive environment.

An alternative Sharing Center activity component is Water Activities for Developmental Enhancement (WADE), with a donated community pool used for enhancing appropriate motor activities.

The 50 children served by the project, ages birth to 3 years, have a wide variety of impairments and degrees of severity—mental retardation, deafness, speech impairment, and orthopedic impairment. Also, the children may be high risk because of such factors as low birthweight and developmental delays of at least 6 months in one area.

Evidence of Effectiveness

From its beginnings, Macomb has emphasized program evaluation. Data have been collected systematically in such areas as child gain, parent change and satisfaction, staff improvement and overall project design. For child gain scores, two formal measures have been used: the Alpern-Boll Developmental Profile and the Bzoch-League Receptive-Expressive Emergent Language Scale (REEL). Children are tested upon entrance to the project and at 6-month intervals. Pre-post multivariate analysis of variance (and other statistical evidence) determined for both measures indicated that the project is effective. Analysis of a parent satisfaction questionnaire, which is administered initially at 3-month and at 6-month intervals thereafter by independent trained observers, found that project activities also led to parent gains. This evaluation data was presented to the Department of Education's Joint Dissemination and Review Panel (JDRP) and the program was validated in May, 1980.

Further evidence of effectiveness is replication and adaptation of project components by other preschools and day care centers in both Illinois and neighboring Iowa. Also, the project has developed and makes available numerous publications and audiovisual products. Finally, the project collaborates with Western Illinois University on a wide range of formal coursework in-service training.

Implementation Requirements

The costs for this home-based rural effort are relatively low. Including initial investment, the cost per child is approximately $2,350 for a 12-month period. This figure is based on one full-time and one half-time child development specialists (CDS) and a caseload of 15 children. Other implementation recommendations include: availability of transportation equipment (from cars to mobile vans, which may be used as demonstration-teaching classrooms when home space is inadequate); use of the core curriculum and measurement instruments; employment of CDSs with majors in special education or early childhood with continuing in-service; access to specialists such as physicians, speech and hearing diagnosticians, and physical therapists—and appropriate manipulative equipment, raw materials, and toys—and finally, access to community facilities for implementing the Sharing Center component and access to a community swimming pool.

Materials Available

An extensive array of print and audiovisual products are available, featuring an entire series of materials under the Baby Buggy label. Contact the project for an order form and product catalog.

For Information, Contact

Patricia Huntinger
Director
Outreach: Macomb 0-3 Regional Project
27 Horrabin Hall
Western Illinois University
Macomb, Illinois 61455
(309) 298-1634

THE MODEL PRESCHOOL CENTER FOR HANDICAPPED CHILDREN/ SEATTLE, WASHINGTON—A Center-Based Program

Background and Program Overview

The Model Preschool Center was one of the first 24 demonstration projects funded in 1969 by the Handicapped Children's Early Education Program, which is sponsored by the federal government. A part of the University of Washington, the center is supported by a mix of state developmental disabilities and Department of Education monies and federal and University of Washington funds. Since 1972, the center has been funded to provide interdisciplinary training and outreach assistance to such varied groups as local education agencies, Head Start, hospital programs, community colleges, and institutions of higher education.

The Model Preschool Center is composed of programs that serve handicapped infants, ages birth to 3 years, who are mentally retarded, visually handicapped, orthopedically impaired, multiply handicapped, and health impaired. The center also serves high-risk infants using some of the following risk indicators: teenage mother, alcoholic/addicted mother, low birthweight, and genetic factors. The approximately 200 children served annually represent a diverse population, that is, Caucasian, oriental, native American, black, and Chicano. The center's service and intervention activities are mainly developmental/educational in nature with a behavioral (diagnostic/prescriptive) theoretical base. Staff work to accelerate and maintain developmental gains in children and to train parents in effective teaching of their own children.

Evidence of Effectiveness

The center has a rigorous, ongoing evaluation effort, part of which is assessing child progress. This is done on a quarterly basis using at least two different appropriate measures—such as the Bayley Scales, Brazelton, and Uniform Performance Assessment System (UPAS). Children in the program make good to excellent progress along the normal developmental continuum in such areas as fine motor, cognitive, social/emotional and self-help skills. The other part of evaluation documents the overall effectiveness of the program. Evidence of the program's effectiveness and contribution to child progress led to the center being recognized nationally in 1972 by Abt Associates as one of eight exemplary projects providing early childhood special education. The program was recognized again by the Battele Institute in 1975. In September 1975, two of the center's programs were approved for replication or adaptation by the Joint Disseminaton Review Panel, USED.

Additional evidence of the center's effectiveness is an extensive list of publications generated by its personnel. Many are available at cost. Numerous motion pictures, videotapes, and slide programs are also available. Finally, center components have been replicated or adapted by many programs, to which it has provided extensive in-service training.

Implementation Requirements

The center comprises different programs, and it is important to differentiate among them. For example, there is an infant or early learning program for children with Down's syndrome that meets in the center for 2 hours, 4 days a week, at an approximate cost of $2,100 per child; this program draws on a staff that does not require special professionals, although support personnel should be available. Another example is the communications program, which includes children ages 2 to 3 identified or suspected of having communication deficits; the program thrives on its concept of professionals from two disciplines (teachers and communication disorder specialists) working together. Average cost per child in the communications program is $1,800 for a 9-month period. The Model Preschool Center should be contacted directly for information about particular programs.

Materials Available

Many diverse products are available from the project, including publications, 16-mm color sound films, videotapes, and slide programs. A catalogue is available.

For Information, Contact

Rebecca Sewell
Model Preschool Center for Handicapped Children
Experimental Education Unit WJ-10
College of Education and Child Development and
    Mental Retardation Center
University of Washington
Seattle, Washington 98195
(206) 543-4011

CONCLUSION

Providing comprehensive educational/developmental intervention services to handicapped and high-risk infants and their families is a relatively young enterprise in the area of human services. The survey results and intervention programs described in this chapter provide an indication of how the knowledge base for exemplary intervention practices, training programs, and print and audiovisual products, has rapidly expanded over the last two decades. This knowledge base has emanated from diverse settings, such as universities, hospitals, and private and public agencies.

As a result of the survey limitations mentioned earlier in the chapter, there are significant restrictions on the generalizability of our findings. However, following are some closing observations by the authors that hopefully will be helpful to those persons who are planning and/or expanding intervention services for handicapped and high-risk infants and their families.

1. It appears that a combination of funds (i.e., local, state, and federal) is helpful in either starting or maintaining intervention programs. Such a funding mix appears to provide more stability over time.
2. Funds for intervention services can be managed by many types of fiscal agencies. The survey results indicate that the highest percentage of programs are supported and managed in universities and in hospitals with institutions of higher education. This higher educational predominance suggests that demonstrating effective practices

and providing community services are activities that dovetail well with the basic university functions of training and research. Other agencies managing project funds are more typically community based. These are private nonprofit organizations and public agencies, such as educational, health, and mental health agencies.

3. Regardless of the fiscal management, intervention programs reflect a variety of theoretical approaches including developmental, behavioral, neurodevelopmental, and eclectic. Often combinations of two theoretical approaches are used. The most popular service delivery option is to provide services for the infant and family in both the infant's home and in the program's center facilities (e.g., classrooms, hospital, etc.). Other options include using only the center facilities, infant's home, or hospital. Reflecting the reported theoretical constructs of programs and their settings for service delivery, almost 60 percent of the respondents indicated they were primarily engaged in developmental/educational intervention services. Other programs indicated they were primarily engaged in specialized therapeutic intervention as well as some combination approaches.

4. All types of impairments and risk conditions were mentioned for the infants served. However, two of the PL 94-142 categories of disabilities were often excluded: seriously emotionally disturbed and learning disabled. Many projects said they would serve infants with these types of disabilities, but they did not think currently available identification and diagnostic procedures are sensitive enough to identify infants who have them. Although a few categorical programs prevail, notably for hearing and visually impaired infants, for the most part multiple risk factors or indicators are used for the determination of need for intervention. This appears logical because many handicapping conditions and developmental delays are not readily diagnosed very early in an infant's life.

5. Family involvement is a key ingredient in all the infant intervention programs. A diversity of activities are utilized, with the majority focusing on the mother. A notable trend is to include other family members (fathers and siblings). Most typically, services to the infants go hand in hand with those to the family.

6. All intervention programs reported that they supported education and health professionals. On the education side, common roles were teachers, aides, and therapists, who usually tended to be full-time employees as compared to specialists, such as physical therapists, occupational therapists, and physicians, who tended to be part-time.

7. Although most programs reported having available print and audiovisual products about their practices and indicated involvement in total and/or partial replication activities, the area of program

evaluation did appear somewhat weak. Half of the responding programs are not currently conducting program evaluations. This evaluation weakness reflects the fact that methods for documenting outcomes and program practices are still in the developmental stage. On the positive side, responding programs indicated they are demonstrating to their funding sources the type of evaluation data that are necessary to obtain continuing financial support.

Clearly, there is an accumulation of experience and materials that planners and policymakers can tap as they plan or expand programming for handicapped and high-risk infants and their families. The authors hope that this chapter has shared some insights concerning the development and the implementation of responsive and effective intervention programs.

Planning Evaluation of Programs for High-Risk and Handicapped Infants

Tanya M. Suarez

The dictionary definition of a plan is "a detailed formulation of a program of action." A plan for evaluation is a detailed formulation of the procedures and actions by which an evaluation is to be conducted. It involves determining the various problems to be solved, the elements of each problem, and how each element affects the others (Gallagher, Surles, and Hayes, 1973). Therefore, planning is also a process of decision making.

This chapter contains an easy-to-use guide to the formulation of an evaluation plan. The "Planning Guide for the Evaluation of Educational Programs for Young Children and Their Families," reproduced at the end of the chapter, translates evaluation decision points into four sets of questions. Each set represents one of four major planning concerns for a

TANYA M. SUAREZ is associate director at the Technical Assistance Development System (TADS) of the Frank Porter Graham Child Development Center at the University of North Carolina at Chapel Hill.

program considering evaluation: 1) focusing the evaluation, 2) determining the specific evaluation design, 3) reporting and utilizing evaluation results, and 4) implementing the evaluation. Choosing among alternatives and answering the questions create the evaluation plan.

The chapter itself is divided into five sections. The first discusses planning for evaluation in general—the definition of evaluation used, the reasons for planning, and other topics. The remaining four sections parallel the guide, describing in greater depth the four major planning areas and offering descriptions of alternatives that may be considered in decision-making.

AN INTRODUCTION TO PLANNING AND EVALUATION

What is Evaluation?

There are many different definitions of evaluation. Among the most common are those that define it as a process of: 1) determining the achievement of objectives (Gallagher, Surles, and Hayes, 1973; Metfessel and Michael, 1967; Popham, 1972; Tyler, 1942), 2) providing information for decision-making (Provus, 1971; Stufflebeam et al., 1971), 3) determining whether a given treatment or program was the cause of desired outcomes (Rutman, 1977; Suchman, 1967), or 4) determining the worth or merit of a program or activity (Scriven, 1967; Stake, 1967; Worthen and Sanders, 1973).

In concept and practice evaluations have certain common key elements. These elements are contained in the definition of evaluation used throughout this chapter:

> Evaluation is a form of *disciplined inquiry* designed to provide information concerning the *worth or merit* of the object being evaluated for *utilitarian purposes.*

1. *Disciplined Inquiry*   The concept of disciplined inquiry is that evaluation is not a haphazard process, but, rather, a systematic approach designed to inquire about or answer specific questions about a program.
2. *Worth or Merit*   At the core of all evaluation efforts is the search for evidence of the worth or merit of the aspect of the program under study. It encompasses more than the mere description or documentation of programmatic effects. It requires that findings be compared to concepts, standards or criteria that are valued by those who will make judgments of the program.
3. *Utilitarian Purposes*   Evaluation must relate information gathering to some other action, whether it be decision-making, justification of efforts, or program improvement.

Why Plan?

One of the primary reasons for systematically planning an evaluation is to provide a direction or focus for the many activities that must be undertaken. Evaluations should provide valuable information that can be used. Therefore, it is necessary to determine what information would be valuable and in what form it could be used. Investigating and making decisions in these areas provide focus for the selection of specific evaluation strategies and activities.

A second reason for planning an evaluation is to increase the efficiency of the evaluation effort. Evaluation is a process that can be conducted in relation to any program component or activity. It is also a process that takes considerable time and effort. Planning helps to ensure that only the most important evaluation activities are conducted, thereby minimizing the time, effort, and resources needed to accomplish the evaluation.

Another particularly important reason for planning evaluations is to ensure that necessary information will be collected and recorded. It is disheartening to expend time and energy on an evaluation only to find out at the end that key pieces of information are not available.

An often overlooked indirect benefit of planning is the opportunity it provides program staff to participate in the evaluation process. The staff will usually be responsible for gathering data, e.g., conducting infant assessments, maintaining records of parent involvement, and keeping logs of community contacts. Their early participation and resulting commitment to the evaluation is a long-term benefit to the process.

It is also useful to have the plan in writing for several reasons. Among them are:

1. It provides a communication device that can be used to inform various audiences of the intents of the evaluation.
   a. For the program staff, it promotes understanding of the intent of the evaluation, the criteria for choosing particular areas for evaluation, and the evaluation activities for which they are responsible.
   b. For evaluation consultants, it serves as a quick and direct method of professional communication.
   c. It can acquaint external audiences, such as funding and administrative agencies, with the types of information that will be available regarding the program.
2. It provides an operational document which can be used to manage the evaluation.

When Should the Evaluation Be Planned?

Ideally, evaluation activities should be planned while a program is being developed. This early planning is particularly important for those areas in which progress must be measured—the progress of infants, staff development results, and parent change or involvement all may require an assessment of initial status upon which to determine gains. If a plan for evaluation is not developed when program activities begin, an entire year of valuable information may be lost. If the plan cannot be developed when the program is developed, then it should be done as soon as possible after implementation.

Regular updating and refining of the plan is equally important. Evaluations need to be refined so that they can reflect modifications in the program and so more closely meet program needs.

It is suggested in this chapter that evaluations be planned by considering alternatives and making decisions in four planning areas. The Planning Guide at the end of this chapter provides questions and examples for each of the four areas. Although it is not suggested that evaluation plans necessarily be developed in the format given, plans should reflect consideration of and decisions regarding each of the major and specific questions listed.

FOCUSING THE EVALUATION

Among the most important and least practiced aspects of evaluation planning is determining the focus of the effort, the foundation from which all other planning decisions are made.

Three primary sets of planning decisions aid in establishing an evaluation's focus. They are: 1) determining the purpose of the evaluation, 2) identifying the audiences for the evaluation and their information needs, and 3) identifying the key components of the program that warrant evaluation. (Refer to the guide questions about focusing the evaluation, on page 210.)

Determining the Purpose of the Evaluation

There are many reasons why a program might be evaluated. Scriven (1967) provided a useful distinction for classes of purposes in his description of formative and summative evaluation. *Formative evaluation* is conducted with the purpose of improving a program. *Summative evaluation* is conducted in order to demonstrate the program's overall worth or merit.

Formative Evaluation:

I. To develop and/or improve the program
    a. To determine the validity of the program plan
    b. To determine if the program was implemented as planned
    c. To examine, test, or validate specific program components
    d. To determine if projected outcomes were achieved
    e. To determine if unintended outcomes were beneficial
    f. To determine the worth of the overall program

Summative Evaluation:

II. To demonstrate the worth of the program
    a. To determine if the program was implemented as planned
    b. To determine if projected outcomes were achieved
    c. To determine if unintended outcomes were beneficial
    d. To determine the worth of the overall program
    e. To explain the relationships among the characteristics of the
        targets of the program, the intervention and the outcomes
    f. To determine the cost-effectiveness of the program
    g. To document the need for a new program or the expansion
        of the current program. (Suarez and Vandiviere, 1978, p. 11)

Within these broad categories there are many, more specific, reasons why an evaluation might be conducted. These are determined by the interests and needs of those within the program and important outside audiences, e.g., the agency from which funds for the program are received.

**Identifying the Audiences
for the Evaluation and Their Information Needs.**

In order for evaluations to be useful, they must be targeted or be responsive to the individuals or groups interested in the results. It is important, therefore, to identify the audiences for the evaluation early in the planning process. Some of the potential audiences for infant program evaluation are listed below.

1. Program staff
2. Funding and/or administrative agency staff
3. Parents
4. Staffs of similar or related programs
5. Persons who potentially may be involved in similar programs
6. Professionals in the field (e.g., health practitioners, educators, psychologists, social workers, therapists)

7. Potential program sponsors
8. Potential program adopters
9. Potential program advocates
10. Policy makers
11. General public
12. Media personnel

Once evaluation audiences are identified, their information needs must be determined. Just as the purposes for evaluation are unique, so are the information needs of different audiences. This is true for government and other funding agencies, which may often have quite specific information requirements, as well as for other key audiences.

Identifying Key Program Components

Determining a program's effectiveness requires evaluation information about the key areas of program design and operation. Though intervention programs for high-risk and handicapped infants have some elements in common, such as the provision of services to both infants and families, particular programs differ in such areas as: 1) the way in which they are conceptualized, e.g., to use a Piagetian or behavioral approach to intervention, to use staff or parents for providing instruction, 2) the type of handicapping condition addressed, e.g., mental retardation or orthopedic impairment, etc., 3) the location of the program, e.g., community setting or institutional affiliation, and 4) the setting for service delivery, e.g., the home, a center, or a hospital. Evaluation plans must reflect these key characteristics in order to provide a fair picture of a program's work and judgment of its worth.

PLANNING SPECIFIC EVALUATION STRATEGIES

The heart of an evaluation plan is choosing questions to be asked and the procedures and criteria that will be used to provide the answers. This process, which is summarized in the second section of the guide, includes: 1) formulating evaluation questions, 2) determining the overall evaluation approach to be taken, 3) establishing data collection procedures, 4) establishing data analysis procedures, and 5) developing criteria for using results to determine the value or merit of the program.

The Evaluation Questions

The selection of specific questions and procedures is guided by the focus, or intent, of the evaluation. If, for example, one of the intents is to determine the merit of the intervention program by first determining the cognitive development of infants, an appropriate evaluation question might be, Has the cognitive development of infants been enhanced as a result of participation in the program? If purposes and audiences' concerns were more global and less specific, the question might be, What has been the impact of the program upon infants?

Evaluation questions should reflect the focus as clearly as possible, providing guidance to the selection of appropriate designs and procedures. For instance, the first sample question, in the previous paragraph, could be answered with an experimental research design comparing the results for an experimental and control group. The second sample question could be answered with an objective-based evaluation (e.g., Gallagher, Surles, and Hayes, 1973) combined with a goal-free evaluation (Scriven, 1974) to provide information regarding anticipated and unanticipated outcomes.

Determining the Overall Evaluation Design

Following are descriptions of four of the most common types of evaluation designs that might be considered in determining an overall evaluation approach: experimental, objective-based, systems, and naturalistic. (See Table 1).

Experimental Designs   Experimental designs are commonly suggested and used for the evaluation of child progress in early childhood programs. This is primarily because 1) the posing of causal evaluation questions requires the use of experimental methods to produce appropriate answers, 2) the experimental legacy of inquiry into early intervention programs, e.g., Garber and Heber (1973), Gray and Klaus (1970), and Ramey and Campbell (1979), and 3) the familiarity of the approach to a broad segment of professional administrators, program personnel, and evaluators.

Kerlinger (1973) defines an experiment as

"a scientific investigation in which the investigator manipulates and controls one or more independent variables and observes the dependent variable or variables for variation concomitant to the manipulation of the independent variable" (p. 315).

In order to use an experimental design for evaluation, it must be possible to control a number of variables. Controls can only be applied when a program is well designed and implemented (Britan, 1978).

Although not mutually exclusive, these designs can be categorized as: 1) experimental, 2) developmental, 3) quasiexperimental, and 4) single-subject or N-of-1 designs.

True experimental designs focus on behavior, such as that of infants and/or parents, and seek to demonstrate causality by strictly controlling for variables which might otherwise account for observed results. Campbell and Stanley (1963) classify as experimental designs the Solomon four-group design, the pretest-posttest control group design and the posttest-only control group design.

Table 1.   Evaluation designs for programs for preschool handicapped children

Type of design and purpose	Examples
Experimental: to determine the cause of observed outcomes	Developmental designs (Porges, 1979)
	Experimental designs (Campbell and Stanley, 1963)
	Quasiexperimental designs (Cook and Campbell, 1979)
	Single-subject or N-of-1 designs (Kratochwill, 1978)
Objective-Based: to determine if stated objectives were achieved	(Popham, 1972)
	Program planning and evaluation model (Gallagher, Surles, and Hayes, 1972)
	Goal-attainment scaling (Kiresuk and Lund, 1976; Carr, 1979)
Systems: to determine outcomes with the inclusion of data regarding the relationship among outcomes, inputs, and processes	CIPP evaluation model (Stufflebeam, et al., (1971)
	Countenance model (Stake, 1967)
	Discrepancy model (Provus, 1971)
Naturalistic: to describe the program and its impacts	Case study (Stake, 1978; Kennedy, 1978
	Naturalistic inquiry (Guba, 1978; Wolf, 1979)
	Qualitative Evaluation (Willis, 1977)
	Ethnography (Wilson, 1977)

Reprinted with permission from Suarez, T. M., Evaluating Educational Programs for Preschool Handicapped Children. Paper presented at the annual meeting of the American Educational Research Association, Boston, April, 1980.

Developmental designs are quite often used in infancy research because they take into account both the status of behavior and the concept of time. They also include the four-group design as well as trend analysis, spectral analysis, and operant designs (Porges, 1979).

Quasiexperimental designs may be used when certain requirements for true experimental designs cannot be met. They include nonequivalent control group designs, cohort designs, regression-continuity designs, time-series designs and correlational designs (Cook and Campbell, 1979).

Single-subject or N-of-1 designs are experimental in nature. They are most appropriate for: 1) programs with a small number of individuals, 2) programs in which the individuals vary dramatically from one another, 3) programs having different goals for individuals served, and 4) data-based intervention approaches, e.g., behavioral. Included in single-subject designs are time-series designs, the analysis and presentation of graphic data, and sequential analysis of observational data using Markov chains (Kratochwill, 1978).

Regardless of the type, all experimental designs require that the program being studied be well developed and operational. For this and other reasons there are those, e.g., Britan (1978), Patton (1978), Reichardt and Cook (1979), and Stufflebeam et al. (1971), who doubt their applicability to particular and, in some cases, any evaluation efforts. Although these cautions do not preclude the use of experimental approaches, they should be noted. Experimental approaches should be used when they are most appropriate—not because they are popular or well known.

Objective-Based Designs   In the objective-based evaluation approach, a program is said to be effective if its objectives are met. As described by writers such as Gallagher, Surles, and Hayes (1973), Popham (1972), and Tyler (1942), procedures for conducting such evaluations require specification of program objectives, gathering of data relative to the objectives, and comparison of results with established criteria to determine whether or not the objectives were achieved.

Not only are objective-based designs appropriate for evaluating total programs based on a series of goals and objectives, they are also useful in evaluating intervention for individuals. This is especially true when interventions are based on individually established objectives, such as those for the handicapped in which individual educational programs (IEPs) are developed for each child. Procedures such as goal-attainment scaling have been developed to combine the results of objective-based evaluations for individuals (Carr, 1979; Kiresuk and Lund, 1976).

Though objective-based evaluations are a logical choice for many programs, a limitation on their use is their focus solely on programmatic outcomes. They are not particularly well suited to formative or summative evaluation of programmatic aspects other than outcomes unless objectives have been developed for these areas. A more serious concern, however, is the issue of the validity of objectives. Unless the objectives can be demonstrated to be validly indicative of programmatic effectiveness or success, the evaluation results produced are subject to question.

Systems Design   Systems types of evaluation designs are based on the process of describing program inputs, processes, and outcomes and the relationship among these programmatic aspects. It is an holistic approach that takes into account the total program—not just particular dependent and independent variables or outcomes. Stake (1967), in his "countenance model" of evaluation, advocates systematic data collection efforts that provide information about a program's antecedents, transactions, and results. Stufflebeam et al. (1971) suggest evaluation of program "context, inputs, processes, and products" in their CIPP model.

The "discrepancy model" of Provus (1971) compares standards to actual status in many programmatic areas.

Systems designs have as one of their basic characteristics the applicability of information for decision-making. They are particularly useful in formative evaluations because they examine program designs and implementation as well as outcomes. By viewing the program as a whole, they are comprehensive and provide a great deal of descriptive information useful for program and report development. Their major drawback is one of their strengths—comprehensiveness. Full implementation can be a formidable task for a small program staff. However, portions of a systems design, e.g., process evaluation, or a complete systems design for only one component of a program, can be used in programs with limited evaluation resources.

Naturalistic Designs Naturalistic approaches to evaluation are emerging as a response to problems encountered with other types of evaluations. Their main characteristic is the attempt to describe the larger context in which a program is set, the events which took place, and the program's effects—all in its own setting. Examples include naturalistic inquiry (Guba, 1978), ethnography (Wilson, 1977), case studies (Kennedy, 1978; Stake, 1978), and qualitative evaluation (Willis, 1977).

As is true for experimental approaches, there is considerable criticism of the naturalistic approaches. Chief among them is that they lack controls, which affects the internal validity of the findings and the extent to which the results can be generalized. Proponents argue, however, that other methods provide results in isolation of the actual program and that this approach provides sufficient information for accurate interpretation of results.

Other Approaches In addition to these four major categories of evaluation design, there are other approaches that might be considered for programs for high-risk and handicapped infants and their families. Takaneshi (1978), for example, argues for the use of evaluation designs with a more pronounced developmental perspective than those currently in use. Scriven (1974), in his description of goal-free evaluation, makes a case for gathering evaluation data regarding unanticipated effects of programs. Finally, Patton (1978) provides suggestions in his utilization-based approach to evaluation that are designed to enhance the usefulness of evaluation.

Specifying Collection Procedures

Table 2 lists types of data collection procedures that commonly are used for evaluation by programs for preschool handicapped children. Such sources as Chapter 6 in this book provide valuable information upon which to base decisions regarding the selection and use of specific

Table 2.   Data collection procedures commonly used in the evaluation
of programs for preschool handicapped children

Assessment area	Types of data collection procedures
Child development	Standardized developmental scales Instruction-referenced scales Observations Parent reports Anecdotal records
Interactions between child and others	Observations Sociometric devices Critical incidence techniques
Parental attitudes, knowledge, and skills	Tests Questionnaires Rating scales Observations Interviews
Environments	Observations Anecdotal records Unobtrusive measures
Placement	Agency records Parent interviews
Staff attitudes, knowledge, and skills	Tests Questionnaires Rating scales Observations Interviews
Unanticipated outcomes	Anecdotal records Program records and documentation Tests Observations Interviews
Cost-effectiveness	Outcome measures Program costs records

Reprinted with permission from Suarez, T. M., Evaluating educational programs for
preschool handicapped children. Paper presented at the annual meeting of the American
Educational Research Association, Boston, April, 1980.

instruments. General criteria for instrument/procedure selection include:

1. The content of the data collection instrument/procedure should
    match the content and intents of the program being evaluated.
2. The content of the data collection instrument/procedure should pro-
    vide an appropriate answer to the evaluation question being asked.
3. Instruments/procedures should be selected that are sufficiently sen-
    sitive to changes in behavior that are of interest.

4. The instruments/procedures should provide reliable and valid information.

5. Instruments/procedures chosen should be feasible in terms of: 1) staff expertise in administration, 2) planning, 3) administration time, and 4) resources (personnel, time, and money) available to gather the data.

For instance, screening instruments are not appropriate for the assessment of the developmental progress of infants. The items are too general to pick up the extent of change in development that may have occurred as a result of intervention. For the same reason, it may be necessary to choose instruments other than standardized developmental assessment scales, for programs serving severely and profoundly handicapped infants. These types of instruments are often not sufficiently sensitive to the minute changes in development of these infants.

Data Analysis Procedures

The key to decision making is to choose the procedure that synthesizes the results into precisely the information that is needed. Most data analysis procedures can be categorized into those which provide: 1) a description of the program and its results, 2) information regarding relationships among various programmatic characteristics and/or outcomes, and 3) information regarding the strength of differences found in the results.

1. *Description*   Synthesizing information that describes a program, participants in the program, the way in which the program was implemented, or the results of the program, is a valuable process. It provides an information base from which other analyses may be interpreted. In many cases, descriptive information alone can answer the important questions regarding a program, e.g., What did it cost to provide services to an infant and his/her family? Where were infants placed after participation in the program? Were parents satisfied with the services they and their infant received? Descriptive techniques, such as exploratory data analysis (Tukey, 1977), also can be used to investigate results and identify areas in which further analysis would be useful. Depending upon the size of the data set and the results, descriptions of programs may be determined by direct review of the data or statistical analyses.

2. *Relationships*   For some questions, it is important to show the relationships among results. If, for example, a program is designed to enhance child development by increasing the quality of mother/infant interaction, data showing the relationship between the two

would be important supporting evidence. The relationship of several outcomes to an intervention strategy could also be beneficial. The techniques that can be used to identify activities that contribute to desirable outcomes for children are mostly statistical in nature, e.g., correlation, regression, and factor analysis, and require statistical expertise to choose the most appropriate procedure.

3. *Differences*   It is often important to determine the extent of the difference among results. Questions such as, Which is the most effective approach for teaching gross motor skills? require gathering similar information about all approaches under consideration. Then results are tested to determine if there are any differences that indicate one is more effective than the others. These are the techniques which most often are appropriate for experimental studies. They are also useful in comparing descriptive information to answer questions such as, Has there been a significant increase in parent participation in the program? Again, these procedures are statistical in nature and include such analyses as t-tests and analysis of variance.

Establishing Evaluation Criteria

In order to determine the worth or merit of a given process or outcome, it must be compared to some criterion. Without such a criterion, it would be impossible, for instance, to determine the importance of an overall 8-month gain for infants on the Bayley Scales of Infant Development (Bayley, 1969).

It is most common to find discussions of criteria including the consideration of statistical and/or programmatic (educational, developmental, therapeutic, and medical) significance (Tallmadge, 1977). Statistical significance is obtained by the use of statistical tests and indicates that the results that are observed are greater than would be expected by chance (Kerlinger, 1973).

Programmatic significance refers to the importance of the result in the benefit it provides to the object of the evaluation, i.e., infants, parents, program staff. There are several sources for information regarding the establishment of criteria for programmatic significance. The first is the knowledge base regarding the phenomena—for example, how infants with certain conditions behave at given ages. Another source is knowledge about the development of normal infants. Prior experience also can be a good basis for criteria setting.

In some cases, particularly for new efforts, criteria for effectiveness may not be evident. In these cases, a best guess is appropriate. It then can be tested and the results used to set future criteria.

PLANNING FOR COMMUNICATING
AND UTILIZING EVALUATION RESULTS

Effectively communicating and using evaluation results requires making decisions regarding: 1) the purposes for communicating and evaluating, 2) the audience(s) that will be addressed, 3) the evaluation results appropriate for each use, and 4) the methods of communicating or using the results. These decision categories are direct extensions of those for focusing the evaluation.

Determining the Purposes for Communicating and Using Evaluation

The purpose for communication and utilization of results, while similar and related, differ. Bettinghaus and Miller (1973) describe four general categories into which most communication objectives can be grouped. These are: 1) increasing awareness of the program, 2) changing attitudes toward the program, 3) achieving compliance with required tasks, and 4) obtaining supportive behaviors for the program. From these general purposes can be derived purposes such as creating an awareness of the effectiveness of the program for infants and their families, creating positive attitudes toward the provision of services to high-risk and handicapped infants and their families, providing evidence to support a transdisciplinary team approach to providing services for infants, and obtaining support for the effort in the community with parents.

Perhaps the most common purposes for utilizing evaluations are program planning and staff development. Evaluation results can aid in planning by identifying program strengths that can be emphasized and identifying areas of weakness that should be changed. They can also be used to aid in planning priorities for the program, allocating funds, choosing methods and materials that best meet the needs of infants and parents, allocating staff, and identifying staff development needs.

The sharing of evaluation information can be a valuable source of staff development, resulting in a staff that is more knowledgeable about the total program and the role that each member plays in its success. The sharing may also stimulate staff cooperation, provide a sense of direction to staff efforts, and import feelings of accomplishment. Also, the results can be used to identify areas in which future staff development would be helpful.

Identifying the Audiences

If audiences are identified before the design of the evaluation plan, then much of the work in planning for this particular area is already done. However, for communication of results it is important to know specifically who the program wants to reach with this information, the audiences' level of knowledge about the program, their technical understanding of evaluation, their political perspectives, and their attention span (Kniefel, 1975). This type of information has implications for the content of communications, the technical level at which they should be presented, the view that should be taken in presenting the results, and the length of each message.

Identifying audiences for utilization requires greater specificity. Patton (1978) argues that evaluation users have personal reasons for their interest. He suggests, therefore, that evaluation for utilization should be targeted toward individuals rather than organizations or broad groups, such as "parents." However, because planning for utilization is very much an internal activity, it would seem that, contrary to Patton's view, some results should be targeted to the entire staff and other groups.

Determining Which Results To Use

For both the efforts in communication and utilization it is necessary to identify the information needed for each audience or purpose. In some cases interests and needs of audiences may be similar, and therefore, can be addressed similarly. A complete analysis of audiences and needs will allow the determination of the number and types of evaluation reports or messages that are required.

Choosing Methods for Communication and Utilization

Once decisions have been made regarding purposes and audiences, needs and interests, it is possible to select appropriate methods for communication and utilization. A variety of communication methods might be appropriate (Kniefel, 1975; Williams, 1978). Project PRIMES, a school-based project in Ohio, for example, used newsletters, reports, memos, information packets, abstracts, meeting presentations, slide tape shows, consultations, television, radio, newspapers, public service announcements, and other vehicles in communicating their evaluation results (Project PRIMES, no date).

Perhaps the most effective methods for sharing information are those that involve personal consultation or staff training. Another effective method is to provide particular results in brief form, such as one-page memos or newsnotes, to staff members most interested in them.

IMPLEMENTING THE PLAN

A final and critical area requiring planning is determining how the evaluation will be accomplished. This requires answering the following questions: Who will conduct the evaluation? What resources will be available for the evaluation? When will tasks have to be done? How will the evaluation be monitored?

Who Will Evaluate?

The evaluation can be conducted by the program staff or others. Each approach has strengths and weaknesses. Because the staff are knowledgeable about the program, they can describe its operation and how it was implemented and assist in interpreting study results. Also, the staff will be more likely to use evaluation results if they are actively involved in decision-making and implementation. However, if the staff do not have the evaluation expertise, and if their participation in evaluation detracts from services provided to infants and families, then staff-conducted evaluation is not the best alternative.

Another common approach to evaluation is to hire an external consultant or consulting agency. The advantages of this arrangement include: 1) evaluation consultants have the necessary expertise, 2) consultants can assist the staff in the design of the evaluation, and 3) consultants can conduct the entire evaluation for the program. Difficulties in using evaluation consultants may arise from consultants' lack of long-term knowledge of the program. Also, the costs of the service may be high, and it is often difficult to obtain a consultant who is appropriate for the program.

A final organizational arrangement that is becoming available to programs, particularly in large agencies and school districts, is the use of the evaluation or research department in the agency itself. The staff of this department can become more knowledgeable about the program because of their proximity. They also may be able to provide assistance more readily and with greater flexibility than most external consultants while at the same time providing the same level of expertise. Problems of compatibility sometimes do occur with this arrangment, however, if the evaluation consultants are appointed by the agency and not selected by the staff. Occasionally, too, problems in the organizational and political structure of the agency hinder successful evaluation efforts.

Regardless of the personnel approach, however, there is almost always a need for some involvement by members of the program staff in the evaluation. It is therefore necessary to specify roles for: 1) management and coordination, 2) design of the evaluation, 3) selection and development of instruments, 4) collection of data, 5) analyzing of data, and 6) writing of summary reports or preparation of other types of communications.

What Resources Are Available?

It is necessary at the outset to determine whether the resources available are adequate for the evaluation being planned. In fact, it is important during the entire planning process to maintain a perspective on the personnel and resources that are available so that the plan can, indeed, be implemented. Resources other than those mentioned previously include: other consultant assistance, materials, facilities, clerical support, office supplies, computer time (if necessary), and other types of resources that might be specific to the plan being developed.

When Will Tasks Be Done?

Because evaluation plans are usually developed separately from program plans, it is important that a schedule for the evaluation be developed and integrated with the program schedule. This will ensure that all activities can be completed and provide a guide for the implementation and management of the plan. Events that might be scheduled include development of special activities undertaken to utilize results.

How Will the Evaluation Be Monitored?

There is nothing more distressing than to have spent a great deal of time in developing an evaluation plan only to find later that data that should have been collected actually were not. Monitoring activities can maintain checks on the collection of data and other activities by the staff as well as help with the management of contracts with external evaluators.

SUMMARY

It has been the purpose of this chapter to provide a guide for planning evaluations of programs for high-risk and handicapped children and their families by describing planning areas in which decisions should be made. The selection of the areas to be considered, although perhaps at first glance overwhelmingly comprehensive, was deliberate. The expansion of evaluation planning beyond the specific questions to be asked and procedures for data collection and analysis were based on the experience of the author and others. The categories discussed represent areas in which failure to take into account program needs, interests, and/or resources has resulted in major damage to evaluation efforts. They are presented here with the intent of helping the reader and user avoid the mistakes of others.

An important note about the use of such detailed planning is in order. Programs and the environments in which they operate change. As they change, it is important that evaluation plans be reconsidered. An important aspect of evaluation planning is, therefore, its continuous nature. By giving regular attention to areas such as focus, design, communication, utilization and implementation, program personnel can ensure that the evaluations they conduct accurately reflect their specific intents and efforts.

Planning Guide for the Evaluation of Education Programs for Young Children and their Families

Major Concern I. EVALUATION FOCUS: What should the evaluation accomplish?

Purposes	Audiences	Audience information needs	Key program components	Statement of intent
Why is the evaluation being conducted?	*Who are the audiences for the evaluation?*	*What do the audiences need to know?*	*What are the key components of the program?*	It is the purpose of this evaluation to _____ (why it is being done) by providing information regarding _____ (key components and audience needs) to _____ (audiences)
e.g.: to meet funding requirements; to monitor/administer the project; to identify and improve weaker components; to strengthen the information available for dissemination/ competition for funds.	e.g.: project staff; funding agency; administrative agency; community agencies/ leaders; professionals; parents.	e.g.: progress of children; quantity and/or quality of services to children and families; attitudes of children and/or families; program costs.	e.g.: services designed to increase the cognitive, social, and motor development of children; services designed to increase parents' skill in teaching their children; a curriculum designed to increase cognitive development of children; a service which links children and families with assistance available in the community.	
a. _____	a. _____	a. _____	a. _____	a. _____
b. _____	b. _____	b. _____	b. _____	b. _____
c. _____	c. _____	c. _____	c. _____	c. _____

Major Concern II. EVALUATION PLAN: What should be the major components of the evaluation?

Evaluation questions	Evaluation design	Data collection procedures	Data analysis	Evaluation criteria
What information will the evaluation seek to provide?	*What design or set of procedures will be used to gather the information?*	*What instruments or forms will be used to gather and/or record the information?*	*How will the resulting data be analyzed?*	*How will the results be judged or interpreted?*
e.g.: Have children made expected progress during their participation in the program? Are parents better able to teach their children? Have interactions among children and primary caregivers improved? Are attitudes of parents, teachers, other related agency personnel toward the program favorable?	e.g.: Pre-post assessment of the development of children in experimental and control groups; monthly assessments of children's progress on IEPs; survey of parental attitude at end of program; observation of mother/child interaction before, during, and after training.	e.g.: McCarthy Scales of Children's Abilities; staff-developed attitude scale to measure parental attitude toward the program; Caldwell Home Inventory; staff-developed form for recording parental participation.	e.g.: Correlated t-test of difference between pre- and post-test means; comparison of expected level of development (determined using a regression analysis) with actual level of development followed by a test of the significance of the difference; computation of percentages of favorable responses; computation of frequencies of participation.	e.g.: Statistically significant difference between means (0.05 level); 75% of objectives accomplished; participation of 65% of the parents in two or more project activities.
a. _____	a. _____	a. _____	a. _____	a. _____
b. _____	b. _____	b. _____	b. _____	b. _____
c. _____	c. _____	c. _____	c. _____	c. _____

Major Concern III.   COMMUNICATING/UTILIZING PLAN: How will the results of the evaluation be communicated and used?

Purpose	Audiences to be addressed	Results to be used	Method of utilization
Why are the results of the evaluation being communicated and/or used?	*What audiences will be given and/or use the results?*	*What information and results will be communicated and/or used?*	*In what ways will results be shared and used?*
Refer to "Purposes" for evaluation and e.g.: reporting to funding/administrative agencies, parents, advisory boards, etc.; program planning; staff development; communication.	Refer to "Audiences" for evaluation.	e.g.: all results; child progress data; monitoring data; cost information.	e.g.: distribution of print materials such as reports, articles, etc.; presentation of non-print media such as slidetape, videotape, TV/radio, etc.; personal contact, training.
Communication			
a. _____	a. _____	a. _____	a. _____
b. _____	b. _____	b. _____	b. _____
c. _____	c. _____	c. _____	c. _____
Utilization			
a. _____	a. _____	a. _____	a. _____
b. _____	b. _____	b. _____	b. _____
c. _____	c. _____	c. _____	c. _____

Major Concern IV.   IMPLEMENTATION PLAN: How will the evaluation plan be accomplished?

Personnel role specification	Resource allocation	Scheduling	Monitoring
Who will conduct the evaluation?	*What other resources are available for the evaluation?*	*What are the key dates on which tasks need to be accomplished?*	*How will the evaluation be monitored?*
			e.g.: regular staff meetings; regular meetings of Manager/ Coordinator with persons responsible for specific tasks; review of quarterly submissions of information gathered to date.
a Manage/coordinate: ____	a. Consultant assistance:____	a. Evaluation plan:____	a. ____
b. Design evaluation:____	b. Materials: ____	b. Selection/development of instruments: ____	b. ____
c. Select/develop instruments: ____	c. Facilities space:____	c. ____	c. ____
d. Collect data: ____	d. Clerical support:____	d. Data analysis:____	d. ____
e. Analyze data: ____	e. Supplies:____	e. Report writing: ____	e. ____
f. Write summary reports:____	f. ____	f. ____	f. ____
g. Other: ____	g. ____	g. ____	g. ____

REFERENCES

Bayley, N. *Bayley scales of infant development.* New York: Psychological Corporation, 1969.

Bettinghaus, E. P., and Miller, G. R. A dissemination system for state accountability programs. Part III: Developing dissemination procedures for state educational accountability programs. Denver: Cooperative Accountability Project, 1973.

Britan, G. M. Experimental and contextual models of program evaluation. *Evaluation and Program Planning,* 1978, *1,* 229-234.

Campbell, D. T., and Stanley, J. C. Experimental and quasi-experimental designs for research on teaching. In N. L. Gage, *Handbook of research on teaching.* Chicago: Rand McNally, 1963.

Carr, R. A. Goal attainment scaling as a useful tool for evaluating progress in special education. *Exceptional Children,* 1979, *46,* 88-95.

Cook, T. D., and Campbell, D. T. *Quasi-experimentation: Design and analysis issues for field settings.* Chicago: Rand McNally, 1979.

Gallagher, J. J., Surles, R., and Hayes, A. *Program planning and evaluation.* First chance for children series (Vol. 2). Chapel Hill, N.C.: Technical Assistance Development System, 1973.

Garber, H., and Heber, R. *The Milwaukee Project: Early intervention as a technique to prevent mental retardation.* The University of Connecticut Technical Papers. Storrs, Conn.: The University of Connecticut, 1973.

Gray, S. W., and Klaus, R. A. The Early Training Project: The seventh year report. *Child Development,* 1970, *4,* 909-924.

Guba, E. G. *Toward a methodology of naturalistic inquiry.* CSE Monograph Series in Evaluation, No. 8. Los Angeles: Center for the Study of Evaluation, 1978.

Kennedy, M. M. *Generalization of findings from single case studies.* Paper presented at the meeting of the American Educational Research Association, Toronto, March 1978.

Kerlinger, F. N. *Foundations of behavioral research.* (2nd ed.). New York: Holt Rinehart & Winston, 1973.

Kiresuk, T. J., and Lund, S. H. Process and outcome measurement using goal attainment scaling. In G. V. Glass (Ed.), *Evaluation studies review annual* (Vol. 1). Beverly Hills: Sage, 1976.

Kniefel, T. M. *Administrator's guide to evaluation in local school districts.* Raleigh, N.C.: N.C. Department of Public Instruction, 1975.

Kratochwill, T. R. (Ed.). *Single subject research: Strategies for evaluating change.* New York: Academic Press, 1978.

Metfessel, N. C., and Michael, W. B. A paradigm involving multiple criterion measures for the evaluation of the effectiveness of school programs. *Educational and Psychological Measurement,* 1967, *27,* 931-943.

Patton, M. Q. *Utilization-focused evaluation.* Beverly Hills: Sage, 1978.

Popham, W. J. *An evaluation guidebook.* Los Angeles: The Instructional Objective Exchange, 1972.

Porges, S. W. Developmental designs for infancy research. In J. D. Osofsky, *Handbook of infant development.* New York: Wiley, 1979.

Project PRIMES Dissemination Chart. Columbus, Ohio: Project PRIMES, Columbus Public Schools, no date.

Provus, M. M. *Discrepancy evaluation.* Berkeley, Ca.: McCutchan, 1971.

Ramey, C. T., and Campbell, F. A.   Compensatory Education for Disadvantaged Children. *School Review,* 1979, *87,* 171-189.

Reichardt, C. S., and Cook, T. D.   Beyond qualitative versus quantitative methods. In T. D. Cook and C. S. Reichardt, *Qualitative versus quantitative methods in evaluation research.* Beverly Hills: Sage, 1979.

Rutman, L. (Ed.). *Evaluation research methods: A basic guide.* Beverly Hills: Sage, 1977.

Scriven, M.   The methodology of evaluation. In *Persepctives in curriculum evaluation.* AREA Monograph Series on Curriculum Evaluation, No. 1. Chicago: Rand McNally, 1967.

Scriven, M.   Evaluation perspectives and procedures. In W. J. Popham (Ed.), *Evaluation in education: Current applications.* Berkeley, Ca.: McCutchan, 1974.

Stake, R. E.   The case study method in social inquiry. *Educational Researcher,* 1978, *7,* 5-8.

Stake, R. E.   The countenance of educational evaluation. *Teachers College Record,* 1967, *68,* 523-540.

Stufflebeam, D. L., Foley, W. J., Gephart, W. J., Guba, E. G., Hammond, R. L., Merriman, H. O., and Provus, M. M.   *Educational evaluation and decision making.* Itasca, Ill.: Peacock, 1971.

Suarez, T. M.   *Evaluating educational programs for preschool handicapped children.* Paper presented at the annual American Educational Research Association Meeting, Boston, April, 1980.

Suarez, T. M., and Vandiviere, P. (Eds.). *Planning for evaluation—A resource book for programs for preschool handicapped children: Documentation.* Chapel Hill, N.C.: Technical Assistance Development System, 1978.

Suchman, E.   *Evaluative research.* New York: Russell Sage, 1967.

Takaneshi, R.   *Evaluation of early childhood programs: Toward a developmental perspective.* Los Angeles: University of California, 1978.

Tallmadge, G. K.   *The joint dissemination review panel Ideabook.* Washington, D.C.: National Institute of Education and U.S. Office of Education, U.S. Department of Health, Education and Welfare, 1977.

Tukey, J. W.   *Exploratory data analysis.* Reading, Mass.: Addison-Wesley, 1977.

Tyler, J. W.   General statement on evaluation. *Journal of Educational Research,* 1942, *35,* 492-501.

Williams, M. K., et al.   *Educational manager's guide to project evaluation.* Andover, Mass.: The NETWORK, 1978.

Willis, G. (Ed.). Qualitative evaluation. Berkeley, Ca.: McCutchan, 1977.

Wilson, S.   The use of ethnographic techniques in educational research. *Review of Educational Research,* 1977, *47,* 245-265.

Wolf, R. L. *An overview of conceptual and methodological issues in naturalistic evaluation.* Paper presented at the meeting of the American Educational Research Association, San Francisco, April, 1979.
Association, San Francisco, April, 1979.

Worthen, B. R., and Sanders, J. R.   *Educational evaluation: Theory and practice.* Worthington, Ohio.: Charles A. Jones, 1973.

Risk Factors Beyond the Child and Family

David Rostetter and James L. Hamilton

Infancy is frequently described as a perilous time. Untoward events and lack of appropriate stimulation can have a devastating effect upon the developing child during this period of rapid physical and psychological growth. Though not simply a passive recipient of environmental offerings (Bell, 1968; Lewis and Rosenblum, 1974), the infant is more dependent on adults and adult-created environments than will be the case later. This early vulnerability is most apparent in infants who for biological or environmental reasons may not develop normally. These especially vulnerable infants are designated "at risk" because they may exhibit signifi-

DAVID ROSTETTER is Chief, Equal Educational Opportunities Coordination, Special Education Programs, U.S. Education Department.

JAMES L. HAMILTON is education program research specialist in the Research Projects Branch, Division of Innovation and Development, Special Education Programs, U.S. Education Department.

This chapter was written by the authors in their private capacity. No official support or endorsement by the U.S. Education Department is intended or should be inferred. Also, authorship is equal.

cant learning or adjustment problems as they grow.

Designating an infant at risk implies uncertainty about his or her development. To be sure, some infants are at greater risk for delayed or deviant development than are others. But even among infants whose risk status is thought to be established (Tjossem, 1976), such as those with Down's syndrome, the developmental course is far from predictable. The imprecision of the risk terminology in use exemplifies our rather primitive knowledge of just what the risk is. *At risk, high risk, biological risk, environmental risk,* and *established risk*—regardless of the terminology used to describe the infant who is not expected to develop normally, the salient issue is the unknown, but potentially hazardous, effects of one or a combination of factors such as prematurity, low birth weight, delivery complications, substandard home environment, and poor nutrition. And beyond such important child and family factors is a still broader array of societal factors that can affect the infant's developmental course.

Following Sigel's (1979) suggestion that the first issue in discussing at-risk infants is to identify the risk factors, this chapter discusses some risk factors that ultimately must be eliminated before the goal of effectively preventing or remediating infant developmental problems can be achieved. These risk factors exist for the most part independently of specific infant and family characteristics, and can only be reduced or eliminated by society, its leaders, or its professionals. The chapter presents first the risk factors associated with measurement and intervention, then those characteristics of community, state, and federal systems that may compromise the optimal growth and development of the child. Following discussion of risk factors, some recommendations for action are offered.

MEASUREMENT RISK FACTORS

One hallmark of a scientifically advanced field of study is the availability of valid and reliable measures of pertinent phenomena. Even a cursory review of the infancy literature reveals an enormous effort to develop or improve measures of infant status and environmental variables that may affect infant development. Progress has been made. However, currently available measures are largely inadequate and, therefore, constitute a risk factor beyond the child and family.

Detection

For all but the most extreme and severe cases, the detection of the infant who will display significant developmental or learning problems later in life has proved a formidable scientific challenge. Over the past several decades, literally hundreds of studies have been conducted in an attempt to find early indicators. These studies have used a variety of methodologies and have examined a wide range of variables considered potentially relevant. The variables studied include maternal factors (e.g., education, socioeconomic status, age, and medical history), pregnancy and delivery factors, and measures of infant functioning.

The studies have failed to identify a single measure or set of measures that accurately predict later learning problems (see Broman, Nichols, and Kennedy, 1975; Jordan, 1980; Stott and Ball, 1965; Thorpe and Werner, 1974; Yang and Bell, 1975). In their review of perinatal influences on the behavior and learning problems of children, Rubin and Balow (1977) conclude that no clear picture of perinatal influence emerges after 25 years of investigation. They suggest that though previous studies have supported the hypothesis that perinatal complications are related to school learning and behavior problems, the relationships generally are not strong and their nature is not clear.

Similarly, developmental measures of infant status fail to predict accurately later cognitive functioning (see Bayley, 1970; Stott and Ball, 1965; Yang and Bell, 1975). Horowitz and Dunn (1978) have suggested three possible reasons for the poor predictive validity of infant assessments: 1) inherent instability of the infant, 2) the changing nature of the behaviors sampled in intelligence tests across different ages, and 3) insufficiency of the testing technique. Whatever the reasons, neither perinatal factors nor infant measures are adequate in predicting later problems. However, good predictive validity studies have not been undertaken yet for some of the newer infant measures (Vietze and St. Clair, 1976), such as the Brazelton Neonatal Behavioral Assessment Scale (Brazelton, 1973) and the Uzgiris-Hunt Ordinal Scales of Psychological Development (Uzgiris and Hunt, 1975).

Across several studies, one variable that has been moderately predictive of childhood IQ and educational and behavioral outcome is the socioeconomic status (SES) of the child's family. Correlations between parental education or SES and later IQ and related measures generally range between 0.20 and 0.60, accounting for 4 percent to 36 percent of the outcome variance (See Broman et al. 1975; Ireton, Thwing, and Graven, 1970; McCall, Hogarty, and Hurlburt, 1972; Rubin and Balow, 1977). It is not uncommon for investigators to conclude that SES is the best single predictor of later intellectual performance and that adding other indicators (such as perinatal factors or measures of infant status) does not meaningfully increase the prediction (e.g., McCall, Appelbaum, and Hogarty, 1973).

Partly because SES is moderately predictive of later learning problems, investigators have increasingly directed their efforts toward environmental influences and their interaction with perinatal factors (e.g., Sameroff, 1979). For example, in a recent review of research on at-risk infants, Sameroff and Chandler (1975) conclude that environmental factors have the potential for minimizing or maximizing developmental difficulties; that is, high SES appears to dissipate the effects of perinatal complications, while low SES appears to amplify the effects of such complications. Other investigations not only have provided evidence of the potency of the home environment and mother-infant interactions on infant development but also, by implication, have suggested the importance of measuring specific environmental factors in order to detect at-risk infants (e.g., Bradley and Caldwell, 1976; Yarrow, Rubenstein, and Pedersen, 1975).

Continued research has demonstrated that accurate identification of at-risk infants is a far more complicated task than once believed. It has also become clear that individual differences among infants, the nature of the infant environments, and the complex interactions between the infants and their environments across time must be better understood and measured if infants at risk are to be accurately identified.

Intervention

That measurement is a risk factor in intervention stems in part from the traditional role it has played in the education of all children. Educators have relied heavily on a variety of tests and measures both for identifying specific developmental, behavioral, or knowledge deficits in students and for measuring progress in attaining instructional objectives.

Although standardized testing has not been used extensively to determine *how* to teach (Hamilton, 1979), it has significantly directed choices of *what* to teach, and, to the extent that test results are used immediately for instructional purposes, *when* to teach it. Unfortunately for the infant educator, there are relatively few diagnostic and assessment instruments available for use with infants; fewer of these have adequate psychometric properties, and still fewer are designed for educational intervention. Thus, the first measurement risk factor associated with intervention is the limited number and quality of instruments that are appropriate for planning instruction and for measuring the effects of instruction.

Several authorities (e.g., Keogh and Kopp, 1978) have described at length the weaknesses and imprecision of available infant measures when used for planning and evaluating intervention efforts. For example, Greenspan, Nover, Silver, and Lourie (1979) suggest several problems that relate to the measurement-intervention risk factor. First, these authors point out that there has been a tendency for intervention personnel to assess only one or two areas of child development (e.g., cognition) rather than multiple interrelated areas of child development, which more accurately reflect the complexity of the infant's growth and development. Second, they point out the lack of symmetry that commonly exists between the goals of the intervention program and the measures used for evaluation. An example of this lack of symmetry is the use of cognitive measures exclusively in a program that focuses primarily on social/emotional variables in mother-infant interactions. Third, they suggest that many commonly used measures are not sufficiently differentiated or sensitive to capture subtle individual differences among infants at different ages. Fourth, these authors suggest that the use of cross-sectional measures (measures that were normed on different infants at different ages) may have limited validity when used to measure the same infant's development over time. Their final point pertinent to our discussion here is the tendency of intervention personnel to measure what is known at a particular child age, and to use available instruments suited to certain times of the infant's life, rather than measuring longitudinally consistent categories of child development over time. Implied in all or most of these problem areas was the dearth of adequate and available measurement instruments.

The second risk factor of measurement relates to measuring the components of the intervention program. Greenspan et al. (1979) suggest that measuring the ingredients of the intervention program is even more complex than measuring infant functioning. They go on to suggest that without measures of the intervention components, the specific components of the program that lead to changes in the infant and/or family may be obscure. In addition, we suggest that without such measurement of the intervention components, decisions about whether program components should be maintained or modified may be difficult if not impossible.

INTERVENTION RISK FACTORS

A statement that there are risk factors associated with intervention may be viewed by members of the helping professions as heretical if not contradictory. However, an objective appraisal of intervention efforts, especially educational ones, for at-risk infants does reveal another set of risk factors beyond the child and family. Some are related to the measurement factors already discussed. However, others are unique to the current state of intervention knowledge and practices.

Intervention programs vary in their target populations, in the nature of the programs offered (e.g., personnel, content, and procedures) and in the settings where services are delivered. (Refer to Chapters 8 and 9 in this text). In a recent review of 24 federally supported programs, Silver (1979) points out that infant intervention programs may be preventive or remedial; may focus on infants whose risk status reflects one or several risk factors; may focus on one or several infant developmental domains (cognitive, emotional, social, physical); may focus primarily on the child, on the mother (who is trained to be the primary agent of intervention with her own child), or on the mother-infant interaction; and may be offered in a clinic, a hospital, a center, or in the home. Keeping this variability in mind, four intervention-related risk factors are discussed: need, availability and accessibility, appropriateness and effectiveness.

Need

The extent to which infants at risk and their families are appropriately identified and offered intervention services for their needs is dependent upon the accuracy of detection measures and procedures. For the truly at-risk infant and family who escape detection, the consequence is the difference between the magnitude of the child's later learning problems and the degree to which an early intervention program might have prevented or remediated such problems. It is for this infant and family, the so-called "false negative," that members of the helping professions so vehemently and justifiably express their concern.

The consequences may be just as hazardous, however, for the infant and family who are mistakenly detected, the so-called "false positive." Kearsley (1979) persuasively argues that professionals can unwittingly produce "iatrogenic retardation" in the infant and young child by alarming parents about the possible effects of prematurity and other perinatal events. The professional may unintentionally produce serious parental anxieties and lowered expectations for child progress that adversely affect parent-child interactions and relationships. This, in turn, may deter the child's opportunities for normal interactions and normal development. Among several other suggestions, Kearsley argues for more accurate detection measures, especially ones that identify the infant, who, despite other presenting symptoms and histories, is cognitively intact (see Zelazo, 1979).

Availability and Accessibility

The at-risk infant and family who do require early intervention are placed at further risk if a program is not available in the community or in some other way made easily accessible. The reasons an intervention program may not be accessible include factors related to eligibility, costs, transportation impediments, or incompatibility of the family's schedule with that of the program. Of course, the community in which an at-risk infant and family reside may offer no intervention program whatsoever. (A further discussion of the role of the community in creating additional risk for the at-risk infant is discussed in another section of this chapter).

Appropriateness

Assuming that an intervention program is needed, and is available and accessible, the next consideration is whether or not the program is appropriate. The nature of the intervention program (for example, whether it is home-, hospital-, or center-based; infant-, caregiver-, or interaction-focused) should be related to the age and condition of the at-risk infant and the characteristics of the family. For example, Keogh and Kopp (1978) suggest that during early infancy the most promising interventions: 1) focus on parent-infant interactions, 2) emphasize the caregiving quality of the home, and 3) are essentially supportive and nondidactic. Certainly, the intervention program that is available to the at-risk infant and family should be closely aligned to the nature of the risk elements (child or family) that originally prompted risk status assignment; to the extent that such alignment is not present, the appropriateness (or inappropriateness) of the intervention program is a risk factor beyond the child and family.

Effectiveness

It is highly possible that even in a situation where the intervention program is needed, is available and accessible, and is appropriate, the program may not be effective in preventing or remediating the child's learning problems beyond what could have been expected in the absence of the program. (Within the rubric of effectiveness must be included the absence of unwanted effects.)

Although there are many reasons why an intervention program may not be effective for a particular at-risk infant and family, discussion here is limited to four major possibilities.

1. Regardless of the delivery setting for intervention, it is possible that the program is not significantly different from, or an improvement over, the home environment and the parent-infant interactions that would naturally have occurred. Although this phenomenon is rarely if ever discussed in the literature, it not only is a distinct possibility, it may account for some of the meager differences or lack of effect found between infants who do and do not receive intervention from particular programs.

2. For a variety of reasons (inadequate measures, incorrect interpretation of measurement results or a difficult-to-assess child) the child's abilities, delays, or adjustment problems may be incorrectly diagnosed. The error may lead to intervention procedures focused on the wrong behaviors, developmental domains, or levels of functioning within domains. Inappropriate intervention may, in turn, lead to little or no child progress.

3. The intervention procedures may be too weak, inconsistent, or inappropriate to effect progress or adjustment of a particular at-risk infant. For example, the program philosophy about how child development is enhanced may not match the particular infant's needs.

That is, a particular infant may be more responsive to a didactic, structured approach than to one that provides for nonstructured activities and freedom-to-explore experiences.

4. The effects (or lack of effects) of intervention procedures may not be monitored with sufficient frequency or sensitivity for decisions to be made about maintaining or modifying them. Frequent and sensitive measures of infant development across domains and other relevant variables (such as the parent-child relationship), must be made for timely recognition of ineffective instructional procedures and unwanted program effects.

In summary, there are several risk factors beyond the child and family that are tied to the quality and appropriateness of currently available measures and intervention procedures. Inadequacies in measurement and intervention procedures interact with risk factors related to community characteristics and service delivery patterns, to which attention is turned next.

COMMUNITY RISK FACTORS

One of the more prominent assumptions related to the at-risk infant is that the child's future well-being is highly dependent on the community in which it is born and reared. Communities vary in the extent to which they make available early identification and intervention services, and it is tempting to offer a list of community characteristics that may be related to that availability. Community size, population density, wealth, and geographical location are characteristics typically mentioned. These variables *are* important in understanding the variation in service provision across communities; however, an intracommunity conceptualization is more appropriate and potentially more productive for identifying community risk factors. Discussed briefly here are five intracommunity factors that, to the extent they are absent from a community, are risk factors beyond the child and family.

Knowledge

The first, and probably most fundamental, community risk factor is the degree to which community leaders and community members have knowledge of the purposes and potential effects of early identification and intervention with infants at risk. Many authorities in early education (e.g., Bronfenbrenner, 1974; Caldwell, 1970; Hayden and McGinness, 1977), have described the rationale and potential benefits of services for at-risk infants and their families; however, these same authorities frequently suggest that this information has not been adequately shared with community lay persons. For example, Hayden and McGinness (1977) suggest that educating the public about what early intervention can and cannot do should be professionals' first order of business.

In addition to a lack of knowledge about early identification and intervention services, community leaders and members may lack knowledge regarding child growth and development, the effects of the home environment and child-rearing practices, and the effects of the overall community structure and milieu. Although knowledge of child development and the potential effects of different home environments and child-rearing practices may appear to be child and family risk factors, they also have community relevance for two reasons: 1) imparting information about child development and childrearing practices is society's responsibility, and 2) all community members, or at least the vast majority of members, should possess this information (Bronfenbrenner, 1977).

Values

The second community risk factor is the extent to which the community and its leaders place value on providing child and family services. It cannot be assumed that there is a relationship between community knowledge about early identification and intervention and the value assigned to services. Individual and group values are influenced by a variety of factors in addition to knowledge—ingrained beliefs, customs, attitudes, and other competing values.

An example of competing values is that community members may view parental rights to privacy and noninterference in childrearing as more important than providing identification and intervention services. The value conflict associated with parent versus child rights is reflected in our legal system. In a review of court opinions pertaining to child placement outside the home of biological parents, Goldstein, Freud, and Solnit (1973) point out that although the law does intrude in a coarse way in parent and child relationships, it has neither the sensitivity nor the resources to supervise day-to-day happenings between parent and child. They conclude that the law ought to, and generally does, prefer the private ordering of interpersonal relationships over legal intrusions on them. On this and other value issues, the law has been described as a relatively sensitive indicator of public opinion (Begelman, 1978). Competing values are discussed further later in the chapter.

Resources

Assuming that community leaders and members have knowledge of, and value identification and intervention for at-risk infants and their families, the next consideration is whether or not the community has or can obtain the resources (financial, personnel, facilities, equipment) for the task. In fact, lack of resources is probably the most frequently mentioned deterrent to providing services. However, a wide range of costs is associated with different service models, and the range of services any community contemplates is also a function of the interaction of other community characteristics, such as population density, size, age patterns, and the knowledge and values considerations discussed previously.

Commitment

Even a community with the requisite knowledge, values, and resources may not be committed to establishing identification and intervention services. One reason for lack of commitment might be that the community has other competing commitments. Also, political considerations may lead community leaders to expend resources on activities of significantly lower value (in an absolute sense) that will have more immediate or visible outcomes. Such politically expedient actions may also include turning back some resources to community members if fiscally austere actions are deemed popular.

Whether or not available resources are committed to child and family services also is related to the knowledge risk factor already discussed. Community leaders may be unaware of the range of service programs available for adoption and their associated costs. Similarly, they may not be aware of the existing resources in the community (philanthropic groups, vacant space, volunteer organizations, professional skills), in neighboring communities, or in government programs that could help to defray the costs of identification and intervention services.

Choices

The last community risk factor is the extent to which the community makes intelligent choices regarding the infant and family services it establishes. Inappropriate choices could conceivably occur despite the community's status on other risk factors. For example, what community members know about the potential effectiveness of identification and intervention services may be undermined by professional or scientific uncertainties about the accuracy of detection measures and/or the effectiveness of intervention. Whether or not the community has an accurate or distorted picture of what is scientifically known and unknown may affect the community's willingness to commit resources to such services and, most pertinent to the discussion here, the nature and extent of the service models selected.

There are many examples of how service choices can place the at-risk infant at further risk. Following are four examples:

1. The service may be inaccessible to the infant and family due to transportation difficulties, high cost, or other factors.

2. The community may offer a service model that is ineffective or inappropriate for a particular at-risk infant and family.
3. The community may provide a service that unintentionally produces unwanted side effects, for example, alarming parents and adversely affecting a naturally postive social-emotional climate.
4. The community may select services that are insufficient, for example, adding a child development-parenting curriculum in the public school program but providing no intervention for infants. Although many authorities (Anastasiow, 1977; Bronfenbrenner, 1977; Scott, 1978) have cogently argued the case for such a curriculum, this service may not be sufficient for a particular at-risk infant and family.

STATE AND FEDERAL RISK FACTORS

As discussion of at-risk infants moves from the community level to the broader issues of societal structure and governance, one fact becomes increasingly obvious—all infants are vulnerable to the factors that increase the probability of delayed or deviant development. Clearly, the social environment is never neutral, and the extent to which it is supportive or nonsupportive has direct impact on the developing child. Emphasis on the social milieu and related economic and political considerations is based on the belief that society has the capability to reduce the incidence of at-risk conditions by decreasing the number of environmental factors that contribute to their risk.

Viewed from this perspective, the risk factors beyond the child and family that can be identified at the state and federal level are extremely important. Although education has been described as a federal interest, a state responsibility and community operation, these role definitions are not nearly as clear for the at-risk infant and family. The responsibility for infant and family services is diffused among many agencies and organizations at community, state, and federal levels. Such diffusion creates an enormous variation in the availability and quality of services to infants and families. The community share of responsibility for these services is critical. However, the role of state and federal governments in research, demonstration, and service is also substantial.

Before discussing some risk factors at the state and federal level, it is important to note that the expectations and behaviors of state governments and the federal government are not necessarily the same regarding infant and family services. It is entirely possible, and quite likely, that this will remain the case for some time. Yet this variability need not obstruct efforts to reduce or eliminate factors that can negatively affect infants and families. The resolution of service delivery problems at various governmental levels can be accomplished through diverse mechanisms.

Though many factors at state and federal levels can be identified that place infants at risk, the primary factor is public policy, along with the mechanisms and spheres of influence that have an impact on it. Public policy should be viewed as a dynamic and changing phenomenon characterized by conflict over resource utilization and allocation. This perspective is different from that which perceives public policy as a distinct entity, basically systematic, that results from some form of consent and consensus. The conflict perspective has been espoused by many social theorists (Baldridge, 1971; Dahrendorf, 1958; Collins, 1975), and provides an appropriate framework for a discussion of risk factors at the state and federal levels.

This section discusses two broad aspects of public policy related to risk factors: 1) the ability to influence the political system into making decisions favorable to improved services to infants and families, and 2) the ability to influence acquisition and allocation of resources to establish and maintain services. Such control of decisions and resources is currently lacking at both the state and federal levels. Risk factors related to influencing political decisions are discussed in terms of rationale for public policy, structures for influencing public policy, and awareness of the scope of the problem. Risk factors associated with acquiring and allocating resources are discussed in terms of lack of agreement on service delivery mechanisms and fragmentation of services.

Influencing Political Decisions

Establishing comprehensive child and family intervention services requires the ability to influence and control policy making and policy changing. Clearly, however, without the appropriate knowledge, values, resources, and commitment at the community level, such influence and control at the state and federal levels becomes irrelevant. But, the effective combination of social policy at all levels will result in the development of comprehensive services.

Rationales for Public Policy   The apparent lack of compelling reasons for establishing comprehensive services is a critical factor that places at-risk infants at further risk. Without a strong rationale and comprehensive public policy, there is little direction for intervention efforts and no mandate for allocating resources to develop and deliver such services.

Many educators believe PL 94-142 can be an appropriate rationale for creating infant and family services if the mandate is extended downwards in age. However, applying this legislation to at-risk infants may not be feasible or sufficient. The basic rationale for the creation and implementation of PL 94-142 was a civil rights one: handicapped children cannot be denied a free appropriate public education which is available to nonhandicapped children. Although the application of the law in some instances extends beyond its civil rights origins, the dominant theme is a civil rights one, which may be insufficient for influencing social policy regarding services to infants, who typically are not served by public schools.

Another common rationale for influencing public policy is that of economic benefit to society. Regarding early intervention with handicapped children, the case is often made that such an approach is cost-effective because society is saved the massive expense of institutionalization and/or more intensive long-term intervention in later years (e.g., Hayden and McGinness, 1977). Unfortunately, as yet no firm data clearly document the extent of economic benefit to be derived. Although such data should be available in the near future, until they are, the economic benefit rationale is limited to suggestions and assertions.

In addition to civil rights considerations and economic benefits, there is a rationale for service based upon the effectiveness of early intervention, its maximization of human potential, and its reduction of human suffering. However, the fact that a strong public policy for infants and family services is lacking at various governmental levels suggests that these arguments have not been especially persuasive.

Structures for Influencing Public Policy   The structures (agencies, organizations, etc.) for influencing public policy must be capable of identifying the problems and proposing a rationale for change to decision-makers. Currently existing structures have not been effective in creating a comprehensive public policy for infants and families for at least two reasons. First, different goals, activities, and constituencies across the agencies and organizations supporting early intervention tend to impede the development of alliances. Lack of unified effort is exemplified by the often exaggerated differences in goals between the educational and medical professions (Gallagher, 1979). It seems ironic that both professions have exhibited considerable interest in at-risk infants and families, yet they focus on their individual issues and problems rather than jointly working to change public policy.

The second reason that existing structures have not created a comprehensive infant and family service policy is that no lead agency or organization has emerged. This may reflect narrowly defined purposes of various groups or it may reflect the fact that organizational efforts are diffused or focused elsewhere. For example, much of the special education effort has emphasized services for the school-aged child and the critically important task of implementing and monitoring PL 94-142. Also, much of the rehabilitation-medical community is dealing with a strong mandate to provide improved and increased services to severely and profoundly handicapped persons, primarily adolescents and adults. These and other factors tend to deter the mobilization of existing structures to create a comprehensive service policy for infants and families.

Awareness of the Scope of the Problem   The extent to which policy makers and the public in general understand the potential benefits of child and family services is unknown. However, the variation in availability and in the provision of services across the nation suggests limited awareness. Some of this lack of awareness can be attributed to the fact that services for at-risk infants and families is a relatively new effort, and educating the public about it is a substantial task. However, until the public is made aware of at-risk infants and the conditions that can exacerbate their risk status, the necessary momentum for influencing decision-makers is unlikely to develop.

In summary, the absence of a strong and effective rationale, unified organizational structure, and broad public awareness of the issues related to early intervention for at-risk infants and families limits efforts to influence public policy. The phenomena constitute significant risk factors beyond the child and family, which society can influence, yet they have not effectively been addressed.

Resources

The availability of increasingly scarce resources is the other major public policy concern related to intervention for at-risk infants and their families. Influence must not only result in appropriate social sentiment but also in identification and allocation of resources for services. Two basic issues related to resources are discussed.

Lack of Agreement on Service Delivery Mechanisms   Disagreements about where to place resources and how they can be utilized most effectively are common at every level of government and society. Disputes also arise over who should control the resources and deliver the services. Should federal or state governments be the major service deliverers? Should the local community be responsible for establishing and maintaining all infant and family services? Or should a combination of federal and state resources support strong community controlled programs? Lack of consensus regarding services to infants and families continues to be a serious impediment to providing comprehensive intervention services.

Fragmentation of Services   A frequent lament is that existing child and family services are fragmented. At the federal level alone, 268 government programs and policies have been identified that affect family life (Institute for Educational Leadership, 1978). Analogs of this fragmentation also are evident at the state and community levels. For instance, the problem may show up as a lack of continuity in services to the child and family over time—the agency that serves the infant frequently cannot serve the toddler or preschool child. In short, because resources for child and family services are scattered across many agencies and organizations at community, state, and federal levels, there is a splintering of responsibility for services as well as gaps in necessary services. This fragmentation is a risk factor beyond the child and family.

RECOMMENDATIONS

For each of the risk factors described (related to measurement, intervention, and community, state, and federal policy) a lengthy list of recommendations for action could be generated. For example, it is certain that improved measures of child status, development, and progress are needed, as well as improved intervention methods, procedures for describing intervention components, and effective strategies for matching intervention elements with child and family characteristics. Also apparent is the need for more reliable information for policy-making and decision-making, and for better mechanisms for obtaining and intelligently committing resources for child and family services. Just as necessary is improved understanding of the complex interactions, characteristics, and decision-making processes both within and among federal, state, and community agencies. Reducing or eliminating such risk factors beyond the child and family will require a concerted and long-term effort. However, the recommendations that follow emphasize some interim steps that can be taken:

1. Encourage leaders at federal, state, and community levels to designate a lead agency or organizational unit that will be responsible for planning, operating, or coordinating child and family services. This recommendation is not novel; implementing it comprehensively would be. Some diversion of funds from other purposes is required for this and the next two recommendations.
2. Develop a system for providing current information on best practices to professionals who have, or will have, direct contact with infants and families. Information on child development, detection, intervention, and communicating with families should be provided to child care specialists, nurses, social workers, pediatricians, and general practitioners. Such a system for rapidly disseminating new information will reduce the variation in professional knowledge.
3. Develop a system for providing child development and child-rearing information to community members, starting with school-age children and adolescents. The goal is to establish a basic level of knowledge about child development and child rearing among society's members, a base to which more specialized information can be added if appropriate.

4. Develop viable detection and service models for communites with specific characteristics (e.g., knowledge, values, resources) that can be adopted by other, similar communities.

5. Develop probability data for various detection measures and child ages that represent the likelihood that a child will exhibit learning or adjustment problems later in life. These estimates should be based on the most current scientific information available and should be used in communities with characteristics similar to the population from which the probability estimates were originally made. By providing such estimates, community professionals, in collaboration with parents, can decide whether intervention is appropriate.

6. In concert with step 5, above, develop and provide probability estimates about various intervention programs that can successfully prevent or remediate various learning and adjustment problems of infants and families. This recommendation is similar in intent to the second recommendation; namely, that decision making at the community level should be a process based on the most current information available.

The above recommendations cannot really be labeled "interim," and they are by no means modest. However, the implementation of these recommendations should help to ensure that children and families at least have the benefits of current knowledge about child development and child rearing, and that community leaders have current information for making policy decisions about child and family services. The costs for implementing these recommendations should diminish as system establishment is replaced by system maintenance.

Once these interim steps have been taken, priorities should be established for accomplishing longer term objectives. Resolving measurement issues should be the number one long-term priority, because until more accurate detection and assessment measures are developed, it is unlikely that society's leaders can be convinced that intervention services should be provided for any but the most severely and obviously impaired infants. Moreover, until we develop improved measures of intervention components, child progress, and overall program effectiveness, our ability to improve intervention programs and convince others of their effectiveness will be severely limited.

REFERENCES

Anastasiow, N. J.   The need and the potential solution. In N. J. Anastasiow (Ed.), *Preventing tomorrow's handicapped child today.* Bloomington, Ind.: Institute for Child Study, 1977.

Baldridge, J. V.   *Power and conflict in the university.* New York: Wiley, 1971.

Bayley, N.   Development of mental abilities. In P. H. Mussen (Ed.), *Carmichael's manual of child psychology* (Vol. 1.) (3rd ed.). New York: Wiley, 1970.

Begelman, D. A.   Ethical issues for the developmentally disabled. In M. S. Berkler, G. H. Bible, S. M. Boles, D. E. D. Deitz, and A. C. Repp (Eds.), *Current trends for the developmentally disabled.* Baltimore: University Park Press, 1978.

Bell, R. Q.   A reinterpretation of the direction of effects in studies of socialization. *Psychological Review,* 1968, *75,* 81-95.

Bradley, R. H., and Caldwell, R. M.   Early home environments and changes in mental test performance in children from 6 to 36 months. *Developmental Psychology,* 1976, *12,* 93-97.

Brazelton, T. B.   *Neonatal Behavioral Assessment Scale.* London: William Heinemann Medical Books, 1973.

Broman, S. H., Nichols, P. L., and Kennedy, W. A.   *Preschool IQ: Prenatal and early development correlates.* Hillsdale, N.J.: Lawrence Erlbaum Associates, 1975.

Bronfenbrenner, U.   *Is early intervention effective? A report on longitudinal evaluations of preschool programs* (Vol. 2). DHEW Publication No. (OHD) 74-25, 1974.

Bronfenbrenner, U.   *Who needs parent education?* Paper presented at the Working Conference on Parent Education sponsored by the Charles Street Mott Foundation, Flint, Michigan, September 29-30, 1977.

Caldwell, B.   The rationale for early intervention. *Exceptional Children,* 1970, *36,* 717-726.

Collins, R.   *Conflict sociology: Toward an explanatory science.* New York: Academic Press, 1975.

Dahrendorf, R.   Toward a theory of social conflict. *Journal of Conflict Resolution,* 1958, *2,* 170-183.

Gallagher, J. J.   *Early education of the handicapped—The last frontier.* Paper presented at the Handicapped Children's Early Education Program Conference, sponsored by the Bureau of Education for the Handicapped, U.S. Office of Education, held in Washington, D.C., December 5, 1979.

Goldstein, J., Freud, A., and Solnit, A. J.   *Beyond the best interest of the child.* New York: The Free Press, 1973.

Greenspan, S. I., Nover, R. A., Silver, B. J., and Lourie, R. S.   Methodology issues and an approach to assessment in clinical infant programs. In *Clinical infant intervention research programs.* DHEW Publication No. (ADM) 79-748, 1979.

Hamilton, J. L.   Assessment in mental retardation: Toward instructional relevance. In R. B. Kearsley and I. E. Sigel (Eds.), *Infants at risk: Assessment of cognitive functioning.* Hillsdale, N.J.: Lawrence Erlbaum Associates, 1979.

Hayden, A. H., and McGinness, G. D.   Bases for early intervention. In E. Sontag (Ed.), *Educational programming for the severely and profoundly handicapped.* Reston, Va.: Division on Mental Retardation, The Council for Exceptional Children, 1977.

Horowtiz, F. D., and Dunn, M.   Infant intelligence testing. In F. D. Minifie and L. L. Lloyd (Eds.), *Communicative and cognitive abilities—Early behavioral assessment.* Baltimore: University Park Press, 1978.

Institute for Educational Leadership. *Toward an inventory of federal programs with direct impact on families.* Publication No. 31. Washington, D.C.: George Washington University and the Institute for Educational Leadership, 1978.

Ireton, H., Thwing, E., and Graven, H. Infant mental development and neurological status, family socioeconomic status, and intelligence at age 4. *Child Development,* 1970, *41,* 937-945.

Jordan, T. E. *Development in the preschool years; Birth to age five.* New York: Academic Press, 1980.

Kearsley, R. B. Iatrogenic retardation: A syndrome of learned incompetence. In R. B. Kearsley and I. E. Sigel (Eds.), *Infants at risk: Assessment of cognitive functioning.* Hillsdale, N.J.: Lawrence Erlbaum Associates, 1979.

Keogh, B. K., and Kopp, C. B. From assessment to intervention: An elusive bridge. In F. D. Minifie and L. L. Lloyd (Eds.), *Communicative and cognitive abilities—Early behavioral assessment.* Baltimore: University Park Press, 1978.

Lewis, M., and Rosenblum, L. (Eds.). The effect of the infant on its caregiver. In *The origins of behavior* (Vol. 1.) New York: Wiley, 1974.

McCall, R. B., Appelbaum, M. I., and Hogarty, P. S. Developmental changes in mental performance. *Monographs of the Society for Research in Child Development,* 1973, *38,* (Serial No. 150).

McCall, R. B., Hogarty, P. S., and Hurlburt, N. Transitions in infant sensorimotor development and the prediction of childhood IQ. *American Psychologist,* 1972, *27,* 728-748.

Rubin, R. A., and Balow, B. Perinatal influences on the behavior and learning problems of children. In B. B. Lahey and A. E. Kazden (Eds.), *Advances in clinical child psychology* (Vol. 1). New York: Plenum Press, 1977.

Sameroff, A. J. The etiology of cognitive competence: A systems perspective. In R. B. Kearsley and I. E. Sigel (Eds.), *Infants at risk: Assessment of cognitive functioning.* Hillsdale, N.J.: Lawrence Erlbaum Associates, 1979.

Sameroff, A. J., and Chandler, M. J. Reproductive risk and the continuum of caretaking casualty. In F. D. Horowtiz (Ed.), *Review of child development research* (Vol. 4). Chicago: University of Chicago Press, 1975.

Scott, K. G. The rationale and methodological considerations underlying early cognitive and behavioral assessment. In F. D. Minifie and L. L. Lloyd (Eds.), *Communicative and cognitive abilities—Early behavioral assessment.* Baltimore: University Park Press, 1978.

Sigel, I. E. Application of research to psychoeducational treatment of infants at risk. In R. B. Kearsley and I. E. Sigel (Eds.), *Infants at risk: Assessment of cognitive functioning.* Hillsdale, N.J.: Lawrence Erlbaum Associates, 1979.

Silver, B. J. Overview of clinical infant research programs. In *Clinical infant intervention research programs.* DHEW Publication No. (ADM) 79-748, 1979.

Stott, L. H., and Ball, R. S. Infant and preschool mental tests: Review and evaluation. *Monographs of the Society for Research in Child Development,* 1965, *30.*

Thorpe, H. S., and Werner, E. E. Developmental screening of preschool children: A critical review of inventories used in health and education programs. *Pediatrics,* 1974, *53,* 362-370.

Tjossem, T. D. Early intervention: Issues and approaches. In T. D. Tjossem (Ed.), *Intervention strategies for high risk infants and young children.* Baltimore: University Park Press, 1976.

Uzgiris, I. C., and Hunt, J. McV. *Toward ordinal scales of psychological development in infancy.* Urbana, Ill.: University of Illinois Press, 1975.

Vietze, P. M., and St. Clair, K. L. *Infant tests: Measures of cognitive development in the study of high risk infants.* Paper presented at the conference, Premature and Small for Date Infants: The Assessment of Cognitive Competence Among a Population At Risk, sponsored by the Georgia Warm Springs Foundation. Princeton, N.J., September 19-21, 1976.

Yang, R. K., and Bell, R. Q.   Assessment of infants. In P. McReynolds (Ed.), *Advances in psychological assessment* (Vol. 3). San Francisco: Jossey-Bass, 1975.

Yarrow, L. J., Rubenstein, J. L., and Pederson, F. A. *Infant and environment.* New York: Wiley, 1975.

Zelazo, P. R.   Reactivity to perceptual-cognitive events: Application for infant assessment. In R. B. Kearsley and I. E. Sigel (Eds.), *Infants at risk: Assessment of cognitive functioning.* Hillsdale, N.J.: Lawrence Erlbaum Associates, 1979.

APPENDICES

APPENDICES

Annotated Listing of Programs that Screen for High-Risk and Handicapped Infants

UCLA Intervention Program for Handicapped Children
UCLA Rehabilitation Center
1000 Veterans Avenue
Room 23-33
Los Angeles, CA 90024

> All infants and children referred for developmental assessment are seen by a pediatrician with subspecialty training in child development.

Infant Parent Education Project
320 East 111th Street
Los Angeles, CA 90059

> Infants, 0-18 months, who are referred from medical sources, are screened with the Denver Developmental Screening Test. The multidisciplinary staff also looks at parent and family strengths and problems.

CHEER Program (Cherry Creek Early Education Reachout)
Holly Ridge Center
3301 South Monaco Parkway
Denver, CO 80220
>Children (0-5 years) referred to the program are screened individually by an interdisciplinary team for all types of handicapping conditions.

Home Learning Center for Hearing-Impaired Children and Their Parents
305 N. McKinley
Ball State University
Muncie, IN 47306
>This screening program is designed to find hearing-impaired infants before 2 years of age with the Infant Cassette Hearing Screening System and Behavioral Response Audiometry.

Macomb 0-3 Regional Project, A Rural Child/Find Parent Service
27 Horrabin Hall
Western Illinois University
Macomb, IL 61455
>Using the "Step Ups" screening instrument, the project determines eligibility for a 0-3 program including mild delays and high-risk conditions.

Project RHISE/Outreach
Children's Development Center
650 North Main Street
Rockford, IL 61103
>Delays in development are screened in three ways: children referred to the program are screened; children in known high-risk groups are routinely screened; and local mass screening efforts are made three to four times a year.

Special Infant Care Clinic
North Carolina Memorial Hospital
Chapel Hill, NC 27514
>The project exclusively serves infants who have been hospitalized in the Neonatal Intensive Care Unit and who have one or more neonatal problems.

Infant Identification and Tracking Program
Maternal and Child Health Branch
Division of Health Services
Post Office Box 209
Raleigh, NC 37602
>The newborn nurseries in North Carolina hospitals are utilized as the focal point for identification of high-risk newborns in order to ensure necessary care and treatment for high-risk infants and their mothers.

Rural Early Intervention Program
Center for Human Development
Convocation Center
Ohio University
Athens, OH 45701

> The Denver Developmental Screening Test is administered at an initial home visit by any member of the transdisciplinary team to a child from birth to 3 years of age with a suspected developmental delay or handicap.

Infant Stimulation/Mother Training Program
Department of Pediatrics
College of Medicine
University of Cincinnati
231 Bethesda Avenue
Cincinnati, OH 45267

> This program, based in the Cincinnati General Hospital, targets teenage mothers (16 years and younger) and premature infants (those weighing less than 1250 grams at birth) for screening.

Project First Chance—Outreach
252 Kent Hall
Kent State University
Kent, OH 44242

> The Kent Infant Development Scale (KID Scale), a normed caregiver-completed behavior inventory, is the basis for a screening program for children chronologically or developmentally under 1 year of age.

At-Risk Parent-Child Program
Hillcrest Medical Center
1120 South Utica
Tulsa, OK 79104

> The premise of this program is that the primary prevention of poor parenting and child abuse and neglect is possible through the use of hospital and clinic settings and resource centers. Therefore, a screening procedure for identifying parents at-risk for poor parenting was developed.

Developmental Education at Birth Through Two (DEBT)
Lubbock Independent School District
1628 19th Street
Lubbock, TX 79401

> DEBT's screening component includes referral, initial intake, observation, administration of screening instruments deemed necessary, and medical evaluation.

Newborn High Risk Hearing Screening by Birth Certificate
Utah State Department of Health
Speech Pathology/Audiology Section
44 Medical Drive
Salt Lake City, UT 84113

The purpose of this program is to identify all deaf and severely hearing impaired newborns in Utah by 8 months of age. This birth certificate computerized system is used to screen all live births, with audiological intervention for those at risk.

Infant Program/Outreach Project
Child Development Resources
Post Office Box 299
Lightfoot, VA 23090

CDR screens referrals of handicapped, suspected handicapped, and high-risk children, 0-2, to determine whether or not additional evaluation is needed.

Project Home Base
Yakima Public Schools
104 N. 4th Avenue
Yakima, WA 98902

Project Home Base, a Title I program, screens families with children aged 0 to 5 years in order to determine those children who will most benefit from the intervention program.

Early Childhood Program
Madison Metropolitan School District
454 West Dayton Street
Madison, WI 53711

This public school-based program screens for documentable delays in any area of child development. The major screening instrument used is the Minnesota Child Development Index.

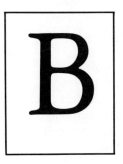

Annotated Listing of Programs that Provide Intervention Services to Infants

Rural Infant Stimulation Environment (RISE)
Area Special Education
Post Office Box 2592
University, AL 35486

> The RISE Project is a day care program for severely multidisabled infants and preschoolers from birth to 6 years. Emphasis is placed on proper care and management in the areas of sensorimotor and reflex development, prespeech and feeding development, language, cognitive, self-help, and gross motor and fine motor activities. Rural areas are targets for the center-based and outreach services with the State of Alabama.

Infant/Parent Education Project
320 East 111th Street
Los Angeles, CA 90059

> This program provides services for children ages birth to 18 months

with a home- and center-based approach. All handicapping conditions except speech impairments, serious emotional disturbances, and learning disability are served.

CHEER Program (Cherry Creek Early Education Reachout)
Holly Ridge Center
3301 South Monaco Parkway
Denver, CO 80220

This program provides services to children ages birth to 5 years old in all categories of handicapping conditions except deaf/blind. A home- and center-based approach is used.

Long Term Follow-Up Clinic
Post Office Box 016820
Mailman Center for Child Development (D-820)
University of Miami
Miami, FL 33101

This program provides center-based services for children ages birth to 6 years old. Children with all types of handicapping conditions are served, with a special emphasis on premature infants from multicultural backgounds (e.g., Black, Hispanic, and Haitian).

Debbie School Early Intervention Program
Post Office Box 016820
Mailman Center for Child Development (D-820)
University of Miami
Miami, FL 33101

This program serves children ages birth to 3½ years old with a center-based approach. Children may have any of the handicapping conditions, except learning disabilities, with special emphasis given to those who have identifiable handicaps at birth.

Teenage Pregnancy Programs
Post Office Box 01680
Mailman Center for Child Development (D-820)
University of Miami
Miami, FL 33101

This program provides services to teenage mothers and their infants ages birth to 1 year old through a home- and center-based approach. The infants are considered at risk due to prematurity or low socioeconomic status of the mother.

Early Childhood Intervention
Illinois Institute for Developmental Disabilities
1640 West Roosevelt Road
Chicago, IL 60608

This program serves children who exhibit all types of handicapping conditions, except learning disability and serious emotional disturbances, ages birth to 3 years old. A home- and center-based approach is used. This project also operates a referral network for high-risk nurseries.

Macomb 0-3 Regional Project—A Rural Child/Parent Service
27 Horrabin Hall
Western Illinois University
Macomb, IL 60455

This home-based program provides services to children ages birth to 3 years old who exhibit any of the types of handicapping or at-risk conditions. This program is a rural infant service delivery model.

Pre-Start Project
Department of Pediatrics
Loyola University
Stritch School of Medicine
2160 South 1st Avenue
Maywood, IL 60153

This is a competency-based program for families of high-risk infants ages birth to 3 years old. Services are provided to infants with all types of handicapping and at-risk conditions through a home- and hospital-based program. Referral and consultation services are provided to other community services.

Peoria 0-3 Replication Project
913 North Western Avenue
Peoria, IL 61604

This program provides services to children ages birth to 3 years old who may exhibit any or all handicapping conditions. A home- and center-based approach is used. Special emphasis is given to the needs of severely handicapped infants and toddlers.

Project RHISE/Outreach
Children's Development Center
650 North Main Street
Rockford, IL 61103

This program serves children ages birth to 3 years old with all types of handicapping conditions. The center-based approach uses a "consultancy model," which is a dynamic interaction between the child's teacher and other clinical staff.

PREPARE
Developmental Training Center
2853 East 19th Street
Bloomington, IN 47401

This project provides services to children ages birth to 3 years old exhibiting any of the handicapping conditions. It is a center- and home-based program using a multidisciplinary approach to develop and implement programs for the children and parents.

Home Learning Center for Hearing-Impaired Children and Their Parents
305 N. McKinley
Ball State University
Muncie, IN 47306

This program, which is both home- and center-based, specializes in services for the hard-of-hearing, deaf, and speech impaired, ages birth to 5. Children ages 18 months to 5 years are mainstreamed in a toddler nursery school, those birth to 3 in a home learning center, and those 3 to 5 years in a preschool class for the hearing impaired. Eight out of 20 of the project's graduates are mainstreamed in the elementary grades.

The John F. Kennedy Institute for Handicapped Children
707 North Broadway
Baltimore, MD 21205

This hospital program serves children, and their families, from throughout the United States. About 300 children from birth on receive comprehensive patient care for a variety of mental, motor, and sensory disabilities. In addition, infants are seen as outpatients in special clinics.

Developmental Evaluation Service for Children (DESC)
12701 Twinbrook Parkway
Rockville, MD 20852

This program provides center-based diagnostic evaluation by a multidisciplinary health and education team for children of birth to 5 years old. These services are for children exhibiting any type of handicapping condition except deaf/blind.

Project TELSTAR
Alpena-Montmorency-Alcoma Intermediate District
1691 M-32 West
Alpena, MI 49707

This home-based program emphasizes services to children ages birth to 3 years old who may exhibit any of the handicapping conditions, except learning disability. This project has been validated in the state of Michigan as a Title IV-C project.

Early Childhood Development Program Institute for
the Study of Mental Retardation and Related Disabilities
130 South First Street
Ann Arbor, MI 48104

This project provides services to children ages birth to 5 years through a center- and home-based program. The parents are the primary service providers with support and guidance from the interdisciplinary project staff. Children with all types of developmental disabilities are served.

Variety Club Infant Development Program
Meyer Children's Rehabilitation Institute
444 South 44th Street
Omaha, NE 68131

This program provides services for children ages birth to 3 years old through a center- and home-based approach. Children with all types of handicapping conditions are served. Almost one-third of children served are multiply handicapped. The majority of children are moderately to severely handicapped.

Special Infant Care Clinic
North Carolina Memorial Hospital
Chapel Hill, NC 27514

This program provides services for children ages birth to 1 year old with all types of handicapping and at-risk conditions except serious emotional disturbances and learning disabilities. This is a hospital-based approach.

Early Childhood Intervention Project
739 Chappel Drive
Raleigh, NC 27606

This program provides services to children ages birth to 3 years old through a home-based approach. Children with all types of handicapping conditions are served, except those who are seriously emotionally disturbed or learning disabled. This program is part of a statewide network of home-based programs.

Western Carolina Infants' Program
Western Carolina Center
Enola Road
Morgantown, NC 28655

This project offers home-based training to parents of children ages birth to 4 years old who are primarily mentally retarded or have health impairments. Interdisciplinary assessments are periodically made at the center.

Rural Early Intervention Program
Center for Human Development
Convocation Center
Ohio University
Athens, OH 45701

This program provides services for children with all types of handicapping conditions, ages birth to 3 years old. A home- and center-based approach is used. Care is provided by a transdisciplinary team, with a case manager assigned to each child.

Parent Infant Program

Nisonger Center

Ohio State University

1580 Cannon Drive

Columbus, OH 43210

> This center-based program serves children ages birth to 3 years old. The served children's primary handicapping conditions are mental retardation, other health impairments, and orthopedic impairments. Other at-risk and secondary handicapping conditions are also served.

Infant Stimulation/Mother Training Program

Department of Pediatrics/College of Medicine

University of Cincinnati

231 Bethesda Avenue

Cincinnati, Ohio 45267

> The purpose of this hospital-based primary prevention program is to identify and serve infants who have social or biological risk factors.

Project First Chance-Outreach

252 Kent Hall

Kent State University

Kent, OH 44242

> This habilitation program provides a responsive residential environment for severely handicapped children whose developmental ages are less than 1 year.

At Risk Parent Child Program, Inc.

Hillcrest Medical Center

1120 South Utica

Tulsa, OK 74104

> This pediatric at-risk project, in conjunction with other programs, provides hospital- and home-based services for children ages birth to 16 years old. Children with all categories of handicapping conditions and at-risk conditions are served.

Center on Human Development Preschool

901 East 18th Street

Eugene, OR 97403

> This program provides home- and center-based services for children ages birth to 6 years old who may exhibit any type of handicapping condition except serious emotional disturbance or learning disability. The center-based program also includes nonhandicapped children.

Teaching Research Infant and Child Center
Teaching Research
345 North Monmouth
Monmouth, OR 97361

This program serves children ages birth to 3 years old with all types of handicapping conditions except learning disabilities through a home- and center-based approach. Emphasis is given to the moderately to profoundly handicapped.

PEERS Project
Special People in the Northeast, Inc.
8040 Roosevelt Blvd., Suite 215
Philadelphia, PA 19152

This program provides services to children ages birth to 4 years old who may exhibit any type of handicapping or risk condition. Both home- and center-based programs are used. The parents are trained each Saturday morning to carry out intervention strategies in the home.

Early Childhood Education—Project OPTIMAL
Whitten Center
Drawer 239
Clinton, SC 29325

This home-based program serves children ages birth to 3 years old who are mentally retarded, deaf, visually handicapped, deaf/blind, and/or orthopedically impaired. The project also provides home-based services on a contract basis with other service providers.

Early Parent and Child Intervention Project
Human Development Center
Winthrop College
Rock Hill, SC 29733

This program provides services to children with all types of handicapping conditions, except deaf and deaf/blind, ages birth to 5 years old. A home- and center-based approach is used. In addition to providing direct services to children, the program offers technical assistance to other people and agencies.

Project MEMPHIS
Department of Special Education and Rehabilitation
Memphis State University
Memphis, TN 38152

This program provides home- and center-based services for children ages birth to 4 years with all types of handicapping conditions except deafness, deafness/blindness, and serious emotional disturbances. Assistance has been provided to over 7,000 other programs in the U.S. and 33 foreign countries in using their materials.

Project KIDS
(Kindling Individual Development System)
Dallas Independent School District
3801 Herschel Avenue
Dallas, TX 75228

This home- and center-based program provides services to children ages birth to 3 years old who exhibit mental retardation, emotional disturbance, learning disabilities, orthopedic impairments, and other health impairments. Parents are integrated into the instructional role in cooperation with the project staff.

Developmental Education Birth through Two (DEBT)
Lubbock Independent School District
1628 19th Street
Lubbock, TX 79401

This home-based program provides services for children ages birth to 3 years old who may have any type of handicapping or at-risk condition. Even though the primary intervention is in the home, some out-of-the-home activities are provided, e.g., parent study groups, specialized therapy, and child play groups.

Center and Homebound Intervention Project for Preschoolers
UMC 68—Exceptional Child Center
Utah State University
Logan, UT 84322

This program provides home-based services for children birth to 3 years old and center-based services for those three to 5 years old. Children with all types of handicapping conditions are served with the exception of learning disabled.

Project SKI*HI Outreach
Department of Communication Disorders—UMC-10
Utah State University
Logan, UT 84322

This program provides specialized services for hard of hearing, deaf, and deaf/blind children ages birth to 6 years old. A home-based approach is used. Emphasis is given to providing training and program support for other programs interested in implementing similar services.

The Winston L. Prouty Center
2 Oak Street
Brattleboro, VT 05301

This program provides home- and center-based services to children exhibiting any of the handicapping conditions, ages birth to 3 years old. In addition to direct services for infants, diagnostic services are provided for other public welfare, social, health, and rehabilitative agencies.

Education for Multihandicapped Infants (EMI)
University of Virginia Medical Center
Box 232
Charlottesville, VA 22908

This demonstration project provides services to infants ages birth to 2 years old and their families through a home- and hospital-based program. Infants may have any handicapping condition.

Infant Program/Outreach Project
Post Office Box 299
Lightfoot, VA 23090

This program serves children ages birth to 2 years old primarily through a home-based approach. All types of handicapping conditions except serious emotional disturbances are served. A center-based parent program is also used.

Model Preschool Center for Handicapped Children
Experimental Education Unit
CDMRC WJ-10
University of Washington
Seattle, WA 98195

Through a center-based approach, this program serves children with mental retardation, visual handicaps, hearing impairments, orthopedic handicaps, and other health impairments who are ages birth to 3 years old.

Project Home Base
Yakima Public Schools
104 North 4th Avenue
Yakima, WA 98902

This home-based program provides services to children ages birth to 5 years old who may have any of the types of handicapping conditions except deaf-blind. The program is also available to all parents living in Title I neighborhoods. This project has ESEA Title III, Title I validation.

Rehabilitation of Families at Risk
Waisman Center
University of Wisconsin
Madison, WI 53706

This program serves children ages birth to 6 years old who are at risk for mental retardation. A home- and center-based approach is used. Research and provisions of technical assistance to other communities wishing to develop a similar program are emphasized.

Early Childhood Program
Madison Metropolitan School District
454 West Dayton Street
Madison, WI 53711

This program serves children ages birth to 5 years old with a home- and center-based approach. Even though all types of handicapping conditions are served, children are only labeled as having exceptional educational needs.

Questionnaire
for Screening Programs

Purposes of the Questionnaire:
To acquire descriptive information about projects that screen for infants who are at-risk and/or handicapped.

Definition of Screening:
For the purpose of this questionnaire, screening is defined as a brief first step measurement activity aimed at identifying exceptional infants who may need an in-depth diagnosis and appropriate, comprehensive services. It should be fast, efficient and economical. The targets of the screening procedure may be either mothers/parents or infants.

GENERAL INSTRUCTIONS: Please answer all questions, using the spaces provided or the backs of pages for those items requiring explanation. We encourage you to make comments and provide explanations for responses as you think necessary. If you have a question as you complete the questionnaire, please contact: Sonya Prestridge, Pat Trohanis or Ruth Meyer at TADS-(919) 967-9221.

DEADLINE FOR RETURNING QUESTIONNAIRE IS OCTOBER 31, 1979

Before you begin the questionnaire, please provide the following information:

Project Name _____

Address _____

_____

_____
                                        Zip Code

Phone _____ / _____
            Area Code

Name of Person Completing Form _____
                                                    Title

**PLEASE NOTE: No information about your individual program
will be used without your prior approval.**

PART ONE—GENERAL INFORMATION ABOUT THE PROGRAM

1. Please describe your screening program including such information as purposes, interdisciplinary nature, and ages and types of children served.

    _____

    _____

    _____

    _____

    _____

2. How many years has your program been involved in screening for high-risk

    and handicapped infants? _____

3. Through what year do you expect to continue services? _____

4. What type of community setting does your project primarily serve?
    (Please check only one.)

    _____ a. urban   _____ c. rural

    _____ b. suburban   _____ d. other (Please specify)

                                 _____

5. How would you characterize the size of your geographic service area? (Please check only one.)

_____ a.   single community   _____ c.   entire state

_____ b.   multi-county region   _____ d.   other (Please specify)

_____

6. What is your program setting?

_____ a.   comprehensive healthcare setting (physician's office, clinic, hospital, neighborhood health center, children and youth project, etc.)

_____ b.   school, preschool or day care program

_____ c.   well-baby or well-child clinic

_____ d.   special site established for screening

_____ e.   home-based

_____ f.   other (Please specify) _____

7. What is the nature of the funding source(s) for your screening project? (If more than one source, please indicate the approximate percentage of funding contributed by each.)

_____ a.   federal grant(s) or contract(s) (% _____)

_____ b.   state grant(s), contract(s) or special program funds (% _____)

_____ c.   local public funds (% _____)

_____ d.   private foundation funds (% _____)

_____ e.   private contributions (% _____)

_____ f.   other (Please specify) _____ (% _____)

PART TWO—THE TARGET AUDIENCE FOR SCREENING

8. Who are the targets of your screening program? (Check either one, or both if applicable.)

_____ a.   mothers/parents

_____ b.   infants

9. Do you provide the following services to identified recipients? (Check all that apply)

_____ a. referral only   _____ c. parent training

_____ b. training for the child   _____ d. other (specify) _____

If you checked item 8a, mother/parents, please answer questions 10 through 22.

If you checked item 8b, infants, please answer questions 23 through 34

QUESTIONS FOR PROGRAMS THAT SCREEN MOTHERS/PARENTS . . .

10.   Briefly describe how mothers/parents are recruited for screening

_____

_____

_____

11.   How many mothers/parents have you screened since your program began?

_____

12.   How many are you expecting to screen this year? _____

13.   What conditions, impairments, environmental factors, genetic traits or handicaps are being screened?

_____

_____

_____

14.   What does your program emphasize as indicators of risk for handicapping conditions? (Please check all that apply.)

_____ a. older mother   _____ g. low parental education status

_____ b. teenage mother   _____ h. mentally retarded parents

_____ c. addicted/alcoholic mother   _____ i. exposure to environmental hazards

_____ d. maternal illness or trauma   _____ j. parental history of abuse/neglect

_____ e. genetic factors   _____ k. other (Please specify)

_____ f. low-income parents

_____

15. What screening instrument(s) and procedure(s) do you use (e.g., interviews, rating scales, indices)? _____

_____

_____

_____

16. Please describe briefly the steps taken by the program to insure the reliability, validity and standardization of the instruments and procedures described in 15 above.

_____

_____

_____

_____

17. Who administers the screening instrument(s)?

_____ a.   trained professionals   _____ d.   self-reporting used

_____ b.   paraprofessionals   _____ e.   others (Please specify)

_____ c.   trained volunteers   _____

18. How much training is needed for personnel to utilize the screening

treatment? _____ hours

19. How much time per mother/parent does the instrument take to adminster?

_____ hours

20. Please describe as briefly as possible any follow-up provided for mothers/parents with one or more possible problems identified.

_____

_____

_____

21. Briefly describe any outreach activities of your project, which may include model replication, professional publishing, print and audiovisual product development, etc.

_____

_____

_____

_____

22.   Do you have unit costs data available for your screening program?

_____ Yes   _____ No

If your answer is yes, please either list the cost of screening one mother, family, or infant or attach your cost data to the questionnaire.

_____

_____

_____

QUESTIONS FOR PROGRAMS THAT SCREEN INFANTS . . .

23.   Briefly describe how your infants are identified.

_____

_____

_____

24.   How many infants have you screened since your program began?

_____

25.   How many are you expecting to screen this year? _____

26.   What conditions, impairments, environmental factors, genetic traits or handicaps are being screened?

_____

_____

_____

_____

27.   What does your program emphasize as indicators of risk for handicapping conditions? (Please check all that apply.)

_____ a.   obstetric complications   _____ f.   neurological problems

_____ b.   low birthweight   _____ g.   developmental problems

_____ c.   postnatal illness   _____ i.   sensorimotor problems

_____d.   prematurity   _____ i.   environmental hazards

_____ e.   physical anomalies   _____ j.   multiple factors

28. What screening instrument(s) and procedure(s) do you use (e.g., rating scales, indices)? _____

_____

_____

_____

_____

29. Please describe briefly the steps taken by the program to insure the reliability, validity and standardization of the instruments and procedures described in 28 above.

_____

_____

_____

_____

30. Who administers the screening instrument(s)?

_____ a.   physicians   _____ d.   paraprofessionals

_____ b.   other health professionals   _____ e.   trained volunteers

_____ c.   non-health professionals   _____ f.   mothers

31. How much training is needed for personnel to use the screening instrument?

_____ hours

32. How much time per infant does the instrument take to adminster?

_____ hours

33. Please describe as briefly as possible any follow-up provided for infants suspected of having one or more possible problems identified.

_____

_____

_____

34. Do you have unit cost data available for your screening progam?

_____ Yes   _____ No

If your answer is yes, please either list the cost of screening one mother, family, or infant or attach your cost data to the questionnaire.

_____

_____

THANK YOU FOR PARTICIPATING IN THE SURVEY

Return completed questionnaire to: Ruth Meyer
Managing Editor
TADS
500 NCNB Plaza (322A)
Chapel Hill, NC 27514

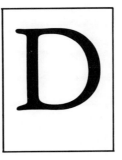

Questionnaire
for Intervention Programs

Purposes of the Questionnaire:

    (1) To acquire descriptive information about projects that provide services for infants (and their families) who are at-risk and/or handicapped.

    (2) To acquire evidence of exemplary status of programs that serve exceptional infants and their families.

GENERAL INSTRUCTIONS: Please answer all questions, using the spaces provided or the backs of pages for those items requiring explanation. We encourage you to make comments and provide explanations for responses as you think necessary. If you have questions as you complete the questionnaire, please contact: Jim Cox, Pat Trohanis or Ruth Meyer at TADS-(919) 967-9221.

**DEADLINE FOR RETURNING
QUESTIONNAIRE IS OCTOBER 31, 1979**

Before you begin the questionnaire, please provide the following information:

Project Name _____

Address _____

_____

_____

Zip Code

Phone _____ / _____
Area Code

Name of Person Completing Form _____
Title

**PLEASE NOTE: No information about your individual program
will be used without your prior approval.**

PART ONE—DESCRIPTIVE INFORMATION

1. What ages of infants does your program serve? (e.g., birth to 12 months,
    birth to 36 months, 12 months to 42 months, etc.)

    _____

2. How many infants did your project serve in the last fiscal year? _____

3. Which of the following Public Law 94-142 categories of handicapping con-
    ditions does your program serve?

    _____ a. mentally retarded   _____ f. deaf-blind

    _____ b. hard of hearing   _____ g. seriously emotionally
                                                 disturbed

    _____ c. deaf   _____ h. learning disabled

    _____ d. speech impaired   _____ i. orthopedically impaired

    _____ e. visually handicapped   _____ j. other health impaired

4. If the infants you serve cannot be described using the categories in item 3,
    please provide what you consider the best description(s) of infants served
    by your project. (Please be as specific as possible, e.g., low birthweight—
    less than 1,500 grams.)

    _____

    _____

5. Which of the following indicators of risk for handicapping conditions does your program *emphasize*? (Please check all that apply)

____ a. older mother   ____ h. low income

____ b. teenage mother   ____ i . low education status
                                                  of parents

____ c. addicted alcoholic mother   ____ j . mentally retarded parents

____ d. environmental hazards   ____ k. low birthweight
         (such as exposure to
         chemicals, lead)

____ e. genetic factors   ____ l. multiple factors

____ f. maternal illness or trauma   ____ m. other (specify) _____

____ g. child abuse and neglect   _____

6. Please indicate the approximate number of infants served by the project who have the handicapping or risk conditions specified in 3, 4, and 5 above.

Primary Handicapping or   Approximate Number
Risk Condition   Served

_____   _____

_____   _____

_____   _____

B. Characteristics of Families or Primary Caretakers Served

1. Please indicate the approximate number of mothers, parents or other primary caretakers served by the project during the last fiscal year.

    Number of families _____

    Number of individual mothers/parents/primary caretakers _____

2. Please characterize the families primarily served by your project, if appropriate, (e.g., low-income, native American, college-educated).

    _____

    _____

    _____

    _____

3.   Please indicate the approximate rate of parental/caretaker participation in the following activities (adding activities which are part of your program but are not listed).

Activity   Percentage of Parents
                                                  Participating

a.   Parents assist in planning, development,   _____
        operation, and evaluation of the
        project.

b.   Parents are trained to teach   _____
        their own children.

c.   Parents participate in educational   _____
        and therapeutic components
        of the project.

d.   Parents advise and assist in information   _____
        dissemination concerning the project.

e.   Other (specify) _____

     _____

f.   Other (specify) _____

     _____

C.   General Information About Overall Program

1.   Which of the following statements best describes the service activities that your project is **primarily** engaged in?
     (Please check only one.)

     _____ a.   developmental/educational   _____ c.   therapeutic intervention
              intervention   (OT, PT)

     _____ b.   medical intervention   _____ d.   other (specify) _____

                                                      _____

2.   What is the single best descriptor of your program's theoretical base? (e.g., behavioral, neurodevelopmental, sensory integration, etc.)

     _____

     _____

     _____

     _____

3. What type of community does your project **primarily** serve?
    (Please check only one.)

    ____ a. urban   ____ c. rural

    ____ b. suburban   ____ d. other (specify) _____

    _____

4. Approximately what service area or geographic target area does your
    project serve? (Please check only one.)

    ____ a. single community   ____ c. entire state

    ____ b. multi-county region   ____ d. other (specify) _____

    _____

5. What is your project's **primary** service delivery mode?
    (Please check only one.)

    ____ a. home-based   ____ d. hospital-based

    ____ b. center-based   ____ e. home- and hospital-based

    ____ c. home- and center-based ____ f. other (specify) _____

    _____

6. With what type of agency is your project affiliated?
    (Please check only one.)

    ____ a. public school (LEA)   ____ f . private non-profit agency

    ____ b. intermediate or regional   ____ g. other public agency
            educational unit   (mental health, public
                                                    health, etc.)

    ____ c. state education agency
            (SEA)   _____

    ____ d. higher education institution ____ h. other (specify) _____

    ____ e. hospital/medical school   _____

7. What is the nature of your project's funding source(s)? (If more than one
    source, please indicate the approximate percentage of each.)

_____ a.   federal grant(s) or contract(s) (% _____)

_____ b.   state grant(s), contract(s) or special program funds (% _____)

_____ c.   local public funds (% _____)

_____ d.   private foundation funds (% _____)

_____ e.   private contributions (% _____)

_____ f.   other (Please specify) _____ (% _____)

8. Please describe your project's staffing pattern. (List all staff positions and approximate percentage of time given to the infant program: e.g., Physical Therapist-50%, Special Educator-100%, Home Therapist-80%, etc.)

_____

_____

_____

_____

_____

_____

_____

_____

_____

9. Is your project involved in interagency activities or agreements?

   _____ Yes   _____ No

   If yes, please describe. _____

_____

_____

_____

_____

_____

10. Does your project have a training program for other professionals or

    paraprofessionals?   _____ Yes   _____ No

    If yes, what is the nature of the training program and to whom is it directed?

    _____

    _____

    _____

    _____

    _____

    _____

11. Please provide any other information that you think would be helpful in describing your program.

    _____

    _____

    _____

    _____

    _____

    _____

    _____

    _____

    _____

    _____

    _____

    _____

    _____

PART TWO—EVIDENCE OF EXEMPLARY STATUS

1. How many years has your project been in existence? _____

2. Through what year do you expect to be funded?

3. Approximately how many infants and/or parents have been served by your project since its inception?

    _____ infants   _____ parents/primary caretakers

4. Please list the names and locations of sites where your project has been replicated (please indicate whether partial or total replication).

    Project Title   City and State

    _____   _____

    _____   _____

    _____   _____

    _____   _____

    _____   _____

    _____   _____

5. Please list the titles of professional publications that have developed out of your project's activities (e.g., published books, chapters in books, journal articles).

    _____

    _____

    _____

    _____

    _____

    _____

    _____

    _____

    _____

6. Please list the titles and a **brief** description of any print and audiovisual products or materials that your project currently has available for distribution. You may wish to attach a publications list if one is available.

_____

_____

_____

_____

_____

_____

_____

7. Briefly describe your program evaluation efforts, impact data, and instruments used to gather the data for your target populations (infants and parents/families). **NOTE:** If your project has prepared an evaluation report, you may wish to include a copy, rather than answer or in addition to answering this question.

Evaluation and impact: _____

_____

_____

_____

_____

_____

Instruments: _____

_____

_____

_____

_____

8. Please provide any other information that you think would be helpful in describing the exemplary status of your program.

_____

_____

_____

_____

_____

_____

_____

_____

_____

_____

_____

_____

_____

_____

THANK YOU FOR PARTICIPATING IN THE SURVEY

Return completed questionnaire to: Ruth Meyer
Managing Editor
TADS
500 NCNB Plaza (322A)
Chapel Hill, NC 27515

Index

Adaptive behavior, of newborn, 8
Advocacy pool, 15
Agencies
  public policy and, 229–230
  referrals from, 73, 122
Alpern-Boll Developmental Profile,
  186
Alpha fetoprotien (AFP) studies, 41
American Academy of Pediatrics
  (Evanston, Illinois), inservice
  training of, 14
Amniocentesis, 41
Anencephaly, 28
  incidence, 23, 27, 28, 29, 30, 37
  risk for, 29, 40
Apgar rating scale, 104
Assessment, 114–115
  accuracy, 219
  background, 101–102
  at birth, 104
  competence areas, 112–113
  developmental scales, 108–112
  inventories of, 113–114
  intervention program effectiveness
    and, 131–132
  intervention program planning and,
    127
  need for, 102–103
  neonatal procedures, 105–108
  prenatal procedures, 103–104
  see also specific assessment tools
Assessment and Management of
  Developmental Changes in
  Children, 113
At Risk Parent Child Program, 85,
  97–98, 241, 248
Attachment bond, handicapped infant
  and, 141–143
Autistic children, family adjustment
  to, 150, 151
Autosomal syndromes, incidence, 27

Bayley, Nancy, 101, 109
Bayley Scales, of Infant Development,
  108, 109–110, 113, 114, 127

Being (state of), parent/child
  in teraction and, 141
Bell, Alexander Graham, 10
Biological risk, 8, 20, 39–40
  see also Risk
Biology, development and, 2–3, 4, 5–6
Birth defect registers, 70
Birth rate, 26
Birth records, as information source,
  25–26
Blacks
  childrearing practices of, 55, 56
  infant mortality and, 24
  see also Low socioeconomic status
Brazelton, see Neonatal Behavioral
  Assessment Scale
British Columbia Health Surveillance
  Registry, 26, 28, 29, 30, 36–37,
  38
  mental retardation and, 34, 35
  risk factors and, 40
Burnout, parents and, 154–155
Bush Institutes for Child and Family
  Policy, The, 15
Bzoch-League Receptive-Expressive
  Emergent Language Scale, see
  Receptive-Expressive Emergent
  Language Scale

California Infant Scales, 101
Case study, evaluation and, 200, 202
Cattell, Psyche, 101
Center and Homebound Intervention
  Project for Preschoolers, 250
Center on Human Developmental
  Preschool, 248
Central nervous system (CNS)
  abnormalities, 26, 27, 28–30,
  41
Cerebral palsy, 21, 26, 27, 31
  etiology, 31–33
  eye contact and, 143
  incidence, 23, 31, 32
  mother/child interaction and, 154
  spastic diplegia, 31

271

M